PRAISE FOR
CHINA'S VISION OF VICTORY
AND JONATHAN D.T. WARD

"The extraordinary rise of China is unprecedented in world history and the biggest geopolitical development of the first two decades of the 21st Century; it is likely to continue to be so for decades to come. Jonathan Ward is very well qualified to document China's extraordinary growth, and he describes it superbly in *China's Vision of Victory*, a powerful work that is sure to provoke thought and serious reflection."

> — **GENERAL DAVID PETRAEUS,** US Army (Ret.), former commander of coalition forces in Iraq and Afghanistan and US Central Command, and former Director of the CIA

"Jonathan Ward is a young scholar with not only all the necessary linguistic and travel credentials, but with something even more important, a vision of history rooted in geography that allows him to espy the future."

> — **ROBERT D. KAPLAN,** author of *Monsoon: The Indian Ocean and the Future of American Power*

"I've long admired Jonathan's determination to get to the truth, on the ground. It is rare to find someone able to combine politics, philosophy, linguistic expertise and hard travel—and bring it to bear on some of the toughest issues of our generation—Jonathan is one of those remarkable people."

> — **RORY STEWART,** author of *The Places in Between* and *The Prince of Marshes*

"This book is a very timely Master Class on China. Everyone with a keen interest in China's political, military and economic policy, past and present, should study this book carefully. Jonathan Ward's gimlet-eyed analysis and prescriptive recommendations should be taken to heart by all."

> —**JACK DEVINE,** U.S. Central Intelligence Agency (Ret.), author of *Good Hunting: An American Spymaster's Story*

"Jonathan Ward has provided an eye-opening analysis of China's strategic ambitions. He effectively demolishes the longstanding expectation in Washington that a prosperous rising China will be content to integrate itself into the Western international order – to the contrary, he demonstrates that Beijing's objectives include nothing less than renovating that order to serve China's own strategic interests. As the United States debates the future of its China policy, *China's Vision of Victory* deserves the widest reading."

— **ASHLEY J. TELLIS**, Tata Chair for Strategic Affairs,
Carnegie Endowment for International Peace

"*China's Vision of Victory* is insightful, compelling, and long overdue. Whether your interest is business, economics, diplomacy, or politics, Jonathan Ward's assessments and analysis are on target. More importantly, his book will help you understand the complexity and interconnection of all facets of America's relations with China. Jonathan has given us a new take on the many challenges we face in addressing Chinese power and its relationship with the world."

— **ADMIRAL SCOTT H. SWIFT**, US Navy (Ret.),
Commander of US Pacific Fleet, 2015–2018

"Dr. Ward tells an absorbing and well-researched story about China's grand strategy to achieve "supremacy among all nations" by 2049 and the role of Western capital in fueling China's rise. *China's Vision of Victory* is a must-read for Western policy makers, intelligence agencies, chief executives, global investors, and globally-minded thinkers. It is a real-life page-turner, if ever there was one."

— **J. KYLE BASS**, Founder & Chief Investment Officer of
Hayman Capital Management

CHINA'S VISION OF VICTORY

CHINA'S VISION OF VICTORY

★

AND WHY AMERICA MUST WIN

JONATHAN D.T. WARD

Printed in the United States of America

First Printing, 2019

ISBN 978-0-57-843810-8

Library of Congress Control Number: 2019902591

ATLAS

The Atlas Publishing and Media Company LLC
www.atlas publishingandmedia.com

To My Fellow Americans

and

Our Friends and Allies Around the World

2019

CONTENTS

FOREWORD

The Need for a New American Grand Strategy in a Time of US–China Competition

ADMIRAL SCOTT H. SWIFT, UNITED STATES NAVY (RET.)
Commander, US Pacific Fleet (2015–2018)
Robert E. Wilhelm Fellow, MIT Center for International Studies

hina's Vision of Victory is insightful, compelling, and long overdue. Whether your interest is business, economics, diplomacy, or politics, Jonathan Ward's assessments and analysis are on target. More importantly, his book will help you understand the complexity and interconnection of all facets of America's relations with China. Jonathan has given us a new take on the many challenges we face in addressing Chinese power and its relationship with the world.

This is an important undertaking. To understand China you have to take a multi-dimensional approach, as Jonathan has done. China's strategy is a *global grand strategy*— dynamic, multifaceted, and utilizing all elements of the nation's government and society. To truly understand China, you have to look at its strategic intentions in all of its parts, as Jonathan has done.

The author notes that China has leveraged its "economic empowerment through engagement with the United States," and China "is now returning to the original ideological intentions of the Chinese Communist Party." I could not agree more. The Chinese have not obscured or hidden their intentions. They have communicated clearly to their citizens their near- and long-term political objectives and their grand strategy for getting there. As Jonathan points out, when Henry Kissinger first visited Beijing, he described China as a "mysterious" country. Through our own shortcomings, we have unnecessarily "mystified" this grand plan. Our lack of knowledge and understanding explains why America thought the best approach for our emerging relationship with China was "engage but hedge." Now, not only are we as Americans beginning to grasp the true nature of China's plans, but the world is as well.

China's grand strategy plays to its advantages and is derived from a vision of its intended relationship with the world. From that grand strategy China has developed regional strategies to guide its actions in every corner of the world.

China has developed military bases on man-made islands in the South China Sea, engineering marvels emblematic of the success of the implementation of Chinese grand strategic outcomes and its resultant transition from a "mysterious" country to one overtly assuming a commanding position on the global stage.

More broadly, and of even greater concern, China has long pursued a strategy of exploiting the international rules-based order when those rules provide Chinese advantage, while also using economic and military coercion, corruption, intimidation, bullying, and outright force when convenient to achieve national objectives.

China's success demonstrates the value of a true grand strategy applied effectively and efficiently. China has done this methodically, with frequent updates based upon changing world conditions, as well as China's assessments of its own ability to advance toward its goals. It has also telegraphed its broad strategic intent, if not its specific objectives. Granted, it has presented goals in much clearer terms to its internal audience than to the international community, but, as Jonathan points out, this is not new and not beyond the view of a careful eye on Chinese discourse.

This reality was reflected in Chinese Premier Zhou Enlai's response to Kissinger's comment about the mystery of Chinese aims when he simply said: "It is not mysterious to us." Nor should it be a mystery to us. Certainly, reading this book will help lift what is the West's largely self-created idea of a Chinese veil of mystery.

From behind this veil has emerged the current debate about China as a competitor with the United States. So what does this competition look like? What is the nature of the core competition between the United States and China? And what are the pitfalls to be avoided in managing it?

First, it is important to note that being competitors is not necessarily bad. We compete in business, politics, government, and in our personal and professional lives. But what is necessary in any competition is a common understanding of the rules and a commitment to follow them, hence, the necessity of a stable international rules-based order.

My view, reinforced throughout this book, is that the primary element of this competition is the divergent views of China and the rest of the world on the value of the international rules-based system designed to mitigate frictions that naturally occur between states. China is challenging the rules-based order in areas it views as impinging upon its national sovereignty. Competitive frictions are occurring globally as other states resist China's refusal to align with the standing international rules-based order, or where China is forcing change merely because it is strong enough to do so.

So what is this "international rules-based order" so many refer to? Some of it is post-Second World War international agreements; some is established international law; some is based on UN conventions and declarations, as well as those of international organizations like the World Trade Organization. Other elements are the result of the evolution of customary business, diplomatic, and military relationships.

What provides the legitimacy of the rules-based order is the value placed on it by international actors. There can and should be differences in views with respect to what constitutes the international rules-based order. This is driven by many factors, not the least of which are the global changes that occur on an increasingly frequent basis. The system itself anticipates this. There are any number of forums in the diplomatic, economic, defense, financial, and law domains where debates discuss the merits of the current rules and consider appropriate changes.

In the Pacific, the system grew from the September 8, 1951 Treaty of San Francisco, which was signed by forty-eight nations and ended the war with Japan. A core motivation behind the convention was to provide mechanisms for peacefully resolving disagreements between the signatory states. The lessons learned from the world's experience with Imperial Japan and Nazi Germany were painful, and there emerged a general international consensus to ensure the hard lessons learned became lessons applied. The core of the new process was rejection of the use of force to resolve claims or to modify the rules themselves, while embracing the stabilizing tenets of diplomacy and dialogue.

In a very general sense, the rules state that disagreements between nations should be addressed via bilateral dialogue. If this fails, then individually or collectively the concerned nations are supposed to turn to the established international institutions for resolution. The result has been seventy-five years of relative stability in the Pacific. An underpinning of that stability has been the incredible rising tide of prosperity that has benefited all the countries choosing to participate in the international rules-based system. It is a simple formula: shared and applied interests in security result in shared stability which, in turn, helps produce shared prosperity.

Exacerbating competition is the fact that the "Global Stage" is not getting any bigger. If anything, with the interconnected nature of the global economy, along with the international nature of state relationships, international law, business practices, and trade, and the effects of local and regional practices on the climate and environment, all factors have helped increase the necessity of an international rules-based system. These same global drivers are shrinking the global stage, driving us closer together, and increasing opportunities for growth and prosperity. But they also feed increased interstate discord. Overall, global stability is not on a positive vector.

China's economic power alone is sufficient to make the case for its inclusion on the global stage. It is in everyone's best interest to welcome and embrace China's assumption of its rightful position. But the global community should also expect China to assume the obligations of a global leader by its acceptance of and adherence to the international rules-based system.

With China's emergence on the global stage, some displacement of those already on the stage will occur. Adjustments will have to be made. Those making adjustments will certainly include the United States. This is not something the United States should fear, but for which it should prepare. The questions we and others should be asking are:

- How do we best understand each of our respective new positions?

- Will adjustments be made through force and coercion, or diplomacy and dialogue?

- Will adjustments be regionally and globally destabilizing, or support international stability and prosperity?

At this point, it is important to note that, as a military practitioner of over forty years, with all of my operational tours originating from and terminating in the Pacific, I believe we are overly focused on the military element of this great power competition. The man-made military fortresses in the South China Sea have significant tactical and operational offensive capability, but are strategically static and defensive in nature. More important, they represent only a small part of China's grand strategy, and they demonstrate China's whole-of-government approach. When it comes to United States Freedom of Navigation Operations, for example, while the Chinese military may respond tactically, the *strategic* response to US actions comes from the Chinese Foreign Ministry.

Freedom of Navigation Operations have been a fixture of US Navy operations for decades, well before my first deployment in the early 1970s. Despite their long history, they are not well understood. They are executed in support of a long-standing United States national commitment to the concept of free and open navigation of international waters. Where national claims are excessive, such operations are conducted by the US Navy on behalf of the State Department to allow State to engage in a dialogue with the subject nation, explaining exactly what element of the United Nations Convention on the Law of the Sea is being clarified. Regretfully, this reinforcement of the value of discourse and dialogue is being subsumed by the military element. Unlike in other arenas of national competition, when it comes to a miscalculation in the military domain, if a tactical action results in crossing a strategic red line, it is much more difficult to walk that action back. In the military domain, consequences tend to be significant, nationally polarizing, and lasting. The watchwords here should be prudence and caution. At best, Freedom of Navigation Operations may reassure what are now skeptical allies, partners, and friends that the United States is committed to an orderly process to evolve the international rules-based order. But let's be clear: Freedom of Navigation operations will not deter a determined and now emboldened Chinese government.

This brings me to my last point: the necessity for the United States to develop a grand strategy of its own. We cannot compete successfully with China without one. There is not sufficient time or space here, nor is this the forum, to advocate for what that United States grand strategy should be. That said, I will take a moment here to discuss how a grand strategy might be drafted and implemented.

The ultimate measure of a grand strategy is whether it generates a *whole-of-government* effort toward common national global goals. By whole of government I mean the organization and alignment of each Presidential Cabinet-level department. The creation and execution of a new American grand strategy should involve not only the traditional strategic departments (Defense, State, and Commerce), but *all fifteen federal executive departments*. All have important contributions to make, roles to play, and resources to apply toward obtaining our national objectives. This means each has to play a role in designing our grand strategy and empowering its execution. Certainly, Congress should exercise oversight and share its insight, experience, and support, as well as ensuring that necessary funding is available to implement the strategy (though my sense is there is sufficient funding in the current budget to do so). A clear grand strategy would help better apply those funds in support of our national goals.

Grand strategy broadly defines and explains how elements of national power are used to achieve internal and external objectives. From this foundation, regional strategies would be developed by the same branches and departments of government. An effective grand strategy would be very broad, with the aim of standing the test of time and surviving political transitions with only minor changes. It would be guided by the long-standing tenets of the Constitution and our other founding documents and ideals. Regional strategies would be more detailed, with specific actions and outcomes for individual departments of government. Metrics would then be applied to assess progress being made toward achieving the stated national goals.

Using regional strategies as a guide and source of authority, branches and departments of government would develop policy to guide the application and implementation of regional strategies. These steps would support moving us away from merely reacting to the current crisis of the day, reduce governmental confusion and chaos, and leverage a whole-of-government alignment that would increase national and international confidence in America's intentions and actions.

Where nations become engaged in activities to challenge and change the international rules-based order through force and coercion, branches and departments of the United States government would be logically organized and engaged in meaningful and much more effective moves to counter not just a rival's actions, but also their strategic intent. From American resolve, a rallying of other nations in support of time-honored ideals and agreements is more likely to rise.

I hope your experience with Jonathan Ward's *China's Vision of Victory* is the same as mine. I am heartened by his fact-based approach to understanding not only China's grand strategy, but also the underlying forces at play galvanizing China as a nation to embrace and support the strategy defined by Xi Jinping and the Chinese Communist Party.

Mysteries survive in the darkness of ignorance. As more academics, policy-makers, diplomats, and business and political leaders begin to understand the nature of the grand strategic game China is playing, the more I expect my confidence to grow that we will continue to enjoy the absence of "Great Power" conflict we have experienced since the end of the Second World War.

Jonathan's book, *China's Vision of Victory*, is an excellent place to start this learning process as we ask ourselves: "Do we wish the global stage to be defined by the embrace of force and coercion as national tools of choice, or do we wish to continue to value rules-based agreement and the proven practices of diplomacy and dialogue?"

I see work like Jonathan Ward's becoming more and more vital now as we endeavor to find reasonable solutions that address the growing concerns of the international community of nations. His work is a great source of my confidence and optimism. I trust that in reading this book you may reach a similar conclusion.

na in 1949 to Xi
he eyes of Chi-
the world
se power
of a
ion

Forty years ago, when Henry Kissinger first visited Beijing, he remarked that China was a "mysterious" country. His Chinese host said this: "What is so mysterious about China? There are 900 million of us and it is not mysterious to us."

For decades since Dr. Kissinger's first visit, US policy-makers were guided by a beautiful and very American vision. They worked toward an idea that China would eventually liberalize, reform, and otherwise become a "responsible stakeholder," living and working alongside the United States on the world stage. The Chinese people had been our friends and allies once before, fighting against fascism in the Second World War under the Nationalist Party, now exiled to Taiwan. The People's Republic of China was a growing market in which American business could prosper. The rise of modern China would be a force for globalization, and, together, America and China could share the world.

The sum of American policymakers' approach was a strategy called "engage but hedge." This is one of the most consequential strategic approaches in American history — not because it has succeeded, but because it has failed.

Most importantly, this strategy has brought us to the brink of the end of an American-led world. It is an approach that will eventually bring about the end of American power.

The People's Republic of China — its rise built substantially on economic empowerment through engagement with the United States — is now returning to the original ideological intentions of the Chinese Communist Party.

What are these intentions? Where is China going? What does it want, not in our eyes, but in the eyes of China's leaders? This book will answer these questions.

From the founding of the People's Republic of Ch[ina] [to Xi] Jinping's accession to power in the twenty-first century, in t[he eyes of Chi]nese leaders China's rise has never been about sharing Asia o[r the world] with the United States. It has been about the restoration of Chin[a's power] and the road to unrestricted power among nations. It is the buildi[ng of a] superpower, and the restoration, as China's leaders see it, of China's *posit[ion] of supremacy among all nations.* Only from this supreme position can Chi-na's destiny be fulfilled.

For a long and trusting moment, over more than thirty years, American policy-makers empowered this rise, perhaps not knowing where it would lead, perhaps knowing only that the Communist Party would lead China.

Our present moment of engagement is finally breaking. The intentions of the Communist Party and the objectives of China's rise are becoming clearer in America. The US national security community deals on a daily basis with a growing Chinese military that is designed to defeat the United States. Members of our Congress are waking up to the dangers for American prosperity as job losses and deindustrialization imperil the future of this country. The international community has begun to recognize the dystopian landscape of human rights abuses inside and even outside China as new technological breakthroughs enable the Communist Party to build a high-tech surveillance state unlike anything seen in history.

But what is most troubling is not what China does today. It is what the Communist Party plans on for the future of the world.

If China were to settle in as a large East Asian nation with arcane territorial claims against its neighbors, a modernizing military, an anachronistic ideology, and broad economic potential to capture the imaginations of businesspeople and financiers around the world, then perhaps it would remain nothing more than a distant, perhaps fascinating country— or, in Kissinger's phrasing, a "mysterious" place.

But China's ambitions have only just begun.

As Chinese Premier Zhou Enlai said to Dr. Kissinger in 1971: "It is not mysterious to us."

In November 2018, former US Treasury Secretary Henry Paulson spoke words that will echo for many years:

There's this . . . myth that some of us who worked to engage China thought it would become a Jeffersonian democracy, or espouse a liberal Western order. We never thought that. We always knew the Communist Party would play an important, dominant role.[1]

Mr. Paulson *knew* that American engagement with China would bring about a globally empowered China and a globally empowered Chinese Communist Party.

The question, then, is how well did Mr. Paulson and others around him understand the forces that they were working to empower?

How well did he and others understand the Chinese Communist Party?

How well did he and others around him understand China?

Did Mr. Paulson and his colleagues understand the new balance of power that they were bringing about and what it would mean for the world?

What we are verging on for our country—even for our world—is the prospect of a "Chinese Century."

A litany of speeches, strategy documents, and policies have poured forth from the Communist Party in recent years. All of them explain China's near- and long-term ambitions. From outer space to the deep sea, from Africa to the Arctic, from artificial intelligence to hypersonic missiles that can "kill" American aircraft carriers, the Chinese Communist Party has mobilized its country and its people to become the global leaders in virtually every form of economic, military, technological, and diplomatic activity on earth. This is not an exaggeration. These are stated goals. This book will explain them in detail.

China's leaders are proud of their achievements and exuberant about their future.

As Chairman Xi Jinping explained to his country in 2017:

Rooted in a land of more than 9.6 million square kilometers, nourished by a nation's culture of more than 5,000 years, and backed by the invincible force of more than 1.3 billion people, we have an infinitely vast stage of our era, a historical heritage of unmatched depth, and incomparable resolve that enable us to forge ahead...[2]

As China's state news agency proclaimed:

> By 2050, two centuries after the Opium Wars, which plunged the "Middle Kingdom" [China] into a period of hurt and shame, China is set to regain its might and re-ascend to the top of the world.[3]

And among China's citizens, whether by survey or by anecdote, the consensus is that China will replace the United States as the world's leading superpower.

Here is how one of the leading China scholars in Britain put it: "The way the Chinese look at it is, why shouldn't they have a go? The British had their turn. America had its turn. Now it's ours." In other words, what we are witnessing, in word and deed, is China's ambition to become the world's supreme power and, in doing so, to transform human history.

As America churns with division and internal strife, China's leaders are designing and executing an ascendance to power on a global scale not seen since the British Empire.

The time frame is important. As described by China's leadership, the completion of China's rise will take shape by 2049, on the hundredth anniversary of the founding of the People's Republic of China. At this point, China would be accepted as the dominant power on Earth, without rival, without peer.

However, in practical terms, the time frame is much sooner.

The next ten years will see a tipping point in the global balance of power from which the United States may never recover.

By 2030, if current trends hold, China will surpass the United States as the world's top economic power in absolute terms.

Many organizations, from the World Economic Forum to the US National Intelligence Council, to a variety of global investment banks, already take this as an unavoidable outcome.

From that point forward, however, when China reaches a position of economic supremacy, America will enter into a losing contest with China.

Today, in 2019, China's ability to build global influence, to wield military and industrial power, and to project ideological influence is second only to the United States. Today, China's economy has grown to be roughly 65

INTRODUCTION

Forty years ago, when Henry Kissinger first visited Beijing, he remarked that China was a "mysterious" country. His Chinese host said this: "What is so mysterious about China? There are 900 million of us and it is not mysterious to us."

For decades since Dr. Kissinger's first visit, US policy-makers were guided by a beautiful and very American vision. They worked toward an idea that China would eventually liberalize, reform, and otherwise become a "responsible stakeholder," living and working alongside the United States on the world stage. The Chinese people had been our friends and allies once before, fighting against fascism in the Second World War under the Nationalist Party, now exiled to Taiwan. The People's Republic of China was a growing market in which American business could prosper. The rise of modern China would be a force for globalization, and, together, America and China could share the world.

The sum of American policymakers' approach was a strategy called "engage but hedge." This is one of the most consequential strategic approaches in American history— not because it has succeeded, but because it has failed.

Most importantly, this strategy has brought us to the brink of the end of an American-led world. It is an approach that will eventually bring about the end of American power.

The People's Republic of China— its rise built substantially on economic empowerment through engagement with the United States— is now returning to the original ideological intentions of the Chinese Communist Party.

What are these intentions? Where is China going? What does it want, not in our eyes, but in the eyes of China's leaders? This book will answer these questions.

From the founding of the People's Republic of China in 1949 to Xi Jinping's accession to power in the twenty-first century, in the eyes of Chinese leaders China's rise has never been about sharing Asia or the world with the United States. It has been about the restoration of Chinese power and the road to unrestricted power among nations. It is the building of a superpower, and the restoration, as China's leaders see it, of China's *position of supremacy among all nations*. Only from this supreme position can China's destiny be fulfilled.

For a long and trusting moment, over more than thirty years, American policy-makers empowered this rise, perhaps not knowing where it would lead, perhaps knowing only that the Communist Party would lead China.

Our present moment of engagement is finally breaking. The intentions of the Communist Party and the objectives of China's rise are becoming clearer in America. The US national security community deals on a daily basis with a growing Chinese military that is designed to defeat the United States. Members of our Congress are waking up to the dangers for American prosperity as job losses and deindustrialization imperil the future of this country. The international community has begun to recognize the dystopian landscape of human rights abuses inside and even outside China as new technological breakthroughs enable the Communist Party to build a high-tech surveillance state unlike anything seen in history.

But what is most troubling is not what China does today. It is what the Communist Party plans on for the future of the world.

If China were to settle in as a large East Asian nation with arcane territorial claims against its neighbors, a modernizing military, an anachronistic ideology, and broad economic potential to capture the imaginations of businesspeople and financiers around the world, then perhaps it would remain nothing more than a distant, perhaps fascinating country— or, in Kissinger's phrasing, a "mysterious" place.

But China's ambitions have only just begun.

As Chinese Premier Zhou Enlai said to Dr. Kissinger in 1971: "It is not mysterious to us."

In November 2018, former US Treasury Secretary Henry Paulson spoke words that will echo for many years:

percent of the size of the US economy, as measured in real terms gross domestic product. China's economy is still growing quickly, at more than twice the speed of the US. Ten years from now, China's economic might will be double what it is today—equal to, and then with every passing year greater than, America's. From that point forward, we will have reached a turning point in history. From here, the possibilities for a global China begin to take shape in earnest, and the end of the American era will be accomplished.

China's economy is the foundation of its power. It is the foundation of its military buildup, its technological advances, and its global influence. While this may have been lost on a generation of American policy-makers, it is not at all lost on the Chinese Communist Party. As an advisor to the Communist Party stated to me in Beijing in 2018, "Chinese strategy is built on China's economic situation." Clear and simple. In Chinese aphorism it is this: 富国强兵 "A rich country and a strong military." These are China's global goals.

The leaders of the Chinese Communist Party have known for decades that the day would come when America questioned China's rise. Thinking on a multi-decade time frame out to 2049, they have called 2000 to 2020 the "period of strategic opportunity." This was the time, which is ending now, in which "the international situation" would be favorable to China. The next decade is what some have called a "decade of concern," the time when the world begins to question and to resist China's rise to global power.

Within the next ten years, 2020 to 2030, a series of major contests that are already underway will gain even greater momentum: military, technological, industrial, financial, and diplomatic— region by region around the world, sector by sector across the economy, breakthrough by breakthrough across new technologies, domain by domain across the military balance. Within these contests, if China should surpass America, as it intends to do, the bedrock for a Chinese century will be laid in earnest.

These are contests for which the Communist Party has been preparing for quite some time, and in which China is securing victory after victory as America argues and deliberates over the meaning of China's rise. They are contests in which China has set clear goals and made extraordinary gains.

The United States stands to witness a colossal turning point in less than a generation's time.

All who are alive today in America were born into a superpower.

Those who are alive today may also be the ones to watch this power perish.

And if this Chinese victory is complete, we will live in a "brave new world" indeed.

What will it mean for America's democratic process to be manipulated from another continent? Not by a weaker nation, such as today's Russia, but by a far more powerful global empire ruled by authoritarian China? What will it mean for the prevailing norms in international relations to be decided by an authoritarian state where freedoms of speech, press, and assembly are extinguished for its citizens and those under its power? What will it mean for religious freedom to exist only if it is subordinated to the power of the Communist Party?

In today's China this isn't a set of imaginary questions. These are realities of daily life.

In China, in addition to the repression of speech and the press, to forced detentions and even executions of political dissidents, and other continual human rights violations, the Communist Party is unrolling a "social credit system" which aims to monitor the "untrustworthy" behavior of citizens, assigning them a "credit score" as part of the Communist Party's program of "social management." The Party is also developing a "youth credit system" in which "dossiers will be created to carry good credit records of trustworthy young individuals."[4] Today, in the western province of Xinjiang—a vast expanse of land brought under control by China's former emperors—the Communist Party has built numerous concentration camps for the Uighur ethnic minority population, and as many as a million people are undergoing "political re-education." The Party has even, by some accounts, sent a million Chinese citizens to occupy the homes of the Uighur minority people in order to report on their behavior and assist the Party in choosing which ones will be sent to the camps.[5]

The troubles of modern China are one thing when they exist inside China's borders. It is quite another thing for this country to plan to become the world's most powerful nation. As China's corporations, financial institutions, and military expand their reach, we will see what Chinese influence really means.

Today, in America, we have to work again for the things that have been given to us by the past. We have to protect our heritage and our progress from a challenger on a scale not seen in several generations.

Our adversary today understands everyone's desire to sleep through difficulties. They understand us well. Meanwhile, they work quietly, thoroughly, and with extreme dedication. In the end, the objective is to secure their global power without awakening the United States, or awakening us only when it is far too late to stop them.

The purpose of this book is to provide the needed wake-up call. To inform you, so that you will understand and be ready.

If our power is ultimately broken, it will be a danger not only to Americans, but to the world.

The United States, its liberties, its diversity, its opportunity, its creativity, and unlimited potential—all of this cannot be finished simply because, in the Pacific, a dictatorship grows rich and lethal, and its ambitions swell.

America stands in striking contrast to the things for which this new power stands. But the promise of the United States, its commitment to our people, and to many, many nations around the world, cannot be maintained without clear vision and strenuous effort.

There are three things we must do to win:

First, the United States must remain the world's top economic power.

Second, the United States must work with the world's democracies—with nations around the globe who share our values and our political systems—in order to preserve an international system of power superior to anything which China can achieve.

Third, the United States must maintain military and technological superiority over China, both on its own, and when combined with the power of its primary authoritarian partner, Russia.

Finally, we must recognize that these are not just short-term problems. These are goals we must sustain over a long-term competition with China, lasting well into the twenty-first century.

These three things can lead us to a victory of our own, to lasting security and prosperity in this new century. Most importantly, if we maintain our power on these three fronts, we can keep the peace and avert the wars which China's leaders are already calling for.

These three objectives can secure and sustain America, along with our friends and allies around the world.

But first, we must understand our adversary. What it wants. What it has already achieved. Why it does what it does. What it plans to do.

First, we must understand China.

起来!不愿做奴隶的人们!
把我们的血肉,筑成我们新的长城!
中华民族到了最危险的时候,
每个人被迫着发出最后的吼声。
起来!起来!起来!
我们万众一心,
冒着敌人的炮火,前进!
冒着敌人的炮火,前进!
前进!前进!前进!

Rise! Those who will not be slaves!

From our flesh and blood, build our New Great Wall!

The time of greatest danger to the Chinese people has arrived,

Forcing the final howl to erupt from each person.

Arise! Arise! Arise!

We are ten thousand crowds with one heart,

Facing the fire of the enemy, advance!

Facing the fire of the enemy, advance!

Advance! Advance! Advance!

NATIONAL ANTHEM OF THE PEOPLE'S REPUBLIC OF CHINA

"THERE ARE JUST TWO COUNTRIES THAT I WANT TO ERASE FROM THE Earth," she said.

I looked at her and waited for her to continue.

"Japan and the United States," said Xiao Qing.

She was a few years older than me. We were in Shanghai. I had returned from months of travel in China's desolate western regions and in Southeast Asia.

"It is not you, Jon," she said. "It is only that I want to drop a nuclear bomb on Washington to destroy your government."

"I like you," she said. "But in a war, I would have to kill you for my country."

It was my first year in China.

The Purpose of This Book

I had just presented on the role of nuclear weapons in Chinese global strategy at one of America's nuclear research facilities in Northern California. As we chatted afterward, a former senior US Defense Department official offered me a parable. The story tells of many blind men, each touching one object. One feels a tusk, another feels an ear, another a tail. Yet another strokes the rough skin. Each describes in detail what he has found. But none grasps that they are all touching an elephant. "That's the problem," my new acquaintance told me. "People endlessly tell us all about China. But no one is describing the whole elephant."

He fixed his gaze on me. I believed he meant that, based on what I told him in my presentation, I should try to describe the elephant. The idea of this book was born that day. It is about the whole of China's rise: what is really happening, and what it means.

China and Me

In 2006, I was a 22-year-old backpacker travelling in China's remotest regions. I had studied Russian and Chinese language at Columbia University, then went to Beijing University to continue my language study. We had a short break that summer, and I spent it staying in monasteries and workers' camps in China's heartland. When I returned, one of my tutors said, "How did you become fluent in the language?" The answer was simple: immersion among all kinds of people in their daily lives. I spent a year in the region the first time: riding a bicycle across southern China, motorcycling through China's northwest deserts, hitchhiking with truck drivers through Tibet and hiding from the People's Liberation Army under sacks of food and cold-weather blankets at checkpoints on some of the remotest roads in the world. Above all, I came to see and know the people of one of the world's great countries.

It was also the beginning of a belief that only gets stronger: that the rise of China will be the central story of our lifetime. And I found, when I returned to America and Europe, that most everyone around me had it wrong. My travels continued. I spent five years living and travelling in Russia, China, South and Southeast Asia, Latin America, and the Middle East, learning other languages and meeting thousands of people.

gers," which began as dictatorships and then became democracies. What may be true of Taiwan or South Korea is not reducible to a blanket theory of economics and governance applicable to every country on earth.

Instead, China is fulfilling an objective that is nearly one hundred years old called "the resurrection of the ancestral land," or, as the Communist Party puts it: "the great rejuvenation of the Chinese nation." Technology is a part of this. Economics and military prowess are too. Geographical ambitions are central. The end of the current world order is planned.

How to Read This Book

This book is about that great rejuvenation of the Chinese nation: the plans that guide it, the history it comes from, the tenacity which girds it, its geographical and military scope, and the myriad advances that are made every day—whether in economics, technology, military affairs, or diplomacy. We can experience these advances in headlines, news, and book subjects, but they must be pulled together to be truly understood. This book's findings and conclusions come from China's own words and sources, and reveal China's own understanding of itself and of its history.

The reader will find that this book draws heavily on primary sources. This is in order to bring the reader into contact with China's own discourse, using a wide variety of sources which represent the thinking of China's leaders and other major actors in China's political process.

By now, the reader may be questioning the precise meaning of the word "China." You don't need be an expert to appreciate that it's a complex and multifaceted place. By its own measure, the country has 5,000 years of history, fifty-six ethnicities, scores of regional languages, and over a billion people. This complexity can cause us to miss the elephant. And on an opposite extreme, much is said with excessive assurance about "China" as a whole.

What matters here is *China's sense of China as a whole*. Chinese leaders, and many Chinese citizens both in China and around the world, have a deep and readily expressible sense of what China means as a nation, as a revolution, and, essentially, as a destiny. It is part of what makes a book like this possible. China has, arguably, one of the most potent and active senses of national destiny that exists on Earth today, and certainly one of the world's clearest and most active discourses. This discourse is not confined to

Party manuals and speeches. It is expressed daily in Chinese media, in popular culture, civil society, and academia. It is even expressed in the cafés and streets and homes, in countries around the world, where Chinese citizens have "gone out" and now witness the rise of their country from around the globe. Many of China's citizens at home and abroad feel that they are doing their part to make this rise happen. Much about these narratives is fed by China's leadership in the Chinese Communist Party, though many people in China feel that the Communist Party does not go far enough. This sense of national destiny will be described in Part One.

One of the primary features of the "great rejuvenation of the Chinese nation" is the expansion of China's geopolitical footprint, a focus on military power and military technology, and a changing strategic geography that is redefining not only Asia, but other regions in the world. This will be covered in Part Two. It is what defense departments around the world are beginning to struggle with every day as a new reality. But this is not a book about Chinese military power alone. It is also about what Chinese leaders and scholars label "comprehensive national power."

The basis for China's rise has been the disciplined and wildly successful focus on economic growth. Part Three describes the nature and origins of that economic reach and rise to technological eminence, linking the strategies that guide its advances in economic growth and in critical technologies. But this book is not primarily focused on the Chinese economy— it is meant to demonstrate how China's splendid new economy is the foundation for something even larger. China already has an economic and trading presence on every continent and in nearly every country on earth. This is a beginning. Its continued rise cannot be sustained within China's borders. It cannot grow through self-sufficiency . China's economic engines run on the energy and natural resources of multiple continents. This is covered in Part Four. The population is fed by the food and agriculture of other nations. Its manufacturers need access to new markets around the world. These are ordinary truths of a globally integrated country, but they are also the basis for something greater. In Part Five, we will cover aspects of China's governance and views of world order.

The Communist Party has declared its intention to build the world's most powerful military, and to become the world's leader in advanced technologies. China's military has officially been tasked with not only national defense, but protection of China's expanding overseas interests. China will build a globally capable military to secure its access to resources and markets in other continents. A global China will be backed by global military power and influence. The objective of China's rise—if the "China Dream" continues—is simple but consequential for the rest of us. Built on economic power, technological mastery, and military supremacy, China will achieve what its official Xinhua News Agency specified explicitly in 2017:

> By 2050, two centuries after the Opium Wars, which plunged the "Middle Kingdom" into a period of hurt and shame, China is set to regain its might and re-ascend to the top of the world.[6]

Note the historical perspective behind this objective, which is vital. Looking forward first, however, this "re-ascendance" will mean the end of an American-led world order, the end of a world order built and sustained by the world's democracies and *rights-based* societies. It will mean a world in which China is de facto the world's leading superpower, capable of extending its military, economic, financial, and ideological influence and power into every place on earth not limited by other nations or by coalitions of nations.

In order to understand and see what China's rise is and what it means, we will consider these core elements:

1. A Vision of National Destiny
2. Strategic Geography and Military Plans
3. Economic and Technological Ambitions
4. Growing Global Reach
5. A Vision of a New World Order

Each Part is meant to bring the reader to a substantial understanding of each element, in order to understand the larger picture— to see and understand the whole elephant.

PART I

中华民族伟大复兴

THE GREAT REJUVENATION OF THE CHINESE NATION

★

CHINA'S VISION OF NATIONAL DESTINY

Between 500 and 2,000 years ago, there was a period of a thousand years when China was supreme in the world. Her status in the world then was similar to that of Great Britain and America today. What was the situation of the weaker nations toward China then? They respected China as their superior and sent annual tribute to China by their own will, regarding it as an honor to be allowed to do so. They wanted of their own free will to be dependencies of China. Those countries which sent tribute to China were not only situated in Asia but in distant Europe as well.

—DR. SUN YAT-SEN, LEADER OF CHINA'S
REVOLUTION IN 1911, KOBE, JAPAN, 1924

We believe that realizing the great rejuvenation of the Chinese nation is the greatest Chinese dream of the Chinese nation in modern times.

—XI JINPING, 2012

THERE IS A GREAT DREAM IN CHINA NOW. THERE IS A GRAND STORY that is being told.

It is a story that most outside the country do not understand, and many haven't heard.

Like most great stories, its essence is very simple: a great nation was laid low. It was devastated by the outside world. It was torn apart by foreigners. Its people were brutalized. Its lands were scorched. Its treasures were stolen.

But that great nation is returning now, and once again it will be the center of the world. It is a story that has been passed down from generation to generation in China, by its leaders, and among its people. What does it mean for all of us? Now that the ending to this story— China becoming the world's great power— *is beginning to become real.*

To start, let us listen to how this story goes.

NATIONAL RESURRECTION

China's national resurrection goes by many names: "The Great Rejuvenation of the Chinese Nation," "Resurrection of the Fatherland," "China Dream," "Road to Renewal," "The New China."

All of these ideas, handed down from leader to leader, shared among China's people, have come as the result of a single period, known as "One Hundred Years of National Humiliation."

A walk around the National Museum on Tiananmen Square in the center of Beijing brings the visitor through a permanent exhibit called the "Road to Rejuvenation." Winding through the museum, we are brought into history as told by the Chinese Communist Party (CCP).

At its beginning, China was a great and powerful nation, the centerpiece of the known world. A place of splendor, progress, and prosperity. In short, a great civilization. But, as the industrial revolution took shape in Europe, China suffered from stagnation, and "the gap between it and the Western powers constantly grew wider." Then came the Opium Wars in 1840. British gunboats cracked open China's hinterland; foreigners invaded. "The imperial powers descended on China like a swarm of bees, looting our treasures and killing our people."[1] And so began one hundred years of decline and plunder at the hands of foreign nations.

As foreign powers worked to gain control of China, "the national crisis and the people's misery constantly deepened," and the Chinese people "pondered the nation's future and the country's fate and searched for a path to salvation."[2] It was at this exhibit that President Xi Jinping gave a famous speech in November 2012, when he called, as prior Chinese leaders have called, for the "great rejuvenation of the Chinese nation."[3] "We just visited the exhibition, 'The Road to Rejuvenation'," he said. "This exhibition reviews the yesterday of the Chinese nation, displays the today of the Chinese nation, and announces the tomorrow of the Chinese nation."

Xi Jinping, a man whose personal story has been worked into legend by an obedient media, is the first Chinese leader to be born after 1949, when the Founding of the People's Republic of China was formally declared by Mao Zedong, and the "Century of Humiliation," in the Party's telling, finally came to an end. Famously sent to the countryside in Shaanxi during the Cultural Revolution, spending years in manual labor, and even living in a cave, Xi has risen to possess power in China said to be unknown since the time of Mao. He stripped away term limits in 2018, to become, at his pleasure, ruler for life.

At the National Museum, Xi declared that, "Since 1840, we have struggled continuously, and have unfolded a brilliant prospect for the great rejuvenation of the Chinese nation. All of us can feel that we are closer to this objective . . . than at any other time in history, and we have more confidence and more ability to realize this objective than at any other time in history."[4]

Speaking for the whole of China, Xi called for the completion of this China Dream—a dream that "has concentrated and endowed the long cherished wish of many generations of Chinese," which "reflects the comprehensive interests of the Chinese nation and the Chinese people," and "is a common expectation of all sons and daughters of China."

As Xi explained in his November 2012 speech at the National Museum: "This nation of ours suffered very gravely after the beginning of the modern era. It made enormous sacrifices, such as have rarely been seen in the history of the world. But because the Chinese people have never surrendered, and incessantly rose with force and spirit to resist, we grasped hold of our own fate in the end. We began the magnificent process of arranging the construction of our own country."

And so, the "China Dream," and the "great rejuvenation of the Chinese nation," became an ambition, a rallying point for a nation of over a billion people, which China's leaders believe can rouse, as Xi himself puts it, "the magnificent national spirit with nationalism at its core."[5] This dream is, in short, China's *Vision of Victory*. It is the vision of 2049—a world in which, one hundred years after the founding of the People's Republic of China, this nation will take its place again at the top of a hierarchy of the world's nations, having borne all burdens, overcome all obstacles, defeated all enemies, and built its power anew so China's place is at last restored.

But Xi's vision is not new. Not at all.

This vision drives a long, continuous, even programmatic series of *plans* that are the heart of the mission of modern China as seen by the Chinese Communist Party. It is the same fundamental vision that each leader has passed to the next since the founding of the People's Republic of China. Though its elements have taken many forms, its essence remains the same. It is the world's great story, and a great ambition, one being told now, and worked upon, by millions upon millions of people, for over one hundred years.

The idea of humiliation and resurrection captured the minds of successive generations, even before the Chinese Communist Party's existence. In fact, the Communist Party did not bring about the first revolution in China. Rather, in 1911, the collapse of the Qing dynasty led to the founding of a republic under the Nationalists (the Guomindang). They sought the restoration of China's power and place among nations after the nightmare of the stagnant, frail Qing dynasty.

The Chinese revolution began decades before the founding of the People's Republic of China (PRC), with roots in the revolutionary yearnings that were shared across Asian lands. Asia at the time was covered in European colonies or under the control of imperial powers. The desire to throw these off and regain sovereignty was widely shared. In China, this generated a unique relationship to the past. Major writers and thinkers saw their Confucian heritage as the cause of their country's decay as a world power and an impediment to national restoration. Political leaders searched for knowledge, technologies, and political systems and theories, from republicanism to Marxism, that could move their country forward. The Republican period predated a Civil War from 1945 to 1949, one that ended in Communist victory, and was a period of upheaval marked by feuding warlords, the ravages of the Second World War, and economic chaos.

What came next was the rise of Mao Zedong, modern China's "world historical individual." A Hunanese intellectual of peasant birth whose youth was spent as a librarian-schoolteacher, Mao found his life's purpose in the cause of China's restoration. As he led the country from 1949 to 1976, his career spanned guerilla warfare, mass propaganda operations, global diplomacy, multiple wars with China's neighbors, and some of the deadliest pogroms and famines in human history. Mao proclaimed in Tiananmen Square on an October day in 1949 that "The Chinese people have stood up!" From this point onward, in the telling of the Communist Party, the "Century of Humiliation" was over.

Over the seven decades since, from Mao through Xi Jinping, Chinese leaders and the Chinese people have worked on a singular project: the restoration of their nation's power and, with it, the ultimate transformation of the world order. Famous as a Communist leader alongside the Soviet Union's Joseph Stalin, Mao saw socialism as the vehicle through which to build his nation. However, as historians have explained, Communism was the banner, but not the purpose of the Chinese Communist revolution:

> Mao's revolution never took as its ultimate goal the Communist seizure of power in China; rather, as the chairman repeatedly made clear, his revolution aimed at transforming China's state, population, and society, and simultaneously reasserting China's central position in the world.[6]

In order to understand the evolution of this program from a movement that began with agrarian land reform, rural pogroms, and guerilla warfare to an expanding global strategy entailing mastery of high technologies, from artificial intelligence and quantum satellites to the use of overseas military bases in geography new to China's history, we must turn to these major leaders, watch them work and plan, and see how they viewed the world and China's role in it from 1949 to the present day.

"THE NEW CHINA"

MAO ZEDONG
(1949-1976)

When the Communist Party took control of China's revolution, founding the People's Republic of China in 1949, it inherited a country burdened by economic collapse and the ravages of total war. Mao set about remaking the revolution in his own image, delivering new grandiosity and lethality to the vision of national restoration. Violence was now at the core, both in practice and in theory. Two famous edicts emerged from Mao's approach: "The revolution is not a dinner party" and "power grows from the barrel of a gun." Cozying up to Stalin's USSR for protection against the United States, the Party began suppression operations around the country in order to consolidate its hold on power. China's massive territory had not been ruled as a whole since the collapse of the Qing in 1911, and Mao would pull the country's imperial borders together once again.

Mao's theory of violence was essential to the Leninist transformation of China, meaning the dominance of a single political party over a nation's people and the use of the population for the objectives of the state. Mao was responsible for a death toll comparable to those of Stalin and Hitler, well into the tens of millions.[7] Mao was also a prolific writer and has left a rich trail of thoughts on his country, helping us understand the shape he gave to the project of China's destiny, and the impact that his vision retains. Let's not forget that Mao is still revered in China, a kind of totalitarian deity. As recently as 2017, a professor was fired for suggesting that he caused the death of millions, and a newscaster was dismissed for calling him a devil online. In the former instance, people came into the streets with signs that said, "Whoever opposes Mao is an enemy of the people"[8] and, in the latter, the act was considered a "serious violation of political discipline" by China's mass media.[9]

Here is a young Mao, writing in 1917 of the need for national strength, decades before his time as the Great Helmsman of China's revolution:

> Our nation is wanting in strength; the military spirit has not been encouraged. The physical condition of our people deteriorates daily. These are extremely disturbing phenomena . . . If our bodies are not strong, we will tremble at the sight of [enemy] soldiers. How then can we attain our goals, or exercise far-reaching influence?[10]

A kind of philosopher-king figure, who came to regard himself as something of a god among men, Mao also wrote about the need for destruction in order to bring about the new world he dreamed of:

> [A] long period of peace, pure peace without any disorder of any kind, would be unbearable to human life . . . [H]uman beings always hate the chaos and hope for order, not realizing that chaos too is part of the process of historical life, that it too has value in real life . . . When they come to periods of peace, they are bored and put the book aside . . . The destruction of the universe is not an ultimate destruction . . . because from the demise of the old universe will come a new universe, and will it not be better than the old universe![11]

Mao, like Xi Jinping, saw the sheer size of its population as his country's greatest strength. Envisioning a "great union of the popular masses," and embracing the Russian Bolshevik model, Mao and his early comrades established as their goal "the transformation of China and the whole world," while embracing a dictatorial line: "If the people are not able to make themselves happy, let's drag them into happiness with an iron hand."[12]

Anyone visiting China has encountered the Chairman's presence, from his giant portrait in Tiananmen Square in the heart of Beijing, to his image on every banknote, and his photographs and books of quotations that still rest in homes in the remotest towns and villages. As many people have said to me, "Without Mao, there would be no modern China." Mao transformed the Chinese revolution but retained its original objectives: the building of China's power and the restoration of China's place among the world's great nations. During the Maoist era, the Communist Party found its voice in a rhetoric of restoration that was new to the revolution: the idea of the "New China."

This old Maoist program is the real foundation of Xi's present-day "China Dream." But Mao's challenge was different. Unlike Xi, whose primary goal is to turn Chinese wealth into Chinese power, Mao aimed to lift the country first from decay and devastation.

Mao characterized national restoration as a set of two choices between an old China and a new one. Under the heading, "We want to build up a New China," the Chairman wrote that the Communist Party would "change a politically oppressed and economically exploited China into a politically free and economically prosperous China,"[13] later writing:

> Two possible destinies await China, a bright destiny and a gloomy destiny . . . Either a China independent, free, democratic, united and prosperous, i.e. a bright China, a new China with her people liberated, or a China semi-colonial, semi-feudal, divided, poor and weak, i.e. an old China. A new China or an old China: these two prospects lie before the Chinese people, the Chinese Communist Party and our Congress.[14]

This vision of the New China was not only part of economic and development programs, it was also present in military operations. Thus, Chinese soldiers entering Tibet in 1950 carried banners proclaiming "Strengthen national defense and build the New China,"[15] and Mao's speeches explained that "advancing the military into Tibet and consolidating national defense is [our] great and glorious mission."[16] Ahead of military operations against India in 1962, the Chinese Foreign Ministry warned their Indian counterparts that "Regardless of anything, the liberated, new China cannot permit itself to be pushed back once again to the position of suffering that was the old China."[17]

Mao's speeches reflected also on his status *not as the founder of but as an heir to* the Chinese revolution:

> For over a century our forefathers never stopped waging un-
> yielding struggles against domestic and foreign oppressors, in-
> cluding the Revolution of 1911 led by Dr. Sun Yat-sen, our
> great forerunner in the Chinese revolution. Our forefathers en-
> joined us to carry out their unfulfilled will. And we have acted
> accordingly.[18]

When the Chairman famously proclaimed in Tiananmen Square that "the Chinese people have stood up," he set the terms as a stand against the outside world and as a reemergence on the international scene:

> The era in which the Chinese people were regarded as uncivi-
> lized is now ended. We shall emerge in the world as a nation
> with an advanced culture. Our national defence will be consol-
> idated and no imperialists will ever again be allowed to invade
> our land . . . Hail the founding of the People's Republic of
> China![19]

From the beginning, China's restoration was aimed not only at trans-forming China from within, but also, as master historian Chen Jian ex-plains, "reasserting China's central position in the world."[20] As Qiang Zhai, another leading historian of the period, explains, Mao's "vision of China's place in the world . . . aimed at transforming not only the old China but also the old world order."[21]

This is the mission China's current leaders have inherited, one they are determined to fulfill.

National restoration was difficult to achieve in the Cold War world. Mao's China was often at odds with other nations, fighting wars against many of its neighbors during his thirty-year reign. In the Korean War from 1950 to 1953, China backed North Korea's Kim Il Sung, fighting a nearly three-year war against the United States, South Korea, and the United Nations on the Korean peninsula, while simultaneously assisting the Vietnamese with their

military operations against the French in Southeast Asia, and sending the
Chinese People's Liberation Army (PLA) into Tibet, destroying a small Tibetan army and taking control of the Himalayan plateau for the first time
in decades.[22] In the latter case, negotiations and military power worked
hand in glove:

> When one of the Tibetans pressed his Chinese negotiator too
> far, he became angry and made the threat explicit: "Are you
> showing your clenched fist to the Communist Party? . . . It is up
> to you to choose whether Tibet would be liberated peacefully or
> by force."[23]

None of these military conflicts were very new, either. While China in
its long history has never sustained military operations outside of continental Asia, it has clashed frequently with its neighbors throughout the centuries, while adding to its territory under successive dynasties. Mao's attempted
transformation of the world order was less about military conquest or external control— China was still an agrarian society fighting for what its
leaders saw as the country's own territories— and more about mounting a
persistent challenge to the leading powers of that time.

At that time, China was an ambitious if impoverished nation, with a
clear sense of where it belonged in world affairs. Mao took on the USSR,
his superpower patron, soon after Stalin's death, vying for influence within
the Communist bloc, frightening his Soviet patrons into withdrawing all of
their nuclear advisors from China after nearly provoking war with the
United States in the Taiwan Straits in 1958, and making light of nuclear
devastation during banquets with his Soviet colleagues.[24] The Sino-Soviet
split was a period of bitter acrimony between the two Communist rivals—
especially notable given China's diminutive national military power in
comparison with the USSR. Nonetheless, Mao's exuberant sense of confidence in China's destiny was evident even then. As he explained to Soviet
Premier Alexei Kosygin in 1965:

> The US and the USSR are now deciding the world's destiny.
> Well, go ahead and decide. But within the next 10–15 years you
> will not be able to decide the world's destiny. It is in the hands

of the nations of the world, and not in the hands of the imperialists, exploiters, or revisionists.[25]

Mao, of course, sought to position his country, and himself, at the head
of these "nations of the world."

Within this ambition, we can see the roots of China's global program
today.

While it may seem true—and it is—that China today is going global on
an unprecedented scale, the Party is often leveraging relationships and diplomatic experience that go back decades to the crucial and visionary period
during the first decades of the People's Republic of China. This period con-
tains some of the most important similarities to and lessons for the present.

Here, within a world dominated by the superpowers, China sought a
third way by marshalling a range of nations that were also emerging from
under the blanket of European empires. China's leaders sought to create a
"new force in world politics to be comprised primarily of the colonial or
newly independent countries of Asia, Africa, and Latin America."[26] In doing
so, they believed they could offer something the superpowers could not, that
is, a common heritage of resistance to colonization. Doing so brought China
first into cooperation and then to war with newly independent India.

The "New China" coexisted poorly with other major states. In addition
to confrontation and war with both superpowers (the United States in
1950, and the USSR in 1969), China's leadership clashed with India— its
rival for power in the developing world. The China–India relationship went
from a high watermark in the 1950s to a degeneration into Himalayan
warfare in 1962. This contest for power continues today in Asia.

In this struggle between Asia's two giants, Chinese leaders sought to
"teach a lesson" to India because of disagreements over Tibet, Asia, Africa,
and even relations with the United States. An independent India was irrec-
oncilable with the ambitions of the "New China," as Beijing's leadership
feared "encirclement," the loss of territory in the Himalayas, and an unfavorable balance of power in Asia. The ethos of violence at the heart of Mao's
revolution also began to work its way into China's approaches to the outside
world, marking a stark contrast between the ideology of the Communist
Party and a different approach to power and politics taken by India's founders. The Chinese Foreign Ministry railed against, for example, Indian

"propagation of nonviolence and passive resistance" in the decolonizing world, and Indian Prime Minister Nehru's promotion of Gandhian ideals, "saying that the African people can through 'passive resistance, overthrow colonialism without spilling a drop of blood'."[27] There could be no alternative to China's ideological model. Any struggle that threatened Chinese ideology and interests was especially grave if the other power had influence in the developing world.

It emerged that Mao was promoting a kind of political-military grand strategy against both superpowers in his meetings with decolonizing nations. He envisioned a kind of global military front, directed against the United States and Western (still colonial) powers. As he explained to an Algerian delegation in the early 1960s: "We should support you because you are struggling against imperialism. It is the same as our struggle. This is our international mission. Algeria's contribution to the whole world is very big—you can pin down 800,000 French troops."[28]

A year later, he told a Vietnamese delegation: "You are Southeast Asia's front line. We are paying close attention to your situation and to the situation in Laos. You have already grabbed one of America's fingers . . . If the [war in South Vietnam] goes on for five to ten more years, the U.S. will think it is not worth it."[29]

It would be a mistake to consider the wars of the Cold War as relics of an entirely different era.

Mao's China was developing a sense of itself in a new international system, punching above its weight by confronting the major powers of the day, playing games of brinkmanship with both superpowers, all buoyed by a belief that the country would soon find its place among the world's great nations. From the contemporary Chinese Communist Party point of view, the Cold War was a geopolitical backdrop to the first decades in China's restoration, a restoration which would require then, as it does now, a transformation not only of China, but the world around it. As Qiang Zhai explains, "Just as the old international order had helped cause China's suffering and humiliation, so too would the creation of a new order contribute to the rebirth of a strong and prosperous China."[30]

While Mao's time frame was off substantially—he envisioned a Chinese ascendancy that would take place within his lifetime, one boosted by his catastrophic Communist programs—China's appetite for external operations was enormous during the founding decades. The country's role on the world stage was active, and the objective was much the same as it is today— build prosperity and power, thus transforming both the country and the world. What came after Mao was much more subdued— lessons had been learned under this dangerous, damaging, bold, and charismatic leader. By the end of Mao's tenure, China had slipped into the mass violence of the Cultural Revolution, switched sides in the Cold War from the USSR to the United States, and suffered numerous purges of senior leaders and original members of the revolutionary movement. Its leaders eventually decided that a shift away from Maoist absolute power was necessary and that checks and balances must be imposed. These checks and balances largely endured — until their removal by Xi Jinping in 2018.

Pure socialism gave way to reforms which at last transformed the Chinese economy, and the geopolitics of global confrontation gave way to the mantra "Hide your brightness, bide your time." The strategy remained the buildup of wealth and power. But for several decades, the country would play a quiet role, working on its own development and biding its time until China's moment arrived.

"HIDE YOUR BRIGHTNESS, BIDE YOUR TIME"

DENG XIAOPING AND JIANG ZEMIN
(1978–2002)[31]

Deng Xiaoping is known as China's great reformer.

On the face of it, he was Mao's opposite. The "Great Helmsman" had barely left the country, traveling abroad only twice in his lifetime, both times to Moscow, on long train journeys where he devoured classics of Chinese history and literature to glean lessons for his own statecraft. Deng was a far more cosmopolitan Bolshevik (his early political affiliation). He opted for a steamship passage to Marseilles as a 16-year-old, working in the French Communist underground, escaping to the Soviet Union, and attending classes at Moscow's Sun Yat-sen University, before turning to more conventional pursuits, such as establishing rural bases for guerilla warfare in China's war with the Empire of Japan.[32]

Deng's years abroad showed him possibilities that Mao had likely never seen. Later in life, as ruler of China, he pulled the country back from Maoist devastation and began the "economic miracle" that gave China over thirty years of growth, learning from a wide range of other nations:

> He would open the country wide to science, technology, and management systems, and to new ideas from anywhere in the world, regardless of the country's political system. He was aware that the new dynamos of Asia— Japan, South Korea, Taiwan, Hong Kong, and Singapore— were growing faster than any countries ever had.[33]

But Deng was also responsible for iron-fisted cruelties which are well known to the world, particularly the violent suppression of the Tiananmen

Square Uprising in 1989, made famous by a photo of the lone, defiant figure standing with his shopping bags in front of a row of PLA tanks. On Deng's orders, the crowds of young people who had gathered in Tiananmen — petitioning China's leaders for democracy and civil liberties, while raising a giant, handmade Statue of Liberty-like "Goddess of Democracy" — were gunned down by the thousands. As two biographers explain: "Unlike Gorbachev in the Soviet Union, Deng was unable to overcome entirely his totalitarian worldview. He was called on to be the reformer of Chinese socialism, not its gravedigger."[34]

After enduring the trials of the Cultural Revolution, during which he was purged, and his son became paralyzed after leaping from a window to escape Mao's Red Guards,[35] Deng returned to power after Mao's death. He opened up the country and, throughout his rule, he prioritized a foreign policy of nonconfrontation. Deng chose cooperation with the United States and Japan, and integration with global markets, forging a path for fantastic economic growth within the shadows of a waning Cold War world.

Above all, Deng's mission, like those who came before him, was to build China's wealth and power. However, where Mao had brought horrors, Deng moved mountains: "in 1978, China's trade with the world totaled less than $10 billion; within three decades, it had expanded a hundredfold."[36]

To accompany growth and development, Deng did away with the bellicosity of the Maoist era. In a 1982 speech titled "China's Foreign Policy," he stated:

> Some people have alleged that China is bellicose, but in fact China hopes for peace more than anything else. China hopes that there will be no war for the rest of the century. We need to develop the country and shake off backwardness. The primary task we have set as the initial goal for the realization is to create comparative prosperity by the end of this century. If we can accomplish this goal, we will be in a much better position. More importantly, we shall achieve a new starting point.[37]

Deng's vision was modest, inclusive, and nonconfrontational. Unlike Mao, or the current leadership under Xi Jinping, Deng deliberately framed

China's aspirations in a second-tier category, insisting that "Within the ensuing 30 to 50 years, we shall approach the level of developed countries. We do not mean to catch up with, still less do we say to surpass, but only approach the level of developed countries."[38]

This plan was predicated on quiet times in global politics:

> Therefore, we cherish the hope for a peaceful international environment. Should war break out, our plan would be thwarted, and in that case we could not but postpone the plan. During the period up to the end of the century and extending decades into the future, we hope that there will be peace. Our proposals for safeguarding world peace are by no means empty talk, but instead are based on our own needs.[39]

And his total focus on economics was inarguable: "The Chinese people are wholeheartedly concentrating on economic development. Our foreign policy coincides with this magnificent goal. Although this objective may seem modest to some people, we hail it as a magnificent achievement."[40]

Deng's China and its achievements created the China that readers are most familiar with. His reforms brought forth the economic miracle, resulting in the China of "Markets over Mao" and "One Billion Customers," the China of mass manufacturing and global supply chains, the rise of the container ship, and the new globalization at the turn of the twenty-first century.

This is the China that Deng Xiaoping enabled.

However, at the core of these activities, and this total transformation, were long-term goals that would prove to be of extraordinary geopolitical importance.

Deng and his colleagues were careful to downplay the geopolitical consequences of China's economic rise. And few from abroad who participated in the building of China— as Deng himself explained it, China's growth required the investment and participation of those from many nations— anticipated the country growing to the proportions it has now reached.[41]

During Deng's rule, and that of his successor Jiang Zemin, the United States was engaged in bringing about a Cold War victory and building a new postwar world built upon free markets and global institutions. This involved the integration of former Communist states, which the US sought

groups, as well as foreign support for Taiwan, were presented as "efforts to keep China down."[48] "Open up and Reform" sat uneasily with a central tension in the nation's restoration— the need to build a nationalist narrative that continued to set China against foreign powers.

Incidents ranging from the bombing of the Chinese embassy in Belgrade during the Clinton administration's Kosovo campaign in 1999, to the midair collision of a US Navy EP-3 and a PLAN interceptor in 2001 over the South China Sea, sent regular Chinese people into the streets, torching symbols of US–China economic integration. Looters burned McDonald's and Kentucky Fried Chicken franchises around the country, and the Party managed public outrage. In the process, China's sense of destiny and self began to acquire an increasingly anti-American edge, driven in part by state propaganda. The days of the Statue of Liberty-like "Goddess of Democracy" being raised in Tiananmen Square were gone, and, ironically, the more prosperous China became, the more outside countries became targets of a new nationalism.[49]

A new compact emerged between the Communist Party and the Chinese people as China's wealth and power grew. Now the Party's promise was not ideological but economic. If the CCP delivered growth, the people should follow. There were moments of insecurity for the Party elite, something exemplified by the persecution of the Falun Gong, a spiritual group with tens of millions of members that Jiang Zemin believed threatened Communist Party rule. But consolidation of the new social compact between the leaders, the Party, and the people was a guiding priority. Deng and Jiang's period of peace was essential— both inside and outside the country. Despite new economic reforms, Communist Party suppression operations continued, especially in the western provinces— Xinjiang and Tibet— and among political dissidents of all kinds. A now notorious organ-harvesting trade began, where the organs of executed prisoners were sold on the international market. The Party's hold on power during this chapter of China's restoration proved to be secure.

1.4

"THE PERIOD
OF
STRATEGIC OPPORTUNITY"

HU JINTAO
(2002-2012)

The best examples of continuity in China's revolution occurred between the Deng, Jiang, and Hu eras, spanning 1978 to 2012. In this thirty-year period, China consolidated its economic miracle while Deng's mantra "Hide your brightness and bide your time" remained the principle when it came to Chinese power. The nonconfrontational language of the Deng period continued, coupled with a quiet focus on modernizing China's military.

Party leaders also identified a "period of strategic opportunity" from 2000 to 2020, when China's "comprehensive national power" could grow, and the country could work, unimpeded, on the buildup of its economic and military position. A Chinese government think tank defines this "period of strategic opportunity" as "the duration of time during which the comprehensive national strength, international competitiveness and influence of a country are expected to rise consistently."[50]

The country consolidated its borders and emerged on the world stage under Mao Zedong. It began an economic transformation under Deng Xiaoping. This provided a platform for thinking bigger than ever before.

Chinese leaders began to speak publicly of the "two centenaries," giving birth to the idea of "the great rejuvenation of the Chinese nation" by the year 2049. In 1997, at the 15th National Congress, an event which takes place every five years, China's leaders put forward these two dates, which would be used to mark the Party's long-term progress. The first centenary, in 2021, the hundredth anniversary of the founding of the Chinese Communist Party, would be the time by which China's "national economy will be more developed."[51] The second, in 2049, the hundredth anniversary of the founding of the People's Republic of China, would be when "the modernization program will have been accomplished by and large."[52]

Jiang's address in 1997 walked his Party and his nation through the milestones on what we can see was already a "road to rejuvenation." He did so, like all Chinese leaders, by returning first to the history of "national humiliation":

> After the Opium War of 1840, China was reduced to a semi-colonial and semi-feudal country. The Chinese nation was faced with two great historical tasks: to win national independence and the people's liberation, and to make the country prosperous and strong and achieve common prosperity for the people.[53]

Jiang credited not just Mao and Deng, but also Sun Yat-sen, the leader of the first Chinese revolution in 1911, for their work on restoring China's greatness, even invoking the concept of the "old China":

> The past century has witnessed the Chinese people undergoing three historic changes on their road of advancement and the birth of Sun Yat-sen, Mao Zedong and Deng Xiaoping, three great men who stood at the forefront of the times.
>
> The first change was represented by the Revolution of 1911, which overthrew the autocratic monarchy reigning in China for thousands of years. It was led by Dr. Sun Yat-sen. He was the first man who raised the slogan of "rejuvenating China" and pioneered the national and democratic revolution in the true sense in modern times. The Revolution of 1911 failed to change the social nature of old China and free the people from their hard lot, but it opened the sluice-gates for progress in China and made it impossible for the reactionary rule to remain stable any longer.[54]

While Jiang continued to adhere to the mantras of peace, he also made clear that military modernization would be a priority:

In order to adapt itself to the profound changes in the military arena in the world, the army should intensify its education and training, and upgrade its defense capabilities under modern technology and especially high-tech conditions . . . We should strengthen the army by relying on science and technology, put more efforts in the research in defense-related science and technology.[55]

By the time Hu Jintao took power in 2002, the rise of China had become a hybrid economic and military rise, while quietly expanding into different regions of the globe through diplomacy and increased trade. With a new emphasis on military power, the revolution began to rediscover its original purpose.

Hu Jintao was a technocrat, an engineer trained at one of Beijing's finest universities, and a former Party Secretary in Tibet who oversaw the deployment of PLA divisions for suppression operations in Lhasa in 1989.[56] His fundamental job was to pull together economics and military power, and to set the stage for China's transition to global power.

Though Hu coined the slogan "The Peaceful Rise of China," he expressed a clear geopolitical vision in other forums that is not so well known to the world: an inevitable decline in China's relations with the "global hegemonist," the United States.

In a "secret speech" in 1994, he explained that:

The whole Party and the whole army should make full preparations and should be more profoundly aware that Sino–U.S. relations will not be in a normal state in the near future, in the next few years, and even for a longer period to come, and further worsening and confrontations may occur.

According to the global hegemonist strategy of the United States, its main rival at present is the PRC. Interfering in China, subverting the Chinese Government, and strangling China's development are strategic principles pursued by the United States. While facing hegemonism, power politics and the aggressive anti-China strategy pursued by the United States, we have no room for any choices.[57]

Since the end of the Cold War, China's leaders had been focused on the collapse of the USSR. Party leaders wondered how China would avoid this fate as Communist regimes collapsed one after another. In the Hu Jintao era, however, new confidence emerged.

In 2006, a twelve-part documentary series aired on China Central Television called "The Rise of the Great Powers." The series brought together the rise of major nations and empires, from Britain, France, Germany, Japan, Russia, to the United States, through interviews with historians around the world. It was broadcast during prime-time in the Chinese language for two weeks straight. The series took in the lessons of national power, from military mastery of the world's oceans, to scientific research, to the importance of innovation. The origins of the series were in a lecture to the members of China's highest ruling body, the Politburo, on the history of the great powers since the sixteenth century.[58]

In the 2000s, the question became not "how would the Party avoid collapse," but "how would it manage China's ascendancy?"

As trade relations and diplomatic power expanded, a slogan emerged for the outside world: "The Peaceful Rise of China." It was essential to present the country in a nonconfrontational light.

However, the leadership continued to manage the period of strategic opportunity for building up national power. Hu Jintao added "New Historic Missions" for the PLA in 2004. These new missions included "providing powerful strategic support for safeguarding national interests." In other words, China's military would prepare to support the expansion of economic power.

Growth rates held up throughout the Hu Jintao years, and national GDP kept expanding. Discussion began not only in Beijing and Washington, but around the globe of a "multipolar world."[59] While military budgets continued to rise, and territorial disputes with other nations remained, Party leaders largely stuck to a rhetoric of modesty, prosperity, modernity, and a nonconfrontational role in world or regional affairs. The national conversation, as this author experienced it, was largely about modernization versus lagging behind. Migrant workers filled cities at breakneck speed, and Hu Jintao famously told George W. Bush that what kept him awake at night most was the need for job creation. US strategy toward China remained "engage but hedge," as the country's growth and trade were deemed good for the US economy and the American consumer—a welcome relief, as the US spent blood and treasure on two wars—simultaneously—in the Middle East and Central Asia.

China hands in the West wrote much about the country's existential stresses, and the coming pressure for democracy and human rights as the middle class surged. Businesses did their best to enter the country's growing markets. Global supply chains increasingly featured Chinese manufacturing and labor, and China's leaders continued to speak of stability, prosperity, and harmony. In retrospect, this seems sincere. China required the stability of the global community in order to maintain its growth, job creation, and internal stability. The "period of strategic opportunity" proved vital to the "great rejuvenation," though few outside China foresaw its consequences.

Challenging the United States was premature, even if the PRC's founders had envisioned this. However, China's global interests began to emerge. Economic growth created a hunger for raw materials from around the planet. Growth began to drive interlocking commodity and industry cycles, especially in mining, energy, and shipping, as the country's economic contributions to the world were still largely in the refining and creation of inexpensive goods. Additionally, the country rapidly created its own industrial and civilian infrastructure; an industrial revolution at warp speed.

Assessing China's situation at the end of his ten-year term in 2012, Hu saw a country whose power had grown markedly:

> China's economy has risen from the sixth to the second place in the world. The country has undergone new historic changes: Its productive forces and economic, scientific and technological strength have increased considerably, the people's living standards, individual income and social security have improved significantly, and its overall national strength and international competitiveness and influence have been enhanced substantially.[60]

During the Hu era, from 2002 to 2012, substantial changes took place, both in capabilities and confidence, and questions about China's relations with the outside world were asked by many as the country's power grew. The outside world asked good questions. Replace with "As American political scientist Susan Shirk put it in her well-known book, *China: Fragile Super-power*. Was China, a nation of over a billion people and a history of unrest, a superpower or a fragile nation? Dr. Shirk highlighted the difference between Chinese and American responses to her work: In America, people asked, "What do you mean, 'fragile?'" In China, people asked, "What do you mean, 'superpower'? No one questions 'fragile.'"[61] However, from the Beijing Olympics, to the development and testing of new military capabilities that would reshape the Asia-Pacific region, to the Great Financial Crisis that rocked America and the world in 2008, a view was beginning to emerge inside the country: China was ascending, and the United States was in decline.

As the Chinese leadership saw it, however, it was not a rise, but a restoration. The question became: When would China's leaders begin to speak of this restoration of power openly?

"THE CHINA DREAM"

XI JINPING

n 2014 and 2015, a turning point began taking shape in the South
China Sea.

The main events came in the form of an oil rig deployment in Vietnamese waters, and the commencement of island-building—dredging
up sand to build permanent installations which soon proved to be for military purposes—on a series of reefs and islets in the Spratly and Paracel Islands. Note that, while the island-building was new, China's claims were
old. Utilizing maps that predated the PRC, and which diplomats and propaganda organs claimed had a basis in ancient history, China's claims of
nearly the entire South China Sea began to feature as a major piece of
military activity and diplomacy. The country issued new passports and
maps, with the "nine-dash line" or the "cow's tongue" as Chinese territory,
a set of claim lines which stretch across nearly the whole of this body of
water vital to global trade. Between 3 and 5 trillion dollars in trade annually
passes through this sea off China's southern coast—a waterway connecting
the economies of Europe, Africa, Asia, and the United States. In Xi Jinping's first years in office, China chose to work toward control of all of it.

If China's revolution had a Mount Rushmore, with its major leaders
engraved in stone, it would elevate Sun Yat-sen, Mao Zedong, and Deng
Xiaoping, for certain. Jiang Zemin called them China's "three great men."
For Xi Jinping, the mission is simple: gain his place in that grand lineage.
That is likely what motivates him and drives his ambitions for China—to
become the fourth great man of China's revolution by raising his nation to
global power. This will be the next cornerstone on the great rejuvenation of
the Chinese nation, and the next milestone on the road to 2049.

From Deng to Hu Jintao, though Communist Party leadership spoke
frequently of the mission of rejuvenation, the country walked a careful line

between building its capabilities and hiding any appearance of hostility to the current world order.

Under Xi Jinping, all of this has changed.

China's national conversation has changed. China's military priorities have evolved in the open. New economic strategies and the plan for a global footprint have all come to light.

New suppression tactics inside China have emerged with advances in technology. And China's relations with the outside world have begun to change as well.

However, it must be said that many things remain fundamentally the same. The story here is not about China's military rise, or Xi's return to the Mao era, but of the great continuities in worldview between each Politburo, and, even more importantly, of the great continuities between each Politburo and a deeper aspiration to restore, as Chen Jian put it, China's "central position in the world." And this worldview is shared by many in China's population.

It is the real meaning of China's rise that concerns us. Not the rise of China's economic weight, or strengthening of its military power. It is this continuous ambition for revolution and restoration at its core. It is the revolution of returning China to preeminence that is envisioned. And right now the world is doing little about it. China steps into gaps in power and stability in the world, and builds its economic, military, and ideological influence in ways that others have done little to counter. This is what it means for history to witness a rising power. And we are seeing it now.

That this power should have such a clear and visible sense of self is beneficial to our understanding of what is at stake. And no Chinese leader since Mao Zedong— impotent in many ways, given China's lack of real power in his time— has articulated this vision with such clarity and confidence as Xi Jinping. What is perhaps most troubling about Xi's ambitions— as one gets deeper into their purpose— is how the Chinese public has come to embrace this sense of destiny. The caution and in many ways the gracefulness of mild-mannered Hu and his predecessors have been set aside by Xi. Now is a time for expansion of national interests, and, in Xi's words, for being able "to fight and win wars."[62]

This is not a departure. It is simply that China that has realized, at long last, its opportunity for preeminence. Xi envisions the completion of a rise that began long before he started his path to power. This is a return to the founding principles of modern China.

As he put it himself in 2012, "All of us can feel that we are closer to this objective of the great rejuvenation of the Chinese nation than at any other time in history, and we have more confidence and more ability to realize this objective than at any time in history."[63]

1.6

THE "NEW CHINA"
MEETS THE
"CHINA DREAM"

Never forget why you started, and you can accomplish
your mission. The original aspiration of Chinese
Communists is to seek happiness for the Chinese people
and rejuvenation for the Chinese nation.[64]

XI JINPING
19th Party Congress, October 2017

Xi Jinping ties his mission to China's "original aspiration." Here, the "New China" and the "China Dream" combine. It is Mao's mission of restoration that Xi intends to complete. Xi aims to add national power to Deng, Jiang, and Hu's contributions of building national wealth.

Mao's proclamation "The Chinese people have stood up" is clearly echoed in Xi's speech: "The Chinese nation, which since modern times began had endured so much for so long, has achieved a tremendous transformation: it has stood up, grown rich, and is becoming strong; it has come to embrace the brilliant prospects of rejuvenation."[65]

There should be little illusion now about what China under the CCP wishes to achieve. As Xi explains, China has "endured so much for so long." This is a sense of history and national purpose which in modern times until now was essentially a form of misery. Only by national rejuvenation, by the growth of wealth and power, can China's role in the world be complete. It is not a rise but a return of China to the center of the world.

Xi explains that in this "new era," China will move "closer to center stage."[66] In other words, the civilizational concept of the 中国, "Middle

Kingdom," or "Central Kingdom," the geographical and political center of the world, will be restored in today's global politics. Not simply China as a nation state, but China at the center of a world system. What does that mean?

In practical terms, the goal is both economic and military. As Xi explains, "China's overall productive forces have significantly improved and in many areas our production leads the world." Moreover, the Chinese Dream requires the "the Chinese dream of a strong army." And, the closer that China gets to realizing its rejuvenation, the stronger its military must become: "Today," he insisted, "we are closer to the goal of the great rejuvenation of the Chinese nation than any other time in history, and we need to build a strong people's military more than any other time in history."[67]

In short, it is the building up of the things on which a nation's power consists, such that China can become, in many of our lifetimes, a global power, "second to none."

Consider this excerpt from Xi Jinping at his Work Report in the 19th Party Congress in November, 2017. It might be one of the most important statements from a Chinese leader in the past twenty years:

> Rooted in a land of more than 9.6 million square kilometers, nourished by a nation's culture of more than 5,000 years, and backed by the invincible force of more than 1.3 billion people, we have an infinitely vast stage of our era, a historical heritage of unmatched depth, and incomparable resolve that enable us to forge ahead...[68]

It is China's "invincible force of more than 1.3 billion people" that will lead to its unlimited potential on the "infinitely vast stage" that is the world. And all of this is tied to the "dreams" of economic and military mastery, the building blocks of the nation's potential.

Xi Jinping's narrative of China's national destiny at the 19th Party Congress deserves to be read in full. As China builds up its economic and military power, as the country begins to see an open road to preeminence, here is the full narrative that the Chinese people are given, in myriad forms, every day in China. This is, in short, the official narrative. And, should China's leaders succeed, it may become, with no exaggeration, the official story of the history of the modern world:

With a history of more than 5,000 years, our nation created a splendid civilization, made remarkable contributions to mankind, and became one of the world's great nations. But with the Opium War of 1840, China was plunged into the darkness of domestic turmoil and foreign aggression; its people, ravaged by war, saw their homeland torn apart and lived in poverty and despair. With tenacity and heroism, countless dedicated patriots fought, pressed ahead against the odds, and tried every possible means to seek the nation's salvation. But despite their efforts, they were powerless to change the nature of society in old China and the plight of the Chinese people.

National rejuvenation has been the greatest dream of the Chinese people since modern times began. At its founding, the Communist Party of China made realizing Communism its highest ideal and its ultimate goal, and shouldered the historic mission of national rejuvenation. In pursuing this goal, the Party has united the Chinese people and led them through arduous struggles to epic accomplishments.

Our Party was deeply aware that, to achieve national rejuvenation, it was critical to topple the three mountains of imperialism, feudalism, and bureaucrat-capitalism that were oppressing the Chinese people, and realize China's independence, the people's liberation, national reunification, and social stability. Our Party united the people and led them in embarking on the right revolutionary path, using rural areas to encircle the cities and seizing state power with military force. We completed the New Democratic Revolution through 28 years of painful struggle, and founded the People's Republic of China in 1949, thus marking China's great transition from a millennia-old feudal autocracy to a people's democracy.

Our Party was deeply aware that, to achieve national rejuvenation, it was essential to establish an advanced social system that fits China's reality. It united the people and led them in completing socialist revolution, establishing socialism as China's basic system, and advancing socialist construction. This completed the broadest and most profound social transformation in the history of the Chinese nation. It created the fundamental political conditions and the institutional foundation for achieving all development and progress in China today. Thus was made a great transition: The Chinese nation reversed its fate from the continuous decline of modern times to steady progress toward prosperity and strength.

Our Party was deeply aware that, to achieve national rejuvenation, it was imperative to follow the tide of the times, respond to the wishes of the people, and have the courage to reform and open; and this awareness created a powerful force for advancing the cause of the Party and the people. Our Party united the people and led them in launching the great new revolution of reform and opening up, in removing all ideological and institutional barriers to our country and nation's development, and in embarking on the path of socialism with Chinese characteristics. Thus was China able to stride ahead to catch up with the times.

Over the past 96 years, to accomplish the historic mission of national rejuvenation, whether in times of weakness or strength, whether in times of adversity or smooth sailing, our Party has never forgotten its founding mission, nor wavered in its pursuit. It has united the people and led them in conquering countless challenges, making enormous sacrifices, meeting setbacks squarely, and courageously righting wrongs. Thus we have, time and again, overcome the seemingly insurmountable and created miracle upon miracle.

Comrades, today, we are closer, more confident, and more capable than ever before of making the goal of national rejuvenation a reality.[69]

The Party's view remains the same as it was in Mao's day. When Xi mentions the toppling of "the three mountains of imperialism, feudalism, and bureaucrat-capitalism," he draws directly from the struggles not only of Mao and the Communist Party, but from the entire May 4 Movement, which was when Chinese citizens began to call for an end to their "humiliations" and for the restoration of China's national power. This movement was born out of protests over the 1919 Treaty of Versailles, after the First World War, and in which the requests of China's government were trampled on, despite its contributions to the winning side.

From these ashes, Xi Jinping, in keeping with the chain of leadership since Mao Zedong, promises to bring greatness to China, and in no uncertain terms. "This great struggle," he said, "great project, great cause, and great dream are closely connected, flow seamlessly into each other, and are mutually reinforcing. Among them, the great new project of Party building plays the decisive role."[70]

The greatness of China and the power of the Party are thus one and the same: "As history has shown and will continue to bear witness to, without the leadership of the Communist Party of China, national rejuvenation would be just wishful thinking." Therefore, if the Chinese people wish to have this sacred resurrection, it is Xi and his Party that must hold power, for the resurrection and the Party are the same. This was Mao's vision, and Deng's, and that of every Chinese leader until Xi. But the difference between the other three and the leadership of today is what China may be able to accomplish in this century, and what it means for the world not to simply have a rise of China within a generally stable system of nation states, but to have a total transformation of this system as economic and military power accrue to a nation which has such a clear sense of self and destiny, of past wrongs inflicted upon it and its future glory, and which plans to attempt, if Xi's vision is to be realized, "to accomplish the historic mission of national rejuvenation."[71]

The "historic mission" is not a matter of ideology and identity alone. It will carry real and practical consequences for the world. As Xi explains, "Achieving national rejuvenation will be no walk in the park; it will take more than drum beating and gong clanging to get there."[72] Or as Chairman Mao put it: "A revolution is not a dinner party."

Mao's full quotation is yet more ominous: "A revolution is not a dinner party, or writing an essay, or painting a picture, or doing embroidery; it cannot be so refined, so leisurely and gentle, so temperate, kind, courteous, restrained and magnanimous. A revolution is an insurrection, an act of violence by which one class overthrows another."[73]

Time will tell what this next leg of the Chinese revolution will bring. But Xi clearly sees a goal in sight: "Today, we are closer, more confident, and more capable than ever before of making the goal of national rejuvenation a reality. As the Chinese saying goes, the last leg of a journey marks the halfway point."[74]

What Mao began, Xi intends to finish.

I.7

FROM
"THE PEACEFUL RISE OF CHINA"
TO
"FIGHTING THE BLOODY BATTLE
AGAINST OUR ENEMIES"

The Chinese people have been indomitable and persistent,
we have the spirit of fighting the bloody battle against our
enemies to the bitter end.[75]

XI JINPING
March 2018

Let us work together to create a mighty force for realizing the
Chinese dream and the dream of building a powerful military.[76]

XI JINPING
November 2017

When China's leaders set an agenda, it becomes the story of the nation.

From the propaganda organs at home and abroad, from the blogosphere to the *hutong* alleyways where citizens gather over tea or beers, from the newspaper pages to the nightly news, to the taxi cabs and the street, the agenda of the leaders becomes the stuff of national conversation.

China's commentariat has seized on the themes of national rejuvenation and military prowess. A new narrative is emerging of a country with an excellent military, walking a peaceful path thus far, but ready for war if it should come.

Here are some excerpts from the *China Daily* in August 2017:

Excellence of weaponry is no longer a big issue for the PLA. Thanks to decades of strenuous efforts and supported by the robust Chinese economy, the Chinese defense industry has cleared the technological bottleneck and the arms embargo of the West to produce some of the most advanced weapons in the world.

No one can deny that China's rise has been peaceful. And China has reason to maintain and even extend the period of strategic opportunity well beyond 2020, as it aims to realize the great rejuvenation of the Chinese nation by 2049 when the People's Republic of China celebrates its centenary. If China can rise smoothly to the top of the world without firing a single bullet, it will certainly be able to claim the moral high ground.

This may sound harsh, but the truth is that peace is not a godsend. It often has to be earned, sometimes at the cost of war.[77]

On the planning side, Xi has laid out three goals for military modernization. By the year 2020, mechanization will be "basically achieved." By 2035, "modernization of our national defense and our forces will be basically completed," and, most importantly, "by the mid-21ˢᵗ century our people's armed forces [will] have been fully transformed into world-class forces."[78]

The Chinese-language original has generated controversy: Does this mean a military that will surpass or rival that of the United States? In Chinese, *shijie yiliu jundui* (世界一流军队) means a military that is first-rate, top tier, world class, or essentially second to none.

But for what? To challenge the United States? Or China's neighbors? Or to fight new wars in this century as China's leaders did throughout the last one?

J. Stapleton Roy, Founding Director Emeritus of the Kissinger Institute for China and the United States, and former US Ambassador to China, asked a worthy question on November 3, 2017 at the Wilson Center in Washington DC. China doesn't have a global alliance system or global military commitments like the United States, so why, he asked, are China's leaders so focused on military modernization and buildup?[79]

Ren Guoqiang, the Chinese military's spokesman, offered this response when asked, "Is China building a first-class military in order to surpass the US military?"[80]

> The report from the 19th National Congress clearly stated that China will unflinchingly walk the path of peaceful development, pursue a national defense policy that is defensive in nature, and uphold a common, comprehensive, cooperative, and sustainable security concept. Just as in the past [China] will strengthen military exchanges and cooperation with other countries, jointly respond to global security challenges, and make great efforts to actively contribute toward the establishment of a community of common destiny for mankind.[81]

China's military buildup is generally explained in this way: as a contribution to world peace and human progress. Except when it is not. The subversion, appropriation, and manipulation of concepts, speech, and slogans by the Chinese Communist Party should be no surprise. While economic prosperity confuses our ability to understand "Communism," propaganda is one of the core competencies of a Communist or Leninist state, even in today's global system.

Xi himself took on the subject of world peace at the National Party Congress in November 2017, setting the stage for the next five years of CCP rule.

An economic and military rise of China—what does this mean for the rest of us?

> The Communist Party of China strives for both the well-being of the Chinese people and human progress. To make new and greater contributions for mankind is our Party's abiding mission.
>
> China will continue to hold high the banner of peace, development, cooperation, and mutual benefit and uphold its fundamental foreign policy goal of preserving world peace and promoting common development. China remains firm in its commitment to strengthening friendship and cooperation with other countries on the basis of the Five Principles of Peaceful

Coexistence, and to forging a new form of international relations featuring mutual respect, fairness, justice, and win-win cooperation . . .

China remains firm in pursuing an independent foreign policy of peace . . .

China will never pursue development at the expense of others' interests, but nor will China ever give up its legitimate rights and interests. No one should expect us to swallow anything that undermines our interests. China pursues a national defense policy that is in nature defensive. China's development does not pose a threat to any other country. No matter what stage of development it reaches, China will never seek hegemony or engage in expansion.[82]

How does one reconcile this growing military power with the profession of peaceful intentions? While Xi professes "commitment to strengthening friendship and cooperation with other countries," the realities of China's international relations are quite different. Take note of the commentary in the *China Daily*: "No one can deny that China's rise has been peaceful." This comes as China engages in massive military buildup, and regular parades with rows of goose-stepping soldiers and nuclear weapons on display, as well as active threats to nearly all of China's neighbors, from India and Japan to each and every Southeast Asian nation. Those are just the facts. However, in the Party view of history, militarism is part of this great rejuvenation. And China's "legitimate rights and interests" are sacrosanct, to be defended through the use of force. It is up to other countries to accede to this, not for China to bend its own behavior.

This sentiment is at the ideological heart of China's rise. It is not only a new horizon that the country aspires to, but a sense of what was taken from China, and what must be taken back.

1.8

FROM
"THE PEACEFUL RISE OF CHINA"
TO
"ABLE TO FIGHT AND WIN WARS"

All must be done with the ultimate goal of improving
battle command capacities and measured by the
standards of being able to fight and win wars.[83]
XI JINPING
2017

Regardless of anything, the liberated, new China cannot
permit itself to be pushed back once again to the
position of suffering that was the old China.[84]
CHINESE FOREIGN MINISTRY
1962

China's sense of self is defensive. As far as the Party and its adherents are concerned, it is their right to return to preeminence in the world. Whatever gets in the way of this goes against "legitimate rights and interests" and stands in the way of the great rejuvenation. The country will build up its "comprehensive national power," meaning economic, military, diplomatic, and ideological capabilities, in order to ensure that its rise is not resisted. That's the proposition in a nutshell.

Xi Jinping credits Hu Jintao for "valuable experience" in "building our national defense and armed forces," advocating that China "continue to implement his policies and strategic decisions."[85] Under Xi, however, consolidation of the armed forces has taken a new direction, and an emphasis on new missions has arisen: "The whole of the armed forces must have an in-depth understanding of the important role it has in the broad picture of China's national security and development strategies. It must put national sovereignty and security before any other consideration."[86]

It is essential to understand Xi's emphasis on military readiness, "being action ready," and building "real combat capacity" in the service of national sovereignty goals. All of this is tied to the "China Dream":

> We will enhance our combat readiness through full-scale combat simulation exercises, and reinforce the belief that as soldiers our mission is to fight, and as officers our mission is to lead our men to victory . . . The armed forces must be capable of winning regional engagements in the information age. We must follow to the letter such military practices as strictly observing discipline, executing every order and acting in unison.
>
> Achieving the great renewal of the Chinese nation has become the dream of the Chinese people in modern times. This great dream we have is to make our country strong. To achieve these aims we must strive both to enrich the country and build a strong national defense and powerful military.[87]

Xi views this mission, as his forebears did, in keeping with the original goals of restoration. The "China Dream," the "New China," and the "Great Rejuvenation of the Chinese Nation" are all *fundamentally military endeavors*.

In China's modern history, the power of the military, the power of the state, and the power of the Chinese people are ideologically bound together, bound up in the country's ability to fight against the outside world.

As Mao explained in his time, "The era in which the Chinese people were regarded as uncivilized is now ended. We shall emerge in the world as a nation with an advanced culture. Our national defence will be consolidated and no imperialists will ever again be allowed to invade our land."[88]

Several core ideas related to this make up the Party's sense of what was won by their revolution, and what could never be challenged by any outside power now that the country has "stood up."

Most important of all are the principles of "sovereignty and territorial integrity" and "noninterference in internal affairs." These two (along with three others) are enshrined as the Five Principles of Peaceful Coexistence— the pillars of China's diplomatic approach to the outside world.

The Party continues to use these concepts in its external relations, explaining that they comprise the bedrock of peace. These are principles that the country expects other nations to live by when dealing with China. Especially instructive is the case of India, where these principles began as a form of diplomacy, but were eventually used as justification for war.

As a Chinese diplomat explained to his Pakistani counterpart in the Mao era: "I remember, when our army peacefully liberated Tibet in 1950, India sent us a diplomatic note saying China should not advance militarily into Tibet. We replied by explaining that liberating Tibet is China's own matter, and foreign countries have no right to interfere; after that, they did not speak again."[89]

The Chinese official went on to explain that "[India] regarded Tibet as part of India's sphere of influence, or even as Indian territory, and instigated Tibetan rebellion. This is obviously something the Chinese people are unable to tolerate."[90]

China's case against India ahead of the Border War of 1962 included extensive discussion of these values and principles. For example: "China does not interfere in the internal affairs of any other country, nor will it allow any country to interfere in its internal affairs. China does not encroach on the sovereignty and territorial integrity of any other country, nor will it allow any country to encroach on its sovereignty and territorial integrity."[91]

Additionally, in diplomatic correspondences over individual incidents, the Party lashed out at "words and deeds slandering China and interfering in China's internal affairs," also invoking the Chinese people with claims that "650 million Chinese people cannot tolerate" infractions against the Party, its leaders, or China. All of this was tied to the idea of the "New China" or China's restoration. In other words, the country expected other nations to submit to what it considered its legitimate view when it came to a conflict of interests.

These are concepts that, at their core, aim to establish irreversible restoration of Chinese power and the exertion of this power, both internally and externally. In the twentieth century, as we shall see in the next part, this had to do with China's power in its region. In the twenty-first century, this will have to do with China's power both in its region and around the world.

Such is the real nature of the rise of China, and the values at its core. Building up the Chinese military is as essential to this project of national rejuvenation as building up its economy. And eventually, by the very nature of China's growing global footprint, the values at the heart of it—the legitimization of expanding power—will come to matter to all who stand in its way.

This is not a new phenomenon—the military mission of this nation, as with many others, is passed on from generation to generation as the nation's power grows. As Xi Jinping explains, "The heroic armed forces of the people will carry on its great traditions, build on past merits, so as to forge ahead to fulfill the historical responsibilities they shoulder."[92]

In order to "achieve the great renewal of the Chinese nation," it must build its military and uphold these values and tenets both at home and abroad. This is the role that China's armed forces play in the "historic mission of national rejuvenation": building the uncontested sovereignty of Chinese power.[93]

It is possible that this could all take place within China's region, in the West Pacific, with the PLA preparing for and conducting military operations only against its neighbors and against other regional powers such as India, Vietnam, Korea, Russia, Taiwan, and the United States, as it did in the twentieth century. However, China is now a global rather than a regional actor, with expanding global interests.

The Party's commitment to wealth and military power, to the restoration of China's perceived historic place in the world, and to the values by which it understands that place in the modern era, all point toward a global Chinese military, which by China's own admission will be second to none. This is a core feature of China's great rejuvenation. What this military's missions are now, and what they will be in the future, is the subject of Part Two.

PART II

蓝色国土

BLUE NATIONAL SOIL

CHINA'S STRATEGIC GEOGRAPHY AND MILITARY PLANS

All of the people, in each West Pacific country, don't understand, why and with what reason the Americans from so far away come to the West Pacific countries, using their military, political, economic and cultural power, to control these countries? Actually it has no basis in reason. Therefore, one day, sooner or later, America will certainly let go of the West Pacific places and withdraw back home, just like it has had to let go of other regions in the world. If the Americans don't go themselves, there will be a day when the people of each country will unite and throw them out.[1]

—MAO ZEDONG, 1959

We are resolved to fight the bloody battle against our enemies . . . with a strong determination to take our place in the world.[2]

—XI JINPING, 2018

THE SOUTH CHINA SEA IS ONLY THE BEGINNING.

Building these new military outposts is an opening move in a strategy that spans multiple continents and oceans. China's leaders are thinking big, thinking long-term, and building up their nation's military power.

By one account, China is undergoing "the most ambitious military modernization in the world."[3] And Xi Jinping envisions an "infinite stage," a geographical sweep of unprecedented scope, and military power that will be "second to none."

From deployments in Africa, the Middle East, and the Indian Ocean, to investments in space-based systems, artificial intelligence, quantum communications, aircraft carriers, and undersea warfare, China is making strides in military technology and achieving the military prowess that its leadership has worked toward for decades.

It is a military that will overshadow China's neighbors and challenge the United States for supremacy. Most importantly, it is a military whose task will be guarding China's presence around the world.

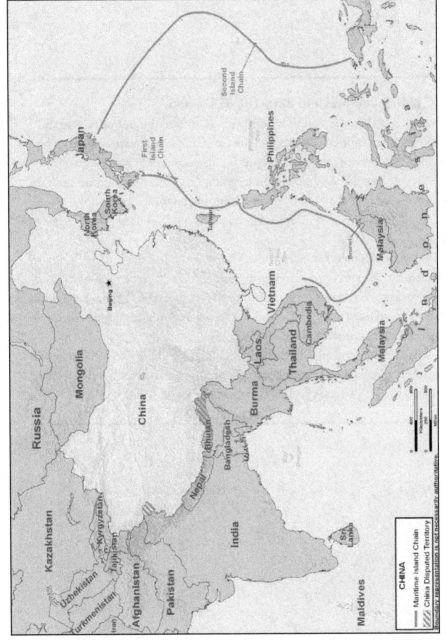

The First and Second Island Chains[4]

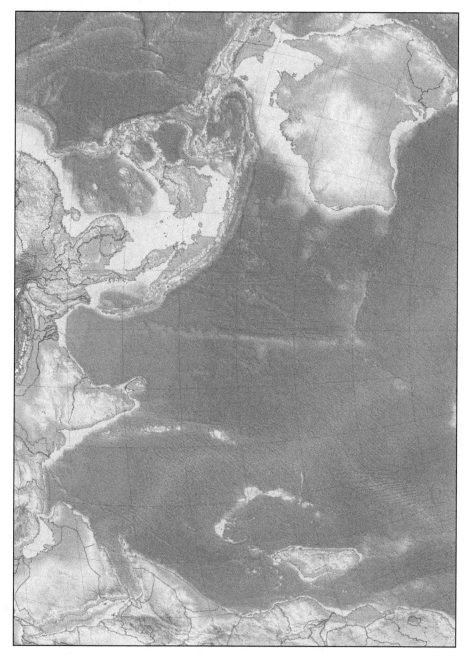

The Indian Ocean Region[5]

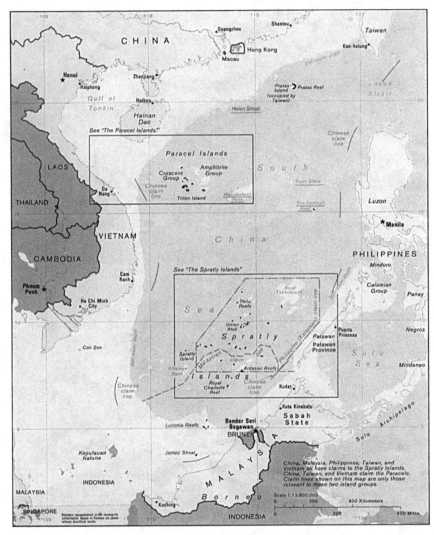

The South China Sea[6]

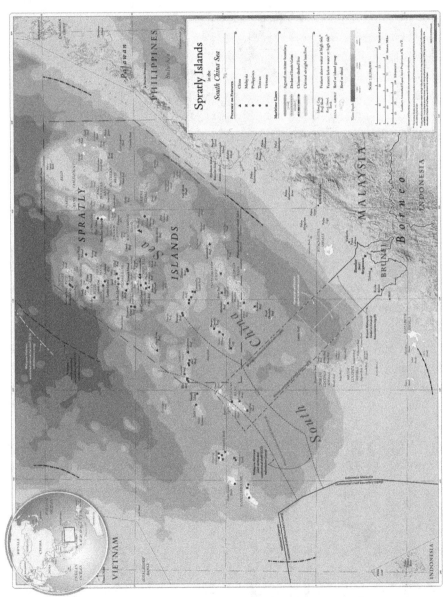

The South China Sea, Spratly Islands [7]

Selected Chinese Territorial Claims [8]

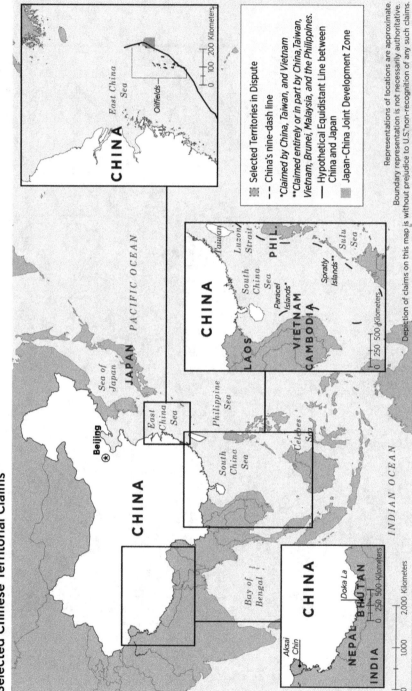

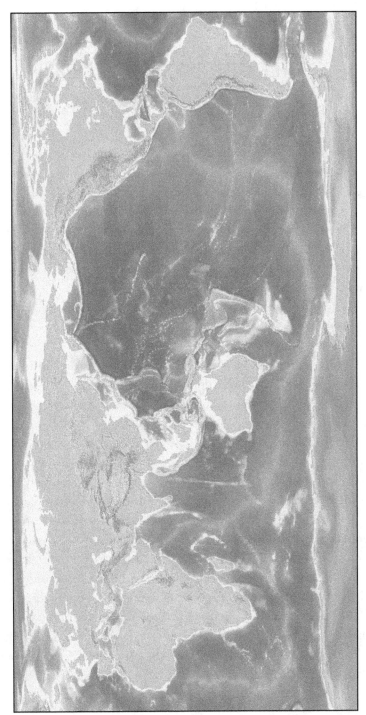

The Indo-Pacific World Map [9]

2.1

THE MILITARY RISE OF CHINA

The world has become accustomed to China as a major economic power. What many do not realize is that the global trading system China has built will be backed by global military power.

Let's zoom out and think about world history. If, a hundred years from now, we were looking back on the time that we are living in today, the years from 2000 to 2025, we would likely see that the most important event was China's progression from an economic power to a major military power.

This progression is happening alongside China's transformation from a *regional power* to a *global power*.

This will change the world.

China's leaders like to speak of having 5,000 years of history—5,000 years of "continuous" civilization. Epigrams from ancient China speak of the country's rule of everything, everything that was "under heaven," and everything between "the four seas."

One important thing is left out: for virtually all of its thousands of years of history, China's *military power* was confined to its region alone.

China has always been a land power, acting within a largely land-based trading system. The silk routes of past centuries connected China, known to itself as the "Middle Kingdom," with other civilizations throughout the Eurasian supercontinent. Silk and porcelain made their way to ancient Rome, to Persia, to the Islamic caliphates. All the world's goods came back on camel trains and caravans to the markets and palaces of Imperial China. For centuries, China captured the imagination of European traders—think of Christopher Columbus setting out to find a westward route to Asia and believing that he had sighted not the "New World," but China's shores.[10]

Today, China's leaders have taken these ancient routes as a new model for global trade. Xi Jinping, standing in Astana, Kazakhstan in 2013, spoke of resurrecting the ancient trade routes, a global program to accompany China's national rejuvenation. He spoke of "the transcontinental Silk Road linking east and west, Asia and Europe."[11] His speech began, "As I stand here and look back at that episode of history, I could almost hear the camel bells echoing in the mountains and see the wisp of smoke rising from the desert."[12]

China's role in the trading system of the ancient and premodern world was substantial.

But China's military power was confined to its own region. Successive dynasties dealt with constant pressure from Mongol tribes on the northern steppes, internal rebellions, punitive expeditions to vassal states such as Korea and Vietnam, and harassment from coastal pirates. While China traded with many of the world's regions, it was diplomatically and militarily separated from the rest of the world, as were virtually all pre-global civilizations. By the time of the first British embassy to China in 1793, the Chinese emperor regarded this ambassador as a foreign pirate who had come to seek the protection of his civilization.

Now, in the twenty-first century, China has emerged as the world's leading nation by volume of trade, surpassing the United States in 2013.[13] This is a world-historical transformation. Not just for the rest of us, but for China itself.

Which brings us to China's military transformation:

The Chinese military has begun a massive campaign to become *a major maritime power*. As the world's top trading nation, China's economic and political survival depends on assured access to the world's resources and therefore to the world's oceans.

The importance of maritime power — the importance of going global as a military — is present in many quarters of Party military planning, strategy, decision-making, and ideology. In the words of the Chinese Academy of Military Sciences, "Today and for a long time to come, our country's national interests are expanding mainly in the sea, national security is threatened mainly from the sea, the focal point of military struggle is mainly in the sea."[14]

Xi Jinping and other Chinese leaders have called for the buildup of maritime power and the transformation of China into a "maritime great power" or *haiyang qiangguo* 海洋强国.[15] A maritime power, as the Communist

Party's policy-making journal defines it, is a country that can "exert its great comprehensive power to develop, utilize, protect, manage, and *control oceans.*"[16]

Many windows into Chinese strategy show that military power and the expansion of global economic interests are intertwined in the minds of strategic planners. As the most recent military strategy, released in 2015, explains:

> With the growth of China's national interests, its national security is more vulnerable to international and regional turmoil, terrorism, piracy, serious natural disasters and epidemics, and the security of overseas interests concerning energy and resources, strategic sea lines of communication (SLOCs), as well as institutions, personnel and assets abroad, has become an imminent issue.[17]

Importantly, China's push to the seas and oceans did not begin with Xi Jinping. It is an evolution of military strategy that dates at least back to the days of Jiang Zemin, when Chinese planners began to recognize the challenges of sea-lane dependence,[18] while having even deeper roots in the vision of Admiral Liu Huaqing, who, in the 1980s, envisioned the creation of a global Chinese navy by the year 2050.[19]

Control of important "Sea Lines of Communication" (SLOCs) is paramount for Chinese military planners. Vitally, over 80 percent of China's oil imports pass through the Strait of Malacca, a narrow waterway in Southeast Asia that is only 2 miles wide at its narrowest point.[20] As minerals flow from Africa, energy supplies make their way from the Middle East, and manufactured goods move across the seas from Asia to Europe, numerous *geographical choke points* jeopardize these trade flows, both to and from China.

Chinese planners believe they must build a military that can guard against all contingencies as these economic interests grow.

When Hu Jintao assumed leadership, he is said to have coined the term "the Malacca Dilemma," drawing his nation's attention to the problem of moving enormous volumes of trade— the lifeblood of the Chinese economy— through a tiny, pirate-infested strait patrolled by the world's largest navy— that of the "hegemonic" United States. Xi Jinping is thinking even bigger.

The "Belt and Road" is Xi Jinping's signature foreign policy and global power initiative.

It is a grand-scale infrastructure and port-building project that spans Eurasia, Africa, and the Indian Ocean Region, financed and designed by the Chinese state, and executed by its instruments of diplomatic, economic, and industrial power.

The "Belt and Road" is usually explained as an economic program. However, it has major geopolitical implications and purposes. In essence, it is the geographical blueprint for China's strategic interests around the world. In a prior century, we would recognize it as a map for empire-building. Today, it is harder for many people to perceive the full ramifications of this multi-continental vision.

Geography is China's Achilles' heel. Surrounded by neighbors with whom China has fought frequent wars, and dependent on trade routes that pass through the world's most infamous maritime choke points, the geographical "Belt and Road," and the military programs and missions that exist within this "Belt and Road," are elements of China's global strategy for security and prosperity. In other words, the full geographical expanse in which the "great rejuvenation of the Chinese nation" will take shape.

While the Chinese military buildup in the South China Sea is well-known, it is only the gateway to a larger set of plans, as Chinese forces will be tasked with military missions all across the "Belt and Road." Several vital geographical concepts come together to form the whole of Chinese military planning: the "First and Second Island Chains," the Strait of Malacca, and the waterways of the Indo-Pacific Region. Economic strategists have mapped out three "blue economic passages" under the 2017 "Vision for Maritime Cooperation under the Belt and Road Initiative." Each of these will link Eurasia's major oceanic trade routes back to China *via the South China Sea*.

These are the "the China–Indian Ocean–Africa–Mediterranean Sea Blue Economic Passage," "the China–Oceania–South Pacific Blue Economic Passage," and a third that "will lead to Europe via the Arctic Ocean."[21] These would be patrolled and defended by an expanded Chinese military that is "second to none" as a maritime power.[22]

Chinese naval strategy and naval operations have long been visible to the world. At present, China plans to field what analysts refer to as a "two-ocean navy," which is meant to operate primarily in the Indian and Pacific Oceans.

In 2007, thinking far ahead, a Chinese admiral once told US Admiral Timothy Keating:

> [H]e proposed, in his words, that as China builds aircraft carriers— he said plural— we can make a deal. You, the US, take Hawaii East and we, China, will take Hawaii West and the Indian Ocean. Then you will not need to come to the western Pacific and Indian Ocean.[23]

In addition to new forays into the Indian Ocean Region, China's naval strategy is focused on what planners call the "two island chains" of the West Pacific. These are the locales that Mao envisioned would be someday stripped of American power.

A strategy was conceived by Admiral Liu Huaqing, known as the "father of the modern Chinese Navy," during his tenure in the 1980s as head of the People's Liberation Army Navy (PLAN). US naval expert Dr. Bernard Cole explains Admiral Liu's plan as follows:

> By 2000, the PLAN would be capable of exerting sea control out to the First Island Chain, defined by the Kurile Islands, Japan and the Ryukyu Islands, the Philippines, and the Indonesian archipelago.
>
> By 2020, sea control would be enforced out to the Second Island Chain, defined by the Kuriles, Japan and the Bonin Islands, the Marianas Islands, Palau, and the Indonesian archipelago.
>
> By 2050, the PLAN would operate globally, with aircraft carrier battle groups.[24]

Today, as Chinese planners envision safeguarding China's "expanding overseas interests" through a massive blue-water navy, and with military forces which, in the words of Xi, are "built to fight," "able to win wars," and "world-class" in size and technological capability, the country remains focused on these geographical lines, as well as its expansion into new maritime regions.[25]

China has begun to make great gains. In the words of US naval expert Rear Admiral Michael McDevitt:

> When one considers all the aspects of maritime power — navy, coast guard, militia, merchant marine, port infrastructure, shipbuilding, and fishing . . . No other country in the world can match China's maritime capabilities across the board. For instance, the United States has the world's leading navy . . . but its shipbuilding, merchant marine, coast guard, and fishing industry pale in comparison to those of China.[26]

As mentioned, the South China Sea, for a maritime China, is the heart of the Indo-Pacific Region. It is the maritime fulcrum where two great oceans meet, and which China *must control* in order to project military power around the world. It is helpful to look at the example of Tibet, a place Chinese military and political leaders decided that they must control in order for their nation to exist as a land power. Qing officials called Tibet "the hand . . . which protects our face."[27] Chiang Kai-shek explained that without the Himalayas China's coastal heartland would be defenseless.

The South China Sea occupies a similar place in the writings of today's Chinese military analysts, some of whom call the body of water China's "blue national soil."[28]

Also, like Tibet, and other pieces of terrestrial Chinese territory in the South China Sea, the CCP's discourse of rights and interests is crucial. As the recent Military Strategy explains:

> On the issues concerning China's territorial sovereignty and maritime rights and interests, some of its offshore neighbors take provocative actions and reinforce their military presence on China's reefs and islands that they have illegally occupied. Some external countries are also busy meddling in South China Sea affairs; a tiny few maintain constant close-in air and sea surveillance and reconnaissance against China. It is thus a long-standing task for China to safeguard its maritime rights and interests.[29]

In official Party propaganda, it is other nations that are "militarizing" the South China Sea, and China is simply acting defensively by building its islands, complete with hardened bunkers, ammunition depots, military-grade runways, surface-to-air missile systems, and anti-ship cruise missiles that can strike vessels within hundreds of nautical miles.[30]

This justification of legitimate "rights and interests" is deployed in the "near seas," but is also likely to be used around the world as China's military reach grows.

The South China Sea, a body of water which sits at the juncture of two great oceans, and at the heart of an explicit vision of global trading routes linked back to China, is a stepping stone, not only to the Indian Ocean and West Pacific, but to the waterways of the world.

And the South China Sea is now *already* under China's effective control. In the words of a testimony before the US Congress by Admiral Philip Davidson, Commander of US Pacific Command, China's "forward operating bases" in the South China Sea "appear complete":

> Once occupied, China will be able to extend its influence thousands of miles to the south and project power deep into Oceania. The PLA will be able to use these bases to challenge U.S. presence in the region, and any forces deployed to the islands would easily overwhelm the military forces of any other South China Sea-claimants. In short, China is now capable of controlling the South China Sea in all scenarios short of war with the United States.[31]

What does control of the "near seas" and their "island chains" achieve for China?

In addition to the ability to "extend its influence [for] thousands of miles," it has an even more immediate effect on China's neighborhood as China lays its *stepping stones* throughout the Indo-Pacific.

Consider the following description of military control of Taiwan— another of the vital places in China's island chain strategy. Just as control of the South China Sea would improve China's ability to seize Taiwan by force, control of Taiwan could carry forward to the blockade and devastation of Japan. A Chinese-language publication from China's Air Command

College explains:

> As soon as Taiwan is reunified with Mainland China, Japan's maritime lines of communication will fall completely within the striking ranges of China's fighters and bombers . . . Our analysis shows that, by using blockades, if we can reduce Japan's raw imports by 15–20%, it will be a heavy blow to Japan's economy. After imports have been reduced by 30%, Japan's economic activity and war-making potential will be basically destroyed. After imports have been reduced by 50%, national economy and war-making potential will collapse entirely . . . blockades can cause sea shipments to decrease and can even create famine within the Japanese islands.[32]

China's aspirations within the first two-island chains, the "blue economic corridors," and the Indian Ocean Region lead to a kind of closed system in which the Party and its military could exert military dominance indefinitely after China's "Great Rejuvenation." Fielding a military that is "second to none" throughout the Indo-Pacific, achieving sea control or sea denial in the island chains, and exerting a massive military presence throughout the "Belt and Road" system is the likely shape of China's aspirations to 2049. However, another crucial dimension to modern military power takes place not on land, air, or sea, but in new domains: space and cyber.

The Chinese military understands the needs to master space and cyber better than almost any other nation.

2.2

NEW TECHNOLOGIES, NEW FRONTIERS

The First Gulf War was China's wake-up call.

With Communist regimes in crisis across Eurasia, US military operations in the Persian Gulf in 1991 dazzled the Chinese leaders, revealing the full effects of America's "revolution in military affairs" across a range of new technologies.

And a generation of Chinese military strategists set to work to figure out how their country could "leapfrog" America.[33]

Today, China's military has been tasked with the following strategic missions:

- to deal with a wide range of emergencies and military threats, and effectively safeguard the sovereignty and security of China's territorial land, air, and sea

- to resolutely safeguard the unification of the motherland

- to safeguard China's security and interests in new domains

- to safeguard the security of China's overseas interests

- to maintain strategic deterrence and carry out nuclear counterattack.[34]

The Chinese military is targeting the development of future technologies, particularly artificial intelligence, quantum computing, biotechnology, and robotics, in order to gain a military edge over its competitors, especially the United States. China's expertise at cybertheft, cyberespionage, and cyberattack is well-known. Its emphasis on military space is perhaps an even more essential piece of the puzzle. Like maritime power, and most other aspects of "comprehensive national power," space plays an important role in Xi Jinping's "China Dream." It is the ultimate destination for a rising power.

In the words of the *White Paper on China's Space Activities in 2016*: "To explore the vast cosmos, develop the space industry and build China into a space power is a dream we pursue unremittingly."[35]

It is a dream of exploration, and also of national power. Advances in space will "protect China's national rights and interests, and build up its overall strength" and "provide strong support for the realization of the Chinese Dream of the renewal of the Chinese nation."[36]

China's space objectives are supported with an extensive list of programs:

> In the next five years China plans to expedite the development of its space endeavors by continuing to enhance the basic capacities of its space industry, strengthen research into key and cutting-edge technologies, and implement manned spaceflight, lunar exploration, the Beidou Navigation Satellite System, high-resolution earth observation system, new-generation launch vehicles and other important projects.[37]

And, as usual, they are phrased in terms of a contribution to human peace and progress:

> It is mankind's unremitting pursuit to peacefully explore and utilize outer space. Standing at a new historical starting line, China is determined to quicken the pace of developing its space industry, and actively carry out international space exchanges and cooperation, so that achievements in space activities will serve and improve the well-being of mankind in a wider scope, at a deeper level and with higher standards. China will promote the lofty cause of peace and development together with other countries.[38]

However, as leading scholars have demonstrated, Chinese space policy "is almost entirely controlled by the PLA."[39] Space takes an important place in *China's Military Strategy*, which explains that "Outer space has become a commanding height in international strategic competition," adding that "Countries concerned are developing their space forces and instruments, and the first signs of weaponization of outer space have appeared."[40] Learning from the United States, China prioritizes the role of space systems in both conventional and unconventional military power.

Anthony H. Cordesman of the Center for Strategic and International Studies (CSIS) explains that "China's growing space capabilities translate into military capabilities that affect all aspects of conventional and nuclear targeting, ground-air-sea operations, precision conventional strike capacities, and missile defense."[41] And, while China states in key documents that it champions "the peaceful use of outer space" and opposition to "the weaponization of and arms race in outer space,"[42] China's civilian and military space programs are intimately linked. Importantly, civilian and scientific programs may have designated military uses: "even China's ostensibly peaceful space developments like the BeiDou SATNAV system, manned space missions, and launch vehicles should be viewed, at minimum, as dual-use capabilities that the PLA will utilize if needed."[43]

As the US–China Economic and Security Review Commission explains, "[N]early every Chinese source describes space as the 'ultimate high ground,' leading many Chinese analysts to assess that space warfare is inevitable."[44] The use of space warfare and anti-space weapons appears to be central to Chinese thinking on military conflict:

> Because of the preeminence of the space battlefield, analysts writing on space argue that it will become *the* center of gravity in future wars and one that must be seized and controlled. In fact, these analysts argue that the first condition for seizing the initiative is to achieve space supremacy.[45]

Modeled on the United States military, China is building an integrated warfighting system that gives space-based support for its navy, army, air force, and a vastly expanded marine corps. Going beyond this, however, both Chinese and Russian military planners have identified space as America's key vulnerability in its global military operations.[46]

Both China and Russia have invested considerable energy and resources in systems that can target American space assets as a way to disrupt—

perhaps decisively— the operations and capabilities of the United States in the event of conflict.[47] As the two leading space powers other than the United States, Russia and China have also substantially increased their military and civilian space cooperation as part of their "strategic partnership."[48] Meanwhile, the US is working hard to avoid a "space Pearl Harbor" that could destroy its military advantages at the start of a conflict.[49]

US concerns are well-founded.

China's vision for space fits clearly within its ideology of national restoration and military dominance. As Lt. Gen. Zhang Yulin, former deputy chief of the armament department of the Central Military Commission explains, "The earth-moon space will be strategically important for the great rejuvenation of the Chinese nation," adding that, "The future of China's manned space program, is not a moon landing, which is quite simple, or even the manned Mars program which remains difficult, but continual exploration of the earth-moon space with ever developing technology."[50] Chinese scientists have expressed their interest in "building a lunar base and long-term residence on the moon."[51] The director of China's Lunar Mission goes so far as to compare the Moon and Mars to islands claimed by China in the East and South China Seas:

> The universe is an ocean, the moon is the Diaoyu Islands, Mars is Huangyan Island [an island in the South China Sea claimed and "effectively controlled" by China]. If we don't go there now even though we're capable of doing so, then we will be blamed by our descendants. If others go there, then they will take over, and you won't be able to go even if you want to. This is reason enough.[52]

Moreover, China's quest in space and its ambitions on the world's oceans and seas combine.

The Communist Party is also funding satellite-based surveillance research, with the goal of detecting submarines from space, a goal which eluded the United States and USSR in the Cold War.[53] As reported in the South China Morning Post, one of the project's researchers explained that, should the satellites succeed, "it will make the upper layer of the sea 'more or less transparent' . . . 'It will change almost everything.'"[54] The Pilot National Laboratory for Marine Science and Technology (Qingdao), tasked with developing space-based ocean surveillance technology lists other research initiatives as supporting "the mission of 'Transparent Ocean,'" and "providing a strong scientific basis for achieving the strategic objective of the "Transparent Ocean."[55] The National Laboratory explains that its "strategic tasks" include "construction of a state-of-the-art ocean observation system" and "establishing the ocean observation system that covers the Western Pacific, South China Sea and the Indian Ocean."[56]

The *South China Morning Post* tells of additional initiatives at the laboratory including a supercomputer called the "Deep Blue Brain" which ties in with space-based surveillance: "data collected by the satellite and other assets in China's global ocean surveillance network will be streamed to the supercomputer in Qingdao . . . [the computer] will then use the masses of data along with artificial intelligence to recreate the world's oceans, in unprecedented detail, in digital form. The Chinese government says it wants to use that 'virtual ocean' to help forecast events ranging from extreme weather to the likely outcome of a sea battle, based on the conditions."[57]

China's oceanic ambitions, from deep sea mining in the Indian Ocean Region, to deploying seabed surveillance networks for subsurface warfare, to deploying acoustic sensors in the Mariana trench, the deepest part of the Pacific Ocean, show an increasing sophistication as a maritime power and an integrated focus on both sea and space as new frontiers for military and economic use. Though technologies such as submarine detection from space have eluded superpowers for decades, China's focus on finding new scientific advantages through the mastery of both frontiers, sea and space, demonstrates, in the words of US Rear Admiral (Ret.) Michael McDevitt, a "comprehensive effort to eliminate their vulnerabilities."[58]

In addition to new Chinese capabilities, official Chinese military doctrine emphasizes "seizing the initiative," including through the possible use of space and cyber warfare.

Here's another important concept in Chinese military doctrine: "war control."

The idea, in the words of a US strategist, is that "war can be controlled as if it were a machine awaiting only the calibration of a skilled engineer bearing the latest in high-technology tools." [59]

As told by a PLA Lieutenant General in *Chinese Military Science*, "war control" means this:

> [I]t is to firmly grasp warfare and dynamically manage warfare. Its substantive connotation is using the minimum cost to safeguard national interests . . . The scope of controlled warfare covers pre-war crisis control, operational control during the war and stability control after the war.[60]

Let's think about what this all means when we consider the role of space, cyberspace, and nuclear weapons. Take this example from a US report on Chinese thinking concerning escalation: "PLA writings . . . reflect the belief that offensive cyberspace and counterspace operations are not only advisable early in a conflict with a major adversary, but that such operations can be undertaken at a comparatively low risk of escalation."[61]

China, like other major powers, is also a nuclear-armed state.

Like Russia, China has invested a great deal in recent years into the expansion and modernization of its nuclear weapons program, including fielding new technologies such as hypersonic glide vehicles designed to defeat American missile defense systems. These systems are meant to provide China with an "assured second strike capability"— the ability to strike back if the nation falls victim to a nuclear strike by a foreign adversary. In any conflict or crisis, two parties have to manage what is called, in military parlance, the "escalation ladder." That is, the escalation of a conflict from the conventional and unconventional, all the way to the possible use of nuclear weapons.

While China views *all of the above* as purely defensive, the Party maintains active territorial claims in its region and is pursuing many forms of geographical expansion. As the Chinese military goes out, frictions will increase with other countries, as is happening already.

The result is expeditionary forces prepared, in Xi Jinping's words, to "fight and win wars," backed by advanced nuclear weapons systems, and a doctrine of possible early use of space and cyberwarfare. Quite the cocktail.

In the words of the Chinese military, nuclear weapons are meant to be defensive only: "The nuclear force is a strategic cornerstone for safeguarding national sovereignty and security."[62]

China's military buildup includes a major nuclear modernization program. What this means is that military power — deterrence as a whole — is a package. So, just as naval patrols in the South China Sea are meant to have an effect on the will of an adversary, the fact that all Chinese military assets are an extension of a nuclear-armed state means that the entire escalation ladder — the risk of escalation — exists any time a nation militarily engages China in its region, and potentially elsewhere in the world.

In the words of an American commentator:

> China today is deploying, not studying, is deploying two new types of ICBMs, one new type of SLBM, and a new class of SSBNs, four of which are in the water. And a new nuclear air-launched cruise missile. Reportedly, a second new type of SSBNs is in development, as is a new strategic bomber. And China also maintains a robust arsenal of shorter-range nuclear forces. These capabilities must be regarded as a key backdrop to China's aggressive maritime policy of seeking to annex the South China Sea.[63]

There is one more concept we should consider. Some Chinese strategists believe it would be possible to turn a crisis situation into "an opportunity to further expand national interests," and that the PLA should "seize the initiative" during a conflict in order to achieve victory against another nation state.[64] Needless to say, this is a dangerous belief, especially with multiple land- and sea-based territorial claims in the West Pacific Region, and as China's "overseas interests" continue to grow.[65]

All of this fits into an even larger ideological view in Chinese military and political thinking that frames nearly all of China's military actions, whether in the South China Sea, Taiwan Strait, Himalayas, or elsewhere as fundamentally "defensive" and the fault of its neighbors, or of other nations.[66]

China's challenges to the US military and to its neighbors in the South China Sea, as well as its challenges to India and Japan, in the Himalayas and East China Seas respectively, all remind us that China's appetite for military confrontation *below the threshold of violence remains high.*

China's neighbors live through regular "gray zone" paramilitary operations — in the South China Sea and East China Sea — as the Party deploys its "maritime militias" and other quasi-military tactics to harass China's neighbors on the seas that the country claims as "blue national soil." The purpose, above all, is to erode the will of other nations and to change the "facts on the water" before China is even ready to fight full-blown wars.

Let us remember that today, despite massive advances, China is not yet the military power that it intends to be.

But Chinese military planners—like those in every military—are actively engaged in *thinking through* just how they would go about the missions given by their leadership—which, in the case of Xi Jinping, is to "fight and win wars." And we have seen here a glimpse of how that thinking goes. As China makes strides into new geographies, its military leaders are planning for the future battlespace, entrusted by their leaders with "the missions and tasks of the new era."

In order to build advantages in emerging technologies from artificial intelligence to robotics in the pursuit of military power, China's leaders have taken a step further, inaugurating a policy of "Civil Military Fusion." This means, in the words of *The Financial Times*, "an instruction by the Chinese Communist Party that new technologies developed by the private sector must be shared with the military." Or, in the words of a senior US official, ensuring "the free flow of technology and material between civilian and military enterprises." Under this program, companies such as China's largest search engine, Baidu, and engineers who were once trained in American companies like Apple, are now working to develop emerging technologies for the Chinese military, even as major Chinese technology companies continue to maintain offices in Silicon Valley.[67]

While "Civil Military Fusion" is largely about building military-industrial collaboration at home, Chinese military technology development initiatives also take advantage of China's access to the outside world. It has recently been estimated that China's military has sent over two thousand military-affiliated scientists abroad to the US, UK, Canada, Australia, and Germany in order to train in science and technology.[68] A collaboration between the PLA National University of Defense Technology and the University of Cambridge in the UK was explained as aimed at producing China's next generation of supercomputer experts, which would "greatly enhance our nation's power in the areas of defence, communications, anti-jamming for imaging and high-precision navigation."[69]

INTERNAL SECURITY AND HOMELAND DEFENSE: CHINA'S TRADITIONAL MILITARY GEOGRAPHY

The "Generalissimo," as Chiang Kai-shek was known, was one of modern China's early revolutionaries.

Educated in Japan, and one of the founders of the Guomindang, he fought to overthrow the Qing dynasty, forced the Chinese Communist Party to take their "Long March" to survive, steered China through the Second World War, and ultimately fled to Taiwan as Communist victory swept the nation in the Chinese Civil War.

An experienced military planner, Chiang understood that the strategic geography of ancient China remained the strategic geography of China in his lifetime. Here is how he saw the security of his country:

> There are no natural frontiers in the areas of the Yellow, Huai, Yangtze and Han rivers where a strong defense line can be prepared. Therefore Formosa, the Pescadores, the Four Northeastern Provinces [Manchuria], Inner and Outer Mongolia, [Xinjiang], and Tibet are each a fortress essential for the nation's defense and security. The separation of any one of these regions from the rest of the country means the disruption of our national defenses.[70]

Indeed, Chinese military planners have been concerned for centuries with these relatively fixed geographical regions in which the country or empire had to maintain its own security.

Whether dealing with nomads from the northern steppes, piracy on the coasts, or eventually more exotic intrusions, such as European gunboat diplomacy and imperialism in the nineteenth century, Chinese leaders have been responsible for an expanse of land surrounding China's three great river systems — the Yellow, Yangtze, and Pearl — each of which runs from the interior heartland interior out to the coast. These rivers fed China's early rise as a civilization built on great agrarian wealth and cultural power.

Chinese forays into the northwest regions along the Silk Road began in the Han dynasty (206 BC—AD 220), but the hold on these regions was tenuous, and subsequent dynasties tended to ebb and flow along the central Yangtze heartlands. More substantial acquisitions of northwestern territories were made briefly in the Tang era (AD 618–906), and then much more substantially by the Yuan dynasty (1279–1368) — Mongol conquerors who formed a "patron-priest" relationship with Tibet and brought the whole of China under Mongol rule.[71] With the acquisition of the Himalayan plateau, Mongolia, and Xinjiang by the Qing dynasty (1644–1912, also steppe rulers of China proper)[72], China's territories expanded just beyond the present-day borders of the PRC, and led to the modern concept of Chinese national security that exists today for military planners focused on China's "internal security."

The concept is reflected today in China's most recent military strategy. Here, Chinese planners reflect on current "challenges" to the Chinese grip on several of the outer regions that Chiang once listed — Taiwan, Xinjiang, and Tibet:

> In recent years, cross-Taiwan Straits relations have sustained a sound momentum of peaceful development, but the root cause of instability has not yet been removed, and the "Taiwan independence" separatist forces and their activities are still the biggest threat to the peaceful development of cross-Straits relations. Further, China faces a formidable task to maintain political security and social stability. Separatist forces for "East Turkistan independence" and "Tibet independence" have inflicted serious damage, particularly with escalating violent terrorist activities by "East Turkistan independence" forces. Besides, anti-China forces have never given up their attempt to instigate a "color

revolution" in this country. Consequently, China faces more challenges in terms of national security and social stability.[73]

Shortly after the founding of the People's Republic of China, the Communist Party and the PLA were active in four crucial regions that were considered essential to the security of China: the Himalayas, the Korean peninsula, Southeast Asia, and Taiwan.

In 1950, Mao sent a small army into Tibet to destroy the Tibetan army near Lhasa and gain control of the Himalayas; the Politburo was simultaneously fighting the United States and United Nations in the Korean Peninsula, while preparing for the "liberation" of Taiwan, an island which by then harbored the remains of the Nationalist government after the Chinese Civil War ended on the mainland. The Communist Party also played an important role in training Vietnamese troops in their war against the French Empire, even cycling veterans from Korean War operations against the United States into Southeast Asia to support Vietnam. In other words, China's ability to exert military force throughout its own region in a systematic, combined manner was evident even in the early decades of the People's Republic of China.[74]

Today, China has set up a series of military commands, described in 2016 by China's Defense Ministry spokesperson at the time as "defensive in nature," which would "better safeguard national sovereignty, security and interests."[75] These commands, like the original assessment of Chiang Kai-shek, comprise five major regions: Western (Tibet, Xinjiang), Northern (Inner Mongolia, Manchuria), Central (Beijing), Eastern (East China Sea), and Southern (South China Sea).

China's homeland defense remains a massive priority for the Chinese military. What is new is the use of a more secure homeland, fought over for centuries, to project power around the world.

China's region is transforming, as the country expands as a regional maritime power, particularly through the addition of military island-building in the South China Sea, "gray zone" intimidation operations in the South and East China Seas, and the buildup of a major submarine fleet, expeditionary "blue water" navy, and vastly expanded marine corps. However, in many ways this is simply an extension of China's traditional geographic security situation into the "near seas" maritime domain. What is far more interesting—and likely more consequential—is the expansion of China's presence overseas outside of its region and outside of its "two island chain" strategy—into the wider world. It is here that we can grasp the totality of the rise of China, its impact, and what this is likely to mean in the future.

2.4

THE NEW WORLD MAP: REGIONAL EXPANSION AND A GLOBAL MILITARY PRESENCE

hina's military already operates globally.

Deep in Argentine Patagonia, the Chinese military operates a satellite support facility for space exploration missions. On the horn of Africa, warships dock at China's first overseas military base. In partnership with Russia, Chinese naval exercises take place from the Mediterranean and Baltic Sea in Europe, to amphibious marine landing exercises in the Sea of Japan. Regular naval exercises take place with Pakistan in the Arabian Sea, and Chinese special forces train in jungle warfare in Venezuela.[76]

China's armed forces are already deploying around the planet.

However, the true blueprint for China's future military presence is in the Indo-Pacific Region, a multicontinental system comprising Eurasia, Africa, and Australia, with the Indian Ocean and West Pacific as the principal waterways. At the heart of this is China's "Belt and Road Initiative."

To meet its economic needs, China requires unbroken access to the world's resources. The military requirements of assuring access to regions around the world necessitates a global mission set that the PLA is already beginning to adjust to. China's resource interests are concentrated in the Middle East, Africa, and Central Asia, while the country's main export markets are Asia, Europe, and the United States.

China must manage this dependency on myriad world regions. Let's have a closer look at what this means. The "Belt and Road Initiative," frequently referred to in Chinese as the "Belt and Road Strategy," has two geographical routes.

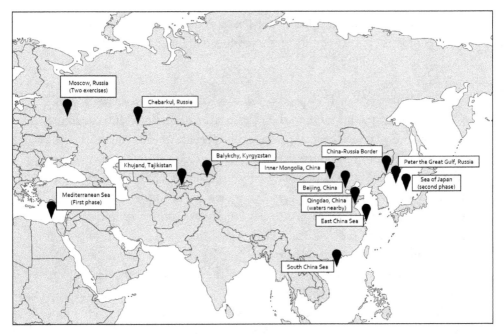

Approximate Location of China-Russia Military Exercises (2012-2016)[77]

First, the "Maritime Silk Road," which passes through the South China Sea, Strait of Malacca, Indian Ocean Region, Persian Gulf, Red Sea, and Mediterranean Sea, connecting China by water to South Asia, Africa, the Middle East, and Europe.

Second, the "Silk Road Economic Belt," which moves along the original Silk Road through Central Asia, the Caucasus, and Russia, and also into Europe.

China's goal with the "Belt and Road"— a projected one trillion-dollar investment program— is to build infrastructure and transportation networks that will link the whole of the Eurasian-African-Australian supercontinental structure more tightly to China. It is a "Middle Kingdom" strategy for the twenty-first century. The "Belt and Road" is— as American author Robert Kaplan put it— "a branding exercise." Many overseas projects and activities existed before Xi Jinping asserted China's intercontinental vision. Nadège Rolland explained in 2017:

> In under three years, the Belt and Road Initiative has become the defining concept of China's foreign policy and is now omnipresent

in official rhetoric. It has established a general direction for the country's efforts to build an interconnected, integrated Eurasian continent before 2050.[78]

The "Belt and Road" is positioned as an economic initiative, a "win-win," and a natural response to the vast, multi-trillion dollar infrastructure needs of emerging Asian and African economies. But it should at this point come as no surprise to notice that it overlaps exactly with China's primary resource interests, and current and future military deployments. Military interests along the "Belt and Road" are of a twenty-first-century nature. China is not concerned with overseas conquest so much as resource and economic security and political influence. Military action could only be a final guarantee of economic growth.

Take, for example, the political crisis in the Maldives, at the heart of the Indian Ocean, in February 2018.

The tiny island nation, known as a white-sand paradise, is made up of over 1,000 islands. Its former president, now in exile, once held the world's first cabinet meeting underwater, in scuba gear, to warn the world that, with rising sea levels, his nation may soon disappear. The British Empire once operated air and naval bases here in remote island outposts. And today, in the shadow of competition for influence between India and China, the island nation finds itself in crisis, caught not between the oceans, but between rising powers.

In 2015, the Maldives amended its constitution to allow foreign nations to own land. In 2017, Chinese naval vessels docked in these islands, and today, the island nation, which has signed on to the "Belt and Road Initiative," may have up to 70 percent of its national debt owned by China.[79] So, in 2018, when a domestic crisis began and the Maldivian president called a state of emergency, a Chinese naval task force, including amphibious ships, entered the Indian Ocean, a move which many interpreted as a warning to India. In the words of a former Indian naval officer, "The message to India was: 'If you come too close to the Maldives, we are not too far away.'"[80] Meanwhile, as a Maldivian cabinet minister explained, "The Chinese interest is purely commercial. They have invested a lot and they have to protect their investments."[81] Ultimately, the crisis was resolved, with the election of a pro-Indian President, but it is likely to be only one of many crises as

China builds its economic and military presence across the "Belt and Road," thousands of miles from the Chinese mainland.

As in many other eras of history, this situation illustrates the old imperial adage in reverse. Where trade once followed the flag, on the "Belt and Road," it is *the flag that follows trade*. The military soon finds its way to where a nation's economic interests are.

As a doctoral student, I sat with the director of a Chinese think tank that was set up to better understand India and its region after the China–India Border War in 1962.

"The Indian Ocean is the most important region in the world for China," he told me, "because China will depend on it *for the next forty years.*"

While global interests matter, it is the Indian Ocean Region — the waterways that form the guts of the Eurasian, African, and Australian intercontinental system — that is the real heart of China's new strategic presence. Half the "Belt and Road" centers on this region where, vaulting ahead of a rising but internally focused India, myriad Chinese plans are underway. China is busy building an extensive system of ports and infrastructure from East Africa and the Arabian Sea to Southeast Asia and the Bay of Bengal, as well as throughout the Indian Ocean islands.

Take, for instance, the China–Pakistan Economic Corridor (CPEC), a $50 billion investment project to give China overland access through Pakistan to the Persian Gulf— thus escaping Hu Jintao's "Malacca Dilemma." The CPEC corridor passes through tumultuous political terrain, in Kashmir, Baluchistan, and in Xinjiang, a region in northwest China subject to continuous human rights abuses and political conflict.

China's determination to integrate the region should be understood as inevitably leading to the presence of expeditionary military forces. Gwadar Port, along with Karachi, is CPEC's key to the Persian Gulf. China Overseas Port Holding Company, a state-owned firm, has a lease on this Arabian Sea port until 2059.[82]

China and Pakistan have been conducting joint naval exercises since 2003.[83] In November 2016, ahead of bilateral exercises, Senior Captain Chi Qingtao, Flotilla Commander Chinese Naval Force, made explicit links between Chinese trade and naval power at Gwadar in the Arabian Sea: "The [fourth] exercise will help improve the naval capability of both countries to protect Gwadar port activities while providing a safe and conducive environment for the movement of merchant ships from there."[84]

China's military expansion is driven by strategic considerations, and also by new security concerns, as Chinese nationals travel by the tens of thousands around the globe to follow and support their nation's expanding economic interests.[85] Bloomberg reports that, by 2018, at least 20,000 Chinese nationals had moved to Pakistan, seeking opportunity as China's economic presence grows. Pakistan has dedicated a military force of 15,000 for protection of CPEC-related projects, but deaths and murders targeting Chinese nationals — for instance, the gunning down in Karachi of an executive from China's largest shipping company — still take place on this new frontier.[86]

In addition to the sea-lane protections envisioned by Chinese admirals of the past, China has begun construction of its first overseas military base. The location is Djibouti, the tiny desert country on the Horn of Africa, at the opposite end of the sea lanes that stretch from the South China Sea across the Indian Ocean into the oil reserves of the Persian Gulf. Chinese naval forces have been operating in the Indian Ocean since 2008 as part of an international antipiracy coalition, docking in the Middle East, Africa, and South Asia, as well as in Indian Ocean island states. Chinese submarines — naval assets which do not have antipiracy uses — have visited Pakistan and Sri Lanka, unsurprisingly, at a Chinese-built terminal in Sri Lanka's port of Colombo.[87]

The web of Chinese ports is often referred to as a "string of pearls," which is meant to guarantee military access to the Indian Ocean Region, and the smooth flow of resources back to China. Though the country denies a concerted strategy of military activity, influence-building, and ownership, the reality is clear.

The port of Hambantota in Sri Lanka, for example, was built and financed by China, and is now controlled by China Merchants Port Holdings, a company controlled by the Chinese state.[88] In 2017, struggling under unmanageable amounts of Chinese debt, Sri Lanka was forced to settle: the island nation, known as "The Jewel of the Indian Ocean," has granted the state-backed Chinese company a 80 percent stake in the port with a 99-year lease which will last until the year 2116. Echoes of the British imperial playbook, with Hong Kong and its adjacent territories on a 99-year lease up to

1997, come to mind. Reports in international media suggest that the Chinese flag was flown over the port of Hambantota for seven days.[89]

Like Gwadar, Sri Lanka is a vital hub on China's "Belt and Road." Chinese companies are building infrastructure around the country, not only in Hambantota, but in Colombo, too, where PLAN submarines have docked on multiple occasions.

In addition to the well-publicized engineering projects across Central Asia, East Africa, Europe, and South and Southeast Asia, lesser-known projects are also underway, with possible political and military value. For example, Huawei, a Chinese telecom company with links to the state and military services, is exploring undersea cables on the Indian Ocean, offering a different map of Chinese regional integration, this time on the seabed. In this scenario, marine cables will link Maldivian islands, and, in a multi-thousand-mile project, Gwadar in Pakistan, Djibouti, and Kenya.[90]

What matters here is that Gwadar and Djibouti are known locations for Chinese military operations. What would the telecommunications infrastructure— built by a company banned from many countries over spying concerns— mean for these Indian Ocean nations?

For now, it should be said that China builds the region's infrastructure as an uncontested power.

Some Chinese analysts are not so careful in their descriptions of the purposes of the "Belt and Road."

Consider these words from two Shanghai analysts in a journal published by the Chinese Academy of Sciences:

> Resources are always scarce; a great nation cannot be stuffed into a narrow space forever. The Eurasian continent is the source where China's national interests are concentrated. It provides a vast stage on which to carry out China's 21st Century geopolitical strategy. As a result of the interaction of the crystallization of the highest wisdom of the Chinese nation and the conditions of the era, the "One Belt, One Road" strategy has announced to the world that the rise of China has arrived, becoming an important starting point for China to go global.[91]

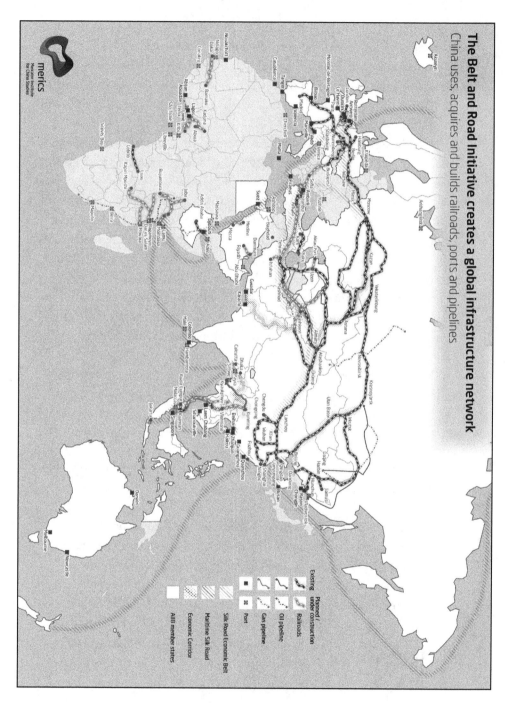

The Belt and Road Initiative creates a global infrastructure network

China uses, acquires and builds railroads, ports and pipelines

The authors also mention that "The 'Belt and Road' concept clearly shows the direction of China's 21ˢᵗ Century global grand strategy." They add that "Many countries along the 'Belt and Road' are rich in natural resources. China already possesses a solid and quickly developing foundation of economic and trade cooperation with these countries. Therefore, they naturally form the optimum target area and an important component of China's global resource supply system."[93]

And here's Professor Shen Dingli of Fudan University, speaking of India, China's regional rival: "China actually has many ways to hurt India. China could send an aircraft carrier to the Gwadar port in Pakistan. China turned down Pakistan's offer to station military units in the country. If India forces China to do that, of course we can put a navy at your doorstep."[94]

Gwadar is one of the primary port and logistics hubs on the "Belt and Road's" "Maritime Silk Road" in the Indian Ocean, and China's gateway to the Arabian Sea and Persian Gulf.

The interconnected Eurasian supercontinent is explained by some Chinese writers as a counter to America's "pivot" or "rebalance" to Asia.[95] The "pivot" was an Obama-era initiative, meant to reorient American strategic focus on the Asia-Pacific, in addition to reducing commitments in the Middle East.

However, the "Belt and Road" strategy is better understood as a new vision of the world map, as perceived in China. The map used by most in China puts the Pacific Ocean at the center, with the Indian Ocean as the core body of water in the Eurasian supercontinent.

American geography has been a fortunate, providential feature, remarked upon by statesmen and historians alike.[96] With open-ocean access to both the Atlantic and Pacific, the United States was secure on its continent from the wars of Europe and the changing empires of Asia.

However, American strategists were aware of an overriding theory that, should any single power come to dominate either Europe or Asia, it would emerge as a continental power capable of challenging American security oceans away.[97] What came to dominate Eurasia could soon come for America. This thinking was a factor in US participation in both World Wars, most visibly in American support for Britain against the Nazi juggernaut after it had rapidly gained control of most of continental Europe.

By the time of the global game known as the Cold War, American thinking became more comprehensive— it was dealing with a far larger adversary. Unlike Germany, which could conquer Europe and North Africa, or Imperial Japan, which spread its dominions across the Western Pacific, the USSR had the potential to dominate *not only Europe but also Eurasia.*

And so American thinking returned to something more fundamental to the quest for power, articulated in what was known as "the Great Game," between the British and Russian Empires in Central Asia. British geographer Halford Mackinder said one hundred years ago that "who rules the Heartland [Central Eurasia] commands the World-Island [Europe, Asia, and Africa]; who rules the World-Island commands the World." Here, the importance of the Chinese superstructure comes into view.

China's structure is not based on the Pacific and the Atlantic. China's view of the world is based on *the Pacific and the Indian Ocean Region.* When analysts speak of China's "two-ocean strategy," it is the Indian and the Pacific Oceans that the nation has in mind.

It is the consolidation of the sea routes that surround the Eurasian-African-Australian supercontinental structure. These are envisioned, as mentioned, by Chinese economic strategists as the three "blue economic passages" in the official "Vision for Maritime Cooperation under the Belt and Road Initiative."[98]

In a future Chinese system, spread across the intercontinental geography of the "Belt and Road," the Indian Ocean would be its maritime core, the primary access route to Africa, Europe, and the Middle East.

The value of Chinese investment and construction in the Indian Ocean Region is without peer and higher than that in any other region of the world: $600 billion between 2005 and 2018. That's double what it has spent in North America or East Asia and $200 billion more than what it has invested or built in Europe.[99] Indian Ocean monies comprise nearly one-third of China's total global investment and construction since 2005. And, as the head of a Chinese think tank explained to me, the country sees itself depending on the region and its resources "for the next forty years."[100]

At present, China's trade routes run from the Pacific to the Americas, overland to Europe ("the Silk Road Economic Belt"), by sea through the Indian Ocean to Europe and Africa ("the Maritime Silk Road"), and

China's Trade Routes [101]

through the Northwest Passage in the Arctic to Europe. The latter is the least developed. However, China has recently announced that *even the Arctic* and its Northern Sea Route is part of the "Belt and Road."[102]

For China, seeking trade with Europe, even the Arctic offers a way around Malacca. But what kind of military presence, if any, is China planning in this unforgiving polar region? This has yet to be seen.

It's impressive to see China attempting to meet a fundamental geostrategic challenge that might have been judged impossible by another nation: creating what the United States has had through the simple grace of geography— global, open-ocean national security.

Instead of America's natural position between the world's two largest oceans, China must transform its larger region—the Eurasian-Indian Ocean supercontinent—to cope with myriad chokepoints that jeopardize trade flows. What even Mao and Deng could not conceive of was the extent of the geographical region that China would depend on as the "great rejuvenation" continued, decade after decade.

Xi understands that a global trade-based China must guarantee access to the global maritime commons, and he aims to tie the world together geographically in ways that will place China, as is the Party's design, at the world's economic and strategic center.

Should Chinese super-strategy be realized, as the "great rejuvenation" proceeds along its benchmarks, from 2021, to 2035, to the future world of 2049, the world's strategic map will have a China of unprecedented power, exerting its influence from the heavens to the ocean floors, in space, cyber, land, air, and sea, and whichever new military domains may come into existence, while projecting its military power across the continents that comprise the geography of the "Belt and Road."

China's economic and therefore political survival depends on assured access to the world's resources, and the project to secure them is fully underway.

TOWARD 2049: CHINA'S VISION OF MILITARY POWER

W hile China's current military structure is focused on "active defense" in the Indo-Pacific, its future presence and capabilities will be far more powerful.

The drive to build a military "second to none" is public.

There has been heavy investment in advanced military technologies: maritime force projection, frontier technologies, space-based systems, and nuclear weapons upgrades, including hypersonic vehicles, all of which will define any future battlespace between major powers.

Clearly, the Party views itself in competition for the first tier.

To offer a flavor of this perspective, here's an excerpt from a key document on China's military and economic future. The State Council's *New Generation of Artificial Intelligence Development Plan*, in a section called "The Strategic Situation":

> AI has become a new focus of international competition. AI is a strategic technology that will lead in the future; the world's major developed countries are taking the development of AI as a major strategy to enhance national competitiveness and protect national security; intensifying the introduction of plans and strategies for this core technology, top talent, standards and regulations, etc.; and trying to seize the initiative in the new round of international science and technology competition.

At present, China's situation in national security and international competition is more complex, and [China] must, looking
at the world, take the development of AI to the national strategic level with systematic layout, take the initiative in planning,
firmly seize the strategic initiative in the new stage of international competition in AI development, to create new competitive advantage, opening up the development of new space, and
effectively protecting national security.[103]

Another core technology is quantum computing.

Quantum technology allows for potentially unbreakable communications links, as well as the related ability to break any encryption keys, given
a quantum computer's processing speeds, superior to the fastest existing
computers by orders of magnitude. Chinese endeavors in quantum technology, assisted at present through access to major research institutions
throughout the Western world, may enable the CCP to achieve what Pan
Jianwei, "the father of Chinese quantum information science," terms *"quantum supremacy."*[104]

Dr. Pan's work has caught the attention of Xi Jinping and other members of the Politburo.

Many are concerned the United States has already fallen far behind in
these areas.

Without the financial resources, clarity of vision, economies of scale,
and sustained focus that China is able to apply to these strategic technologies, it is possible that China may gain a powerful lead in the technologies
of the future, enabling all manner of victories over the United States and
building the ascendency to achieve its aims by 2049.

If successful, mastery of quantum science and its applied technologies
would give China an important edge in any future strategic competition. US
defense technology specialist Elsa Kania observes that, "While quantum communications networks are much more secure against cyber espionage, future
quantum computing has the potential to leapfrog US cyber capabilities."[105]

Prioritization of these technologies evinces both an ambition and an
understanding of the path to a potentially decisive advantage over competitors in any future battlespace. It also reminds us of an approach to military
technology and weapons development that took shape decades ago.

Since the 1990s, awakened by the First Gulf War, Chinese military strategists have aimed to determine the long-term direction of key military technologies, build up "asymmetric" advantages, and "leapfrog" the United States.

What is surprising is how little, apparently, the United States knew about China's military planning just twenty years ago. According to Michael Pillsbury, a China analyst who worked for decades in the US defense system, he was asked in the early 2000s by the then Vice President, Dick Cheney, to determine what exactly China was preparing militarily in order "to learn whether China really had an antisatellite program, a counter-stealth program, or aircraft carrier-killer missiles."[106]

Today, these very programs are not only real, but they have reshaped the military balance of the West Pacific, vastly complicating the operating environment for the US and its allies. To think that, at the highest levels of government, the United States did not know that these investments and programs were happening reminds us of how brilliantly China has moved from a position of total disadvantage to what Aaron Friedberg calls "a contest for supremacy" in less than a generation's time.[107]

PART III

赶上美国，超过美国

CATCH UP TO AMERICA, SURPASS AMERICA

★ ★ ★

CHINA'S ECONOMIC AND TECHNOLOGICAL AMBITIONS

Our objective is to catch up with America and then to surpass America. America only has one hundred million people or more; our population is over six hundred million. We should catch up with America. On the day that we catch up with America and overtake America, then we can let out a breath of air. Now, we are not there and must take the bullying.[1]

MAO ZEDONG, FOUNDER OF THE
PEOPLE'S REPUBLIC OF CHINA, 1955

The U.S. world order is a suit that no longer fits.[2]

CHINESE COMMUNIST PARTY,
FINANCIAL TIMES, 2016

[T]he Party has united and led all the Chinese people in a tireless struggle, propelling China into a leading position in terms of economic and technological strength, defense capabilities, and composite national strength. China's international standing has risen as never before.[3]

XI JINPING, 2017

THE WORLD HAS BEEN LIVING WITH CHINA'S "ECONOMIC MIRACLE" for over thirty years.

Hundreds of millions have been lifted from poverty.

It has become the manufacturing power of the world— approaching the industrial output of the United States and Japan combined.

Over 30 of the world's 100 largest cities are in China, and over 100 cities in China have a population of one million or more.

China has the largest labor force on the planet— over 800 million people.

Operating on "Five Year Plans"—once laughed at in a post-Cold War world—the country has transformed itself, becoming one of only two economies on Earth with a GDP over ten trillion dollars.

Its volume of trade and capture of global commodities are second to none.

China's companies, both state-owned and private sector, have expanded across the Earth, making great gains not only in manufacturing, but in technology, agriculture, infrastructure, and shipping, and in many cases leading entire industries.

From an inward-looking country riven by political dissonance and economic torpor in the twentieth century, China has emerged to trade with all the world's regions, becoming the *top trading nation, ahead of the United States*, and building up massive cash reserves, many times those of other nations.

And that is just today. The *next* thirty years may be far more consequential.

"COMPREHENSIVE NATIONAL POWER"

Comprehensive national power is an economic concept.

Xi Jinping's "China Dream," like the guiding ideas of his predecessors, is based on realizing China's economic potential.

Even as an agrarian, pre-industrial society in the Cold War, Mao and his comrades chose Communism and socialism as their path, not because they expected to produce stagnation and misery, but because they, like their Soviet counterparts, believed that a socialist economy would prove superior to Western capitalism. China and the USSR could *outproduce* the West.

Much is made of China's former glory. Whether it is Xi Jinping referencing China's civilizational brilliance prior to the Opium Wars — "With a history of more than 5,000 years, our nation created a splendid civilization, made remarkable contributions to mankind, and became one of the world's great nations" — or the World Economic Forum sharing a table on China as the world's largest economy in the 1700s, and then anticipating a return to this position in the 2030s, many in China and around the world have bought into the narrative that China's rise is not a rise, but a return.[4]

The Party's narrative of history, as we have seen, is not rise, but restoration.

The important thing is to understand that *economics* will be the foundation for China's power as a whole.

This goes back to an epithet from ancient China: 富国强兵, which translates as "Wealthy country, strong military."

Let's have a look at the idea in modern terms.

One sees the phrase "wealth and power" scrolling on LED lights in China's schoolyards, taught as a mantra to the children of today.

The related concept, "comprehensive national power," is explained by leading scholars at Qinghua University in Beijing in their essay, "The Rising of Modern China: Comprehensive National Power and Grand Strategy."

Hu Angang and Men Honghua begin by quoting Sun Tzu's *The Art of War*. "The art of war is of vital importance to the state. It is a matter of life and death, a road either to safety or to ruin. Hence it is a subject of inquiry which can on no account be neglected."[5] The authors then offer a discussion of "comprehensive national power," which they explain as follows: "[T]he status (or position) of a country in the international community is in essence associated with the rise and fall of its national power, the increase and decrease of its strategic resources," explaining that "[comprehensive national power] . . . means the sum total of the powers or strengths of a country in economy, military affairs, science & technology, education, and resources and its influence."[6]

While China has a profound military culture and a proud military history, throughout much of the history of Chinese civilization, China's massive economy or market generally has been the centerpiece of Chinese power. This has never been lost on China's leaders, even in the most fervent ideological moments of Communism.

As Zhou Enlai, China's Premier under Mao Zedong and himself a staunch Communist, once remarked of China's appeal to Western Europe— in the context of a strategy to weaken American alliances:

> [Western Europe] has to look for a way out by finding a vast [foreign] market in its efforts to restore its economy, and the East–West trade certainly provides that outlet . . . given its 600 million population, China has always been a very large market and thus to trade with China has enormous potential.[7]

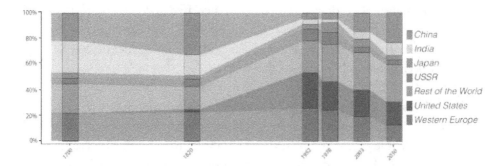

Share of world GDP (% of world total), 1700 – 2030

The appeal of the Chinese market has always been a centerpiece of China's view of its own strength. Much of the patriotic passion that defined the "Century of Humiliation" was directed against the stagnation and technological backwardness that had crushed China in comparison to the rising empires of Europe and Japan.

Even under Mao, a crusade began to restore China's economy, including through the ill-fated Great Leap Forward, the objective of which was not to starve tens of millions in the countryside, but to surpass Britain in industrial capacity.[8]

What was missing was not an objective, but the competence to see it through.

As Richard Nixon remarked of China during the opening of US-China relations, "Well, you can just stop and think of what could happen if anybody with a decent system of government got control of that mainland. Good God. There'd be no power in the world that could even—I mean, you put 800 million Chinese to work under a decent system—and they will be the leaders of the world."[9]

China received that system overhaul under Deng Xiaoping. And China today aspires to what Nixon once predicted, based, quite simply, on the continued success of the economy. Note how Hu Jintao ties together power and economic might:

> The economy has developed steadily and rapidly. China's overall national strength has grown considerably. The gross domestic product (GDP) has reached 47.3 trillion yuan in 2011, and government revenue increased by a wide margin. The overall agricultural production capacity has increased and grain output has gone up year after year. Fresh progress has been made in adjusting the industrial structure, and the infrastructure has been extensively upgraded.[10]

The fixation on technology is now at the heart of Chinese economic planning—and also at the heart of the work of many entrepreneurs and businesspeople—a fixation which began during the Opium Wars as Qing dynasty officials puzzled over how to fight the British invaders, whom they had designated as coastal pirates.[11]

Have a look at Hu's references to technology and innovation while addressing the nation in 2012:

> Notable progress has been made in making China an innovative country, and major breakthroughs have been made in manned spaceflights, the lunar exploration program, and in the development of a manned deep-sea submersible, supercomputers and high-speed railways.[12]

Advanced technology and innovation continue to be at the heart of Chinese strategy, not only for the military industrial base, but to continue to build economic power as the country rises up the value chain and as labor costs increase.

MADE IN CHINA 2025: MASTERING FUTURE INDUSTRIES AND GOING GLOBAL

The most important strategic program today is called "Made in China 2025."

This industrial initiative looks out over a ten-year time frame (it was released in 2015), and is couched in terms of China's national destiny and the grand historical terms of "the rise and fall of world powers":

> Manufacturing is the main pillar of the national economy, the foundation of the country, tool of transformation and basis of prosperity. Since the beginning of industrial civilization in the middle of the 18th century, it has been proven repeatedly by the rise and fall of world powers that without strong manufacturing, there is no national prosperity. Building internationally competitive manufacturing is the only way China can enhance its strength, protect state security and become a world power.[13]

Planners identified "strategic industries" in the Hu Jintao years that China would have to master to sustain economic growth and achieve the superpower status coveted by its leaders. The sectors targeted for mastery are:

- Next Generation IT
- High-end Digital Control Machine Tools and Robots
- Aerospace and Aeronautical Equipment
- Oceanographic Engineering Equipment and High-technology Shipping

- Advanced Rail Transportation Equipment
- Energy Efficient and New Energy Automobiles
- Electric Power Equipment
- Agricultural Machinery Equipment
- New Materials
- Bio-pharmaceuticals and High-performance Medical Equipment

"Made in China 2025" highlights the "urgency" of China's need to catch up with advanced economies in terms of science and technology, linking this to the PRC's original self-conception as the "New China" and to "China's position as a world power":

> Since the founding of New China, and especially following the reform and opening-up period, China's manufacturing sector has maintained rapid development and has built an industrial system that is both comprehensive and independent. It has greatly supported China's industrialization and modernization and significantly enhanced the country's overall strength.
>
> It has supported China's position as a world power. However, compared with the advanced economies, China's manufacturing sector is large but not strong, with obvious gaps in innovation capacity, efficiency of resource utilization, quality of industrial infrastructure and degree of digitalization. The task of upgrading and accelerating technological development is urgent.[14]

The advent of "Made in China 2025" is an "existential" issue, according to my conversations with economists and trade organizations in the United States.

When China enters new export markets, it does so not only with cheaper goods, but also with government support.

As a Chinese telecommunications manager explained to me on a plane ride in India, "China is one giant incubator." In other words, decades' worth of forced joint-ventures, technology transfer, cyber-espionage, and conditional market access given to foreign firms in their quest to enter China's giant market has produced one great outcome: globally competitive Chinese firms.

Chinese firms, especially those known as "national champions," are given priority over foreign firms inside the Chinese market, while benefitting from unconventional methods such as state-supported technology transfers, financing, and espionage—a practice that has lasted decades, but which has begun to reach a tipping point for something even larger.

What happens after "incubation" in China's giant domestic market is that these firms go out into the world—while *continuing* to receive the support of the Chinese state.

The country's objective of turning "national champions" into global actors will mean a new form of competition for multinational companies around the world, something which has never been seen on this scale in history.

When American and other global companies compete with their Chinese competitors, they are competing not only with these companies, but also with the Chinese state.

The investments that are necessary to compete globally are there thanks to massive amounts of capital which the state can deploy to build new "champions" and aid existing companies in both traditional and emerging industries.

This strategy is what enables China to overcome barriers to entry and "leapfrog" not only military technologies, but vital sectors which are the essence of industrial and economic power.

A panelist at the Center for Strategic and International Studies (CSIS) in Washington, DC, explained this phenomenon using robotics as an example:

> Out of the thousand companies that are out there . . . You'll end up with a dozen or half a dozen that will be world class, eventually. And that's where they're going. That's the plan. And it's a very long game. It's not a five-year game, it's not a ten-year game. It's a twenty-year game. And in the end, twenty years later, you've burnt through massive amounts of capital to eventually dominate or have high control of a very high, very important critical industry; the outcome is positive in the end.[15]

Regarding smartphones, he explained that there would be "Lots of losers, a few winners, and eventually the market will concentrate on four or five players, of which two or three will be Chinese. Apple, Samsung, Huawei, a couple other players, and that'll be the smartphone market."[16]

At the heart of this is state strategic planning.

As "Made in China 2025" explains:

> At present, a new wave of technological and industrial revolution is aligning with the transformation of China's economic development and reshaping the structure of the international division of labor. China must seize this historic opportunity to implement a strategy of reinvigorating Chinese manufacturing and reinforce planning and forward deployment in accordance with the requirements of the "Four Comprehensive Points" strategic blueprint (a prosperous society, policy reform, rule of law, party discipline).
>
> We will strive to transform China into the global manufacturing leader before the centennial of the founding of New China, which will lay the foundation for the realization of the Chinese dream to rejuvenate the Chinese nation.[17]

Though some are dismissive of these initiatives, China's acceleration across major industries can already be observed.

Take shipbuilding, for example. In the year 2000, China contributed very little in terms of global ship production. Today, China is the largest shipbuilding nation in the world by compensated gross tonnage.[18] Shipbuilding was explicitly selected for mastery.

"Made in China 2025" provides firm guidance on which sectors the country seeks to master. Consider also those sectors and technologies where Chinese companies have made significant progress of their own, whether through acquisition (take Lenovo's purchase of IBM's personal computer business as an example) or organic growth in technology companies such as Huawei, Xiaomi, Tencent, and Haier. In the case of the latter, Haier was once considered an attractive acquisition target for General Electric. But as the Chinese incubator moved forward, the roles reversed and Haier bought GE Appliances.

Today, China's economic power is visible across numerous industries, and the ambitions of the Chinese state are visible in every major emerging technology of the twenty-first century. Through global acquisitions, state-led strategic investment, and global cyber- and human espionage, China's state and private corporations have made great gains in everything from telecommunications, semiconductors, robotics, aerospace, automobiles, space industry, and agricultural and industrial machinery, and even in major technologies where the US has always been confident in its ability to lead, from artificial intelligence, autonomous vehicle development, big-data processing, smart appliances, to other Internet of Things-driven industries.

The creation of an advanced industrial base is essential to the Communist Party's ambition of catching up with and ultimately surpassing the United States as the leading technological power.

Importantly, China's industrial base doubles as a base for military power. The two, for Chinese leaders, are inseparable, especially given the Party's view of history.

China's sense of decline and fall historically is based on a lack of technological capacity. The country was, in the eyes of generations of Chinese citizens, picked apart in defeat after defeat by the European and Japanese empires. The wide gap in military technology, as well as political and economic stagnation, is often named as the culprit in these defeats, the foundations of the "Century of Humiliation."

In short, in the view of its government and many citizens, China's fall as a nation was the result of lagging technology and a stagnant economy.

In 2006, my first year in China, I could not get away from conversations that hinged on two points: "We are lagging behind" and "We must develop the economy." The two words 落后 (lagging) and 现代化 (modern) featured in hundreds and hundreds of conversations I had in China's cities and countryside.

It's striking how the words from China's leaders were reverberating through the conversations of the whole country, from the cities to the remotest villages—some with barely any electricity, where a single loudspeaker in the village square would blare the party line on economics, and farmers and families would carry on the conversation with me in their homes.

Hu Jintao had seized upon modernization and development as the national narrative. On the other hand, this is an old, old struggle in China.[19] Remember that Mao's Cultural Revolution took as its object of destruction anything that was not fully revolutionary—or anything which spoke of China's past.

The people I met in that first year were visibly confronting anything that was "old," whether it meant tearing down old houses, village structures, and urban districts, or speaking of the importance of wealth and new advances in technology. It seemed that the country was tearing apart its past traditions in order to rush into modernity of a Western kind. I did not know then how long and hard China had struggled against its past. As a saying goes in the country: "If the Old doesn't go, the New will not arrive."

And in China, the New means power.

THE IMPORTANCE OF ECONOMIC POWER: TECHNOLOGY AND NATIONAL STRENGTH

Meiji Japan was famous among twentieth-century Asian leaders as the one country that avoided a fate as a Western colony. This question plagued generations, not only in China, but around Asia and Africa. As European colonialism seeped into the rest of the world, nearly 450 million people came under foreign rule.[20] While resistance movements came and went, only in the twentieth century, after the Second World War, did colonialism begin to end in earnest around the world. Two European wars broke the back of empire, and the "Great Divergence" began to come to an end, giving way to the Cold War between the Soviet Union and the United States. Nearly every Asian and African nation holds this colonial heritage. And many attribute the horrors of colonization to a lack of economic progress and political unity.

China's narrative stands out.

It stands out not for its focus on economic and technological power, but for its emphasis on military power and on violence. This is largely the Communist Party's contribution to decolonization narratives. In the 1950s, Mao Zedong sought to build and lead a forum for decolonizing nations. Importantly, he added China's own national narrative to that of other nations, tying China's "humiliations" to those of others around the world. At the center of this was economics:

> We have a long-term plan. Fundamentally, our plan is to build up economics, and plant the seeds for ten to fifteen years. There are lots of external problems. Taiwan and South Korea have US

bases. Japan, Philippines, Vietnam and Thailand also have US bases. We hope that all Afro-Asian countries will build up their economies. We can all unite and say what we want to imperialism . . .

Other countries like India, Burma, Indonesia, and Pakistan are all about the same, they have no industry. Independent countries can take steps forward, but joining military pacts divides us . . .

In 1900, the Eight Nation Alliance beat their way into Beijing. The armies of the Eight Nation Alliance also included small countries, but they humiliated a big country. Japan was also a small country and it invaded us. This is because they were an industrialized country, and we were agricultural, and our government was corrupt.[21]

The other tool was violence. As decolonization and national liberation movements gained traction, Mao sought to contribute China's ideology to the struggle. Speaking to an Algerian delegation— a nation at war with its French occupants— in 1958, he drew up a map of global struggle:

In the circumstances of anti-imperialism, we here count as one frontline, that is the Eastern frontline, on the West Pacific. You are the Western front line. You are in a period of difficulty . . . We have gone through many setbacks in the last twenty-two years; ultimately we won. India struggled against Britain for decades but won. Egypt has been independent for just a few years. Of course, their methods were different. Your struggle against the French now is a national liberation struggle. The time of the struggle may be long. Hopefully yours won't take as long as ours.[22]

In the early decades of China's revolution, Mao and his compatriots saw economic revitalization, military struggle, and confrontation with the United States as intertwined. Not only in China's region, but around the developing-decolonizing world. It was part of the Party's agenda of overturning what they saw as inequities against China in the existing world order. As John W. Garver, one of the enduring scholars of China's international relations, explains:

> At a minimum, [Mao] hoped to pressure the United States to cease supporting the [Taiwan-based GMD], blocking China's entry into the United Nations, and economically isolating China. Maximally, if several foreign revolutions actually succeeded, China might emerge as the leader of a revitalized world revolutionary movement and the structure of U.S. power in Asia would either collapse or be rolled back.[23]

This approach to the world has softened, to be sure. However, the ideologies at its center are not gone and are likely to reemerge. The central lessons of the "Century of Humiliation" are essentially: build the economy, build technology, build the military, and prepare to fight. Not only in China's region, but around the world. As the country's global reach expands, and as the Communist Party searches for an ideology with international resonance—a message that will appeal to and justify its power to the world—we may see a return to an attempt to make China's sense of triumph over an old system and, of course, its "economic miracle" more attractive to other nations.

China's leaders have already begun to take up messages that are similar to those in Mao's time drawing contrasts between China and the West, between China and democratic systems, and between Chinese leadership and the humiliations visited upon many nations by a prior world order. Many of these arguments will be made, and are already being made, in terms of economic power, often with Chinese leaders, officials, and propagandists attempting to position their country as the champion of other developing nations around the world.[24]

China's new global role comes from its position of economic power. Military and diplomatic power is also built on economic power. If China aims for its military to be "second to none," it aims even higher for its economy. With economic supremacy, the rest will follow.

CHINA'S ECONOMY: REJUVENATION'S ENGINE

L et's turn to the state of China's economy.

There are many narratives, and many myths and misconceptions.

Standard discourse around the world ranges from two extreme poles: from China as an unstoppable juggernaut— soon to pass the US, or having already surpassed it— to narratives of impending doom— China will eventually collapse or hit a wall, and that will be the end of this.[25] Will China rule the world, doubling or tripling American GDP, or is this a repeat of fears over Japan in the 1980s, when numerous Americans believed that Japan would surpass the US in economic and technological capacity? In the latter example, Japanese businesses were buying up properties around Manhattan and in other global cities, exporting cheaper electronic goods and automobiles, and a host of fearful products appeared in American culture (some might remember Michael Crichton's *Rising Sun*). This scenario never materialized, and Japan was hamstrung by aging demographics and enormous debt.

In China's case, it may be neither of these extremes. The GDP increases over the past thirty years are unprecedented in human history, though one must also understand the realities of environmental degradation, human displacement, and debt in China's economic ascendency. It may be most useful to look at China as a case of patient, state-led strategic planning intertwined with a work force many times the size of most other nations, a period of globalization that offered new export opportunities, and a global division of labor that played to China's natural advantages in manufacturing and nascent industrial power. These factors and others converged to bring us the China of today. Whether one (or all) of these elements continues to fuel Chinese growth will tell us much about where China can go tomorrow. The Communist Party understands very clearly that its job is to ensure the maintenance and advancement of this juggernaut, the engine of China's restoration.

We can see it best in China's city skylines. Have a look at Shenzhen and Shanghai. The former was once a fishing village across the river from prosperous Hong Kong. It has since turned into one of the world's top manufacturing and export centers— now a forest of buildings more than forty stories tall. Shanghai's eastern district was once farmland. Today, this Epcot-like cityscape is universal language for the future, and for the Chinese economic meteor.

What we need to understand is how long and hard China's leaders, whether Communists, mercantilists, quasi-capitalists, or all of the above have worked toward a single goal— revitalization. And how successfully they have been in mobilizing their country to achieve these ends. And how accurate they have been in pinpointing and replicating several of what historian Niall Ferguson calls the "killer apps" of the West.[26]

China's success and discipline have led to a transformation, already, of the world order, and an epochal shift in history. That is, the beginning of a transition of wealth and power to Asia from the West. Even if it stalls, a new balance of power is emerging.

However, China's plans are about *anything* but allowing this to stall or stop.

In the views of the leadership, China is just getting started.

Counterarguments about China's ascendency— that is, that it will not happen— stress problems with the economy. And these certainly exist. Think about resource misallocation— epitomized by China's "ghost cities," the ultimate "bridges to nowhere," entire metropolises planned and executed where not a soul resides. Think about a looming housing bubble and aging demographics— "Will China get old before it gets rich?"— and potentially the most important issue of all— the massive debt that has funded growth for years.

China's economy is slowing. The double-digit growth rates that lasted thirty years are over now. Until roughly 2014, China was adding the equivalent of the entire GDP of India every two years.[27] While this is no longer true, China still adds more to its GDP each year than any other nation.

Even with slower Chinese growth, China is on track to surpass the United States in terms of real GDP in the 2030s. The US National Intelligence Council has this factored into its thinking: "China alone will probably have the largest economy, surpassing that of the United States a few years before 2030,"[28] and the idea has become commonplace from international security circles to global investment banks. Not if— but when— will China become the top economy in the world?

Chinese state media, a central location for the Communist Party's conversation with its own people, has changed the tune on breakneck economic growth. It is no longer a national imperative to grow at any speed as it was in prior years. The Party now speaks of "balanced" growth and environmental need, changing the narrative of the 2000s.

Chinese leaders focus as much on managing *the narrative* as managing the economy.

Messaging is a feature of any government. Media briefings, government relationships with journalists, and phenomena such as social media activities by national leaders all massage public perceptions. But in China the nature and level of message management is quite different. Bill Bishop, a leading "China hand" in Washington, explains:

> [This is] all about re-orienting the bureaucracy to focus on greener, more balanced and sustainable development . . . The Party has changed the "principal contradiction" that the Marxists in China believe defines society. Since 1981, near the start of the reform and opening era, the principal contradiction had been "the ever-growing material and cultural needs of the people versus backward social production," which effectively justified growth at all costs. For the Xi era, that contradiction is now "between unbalanced and inadequate development and the people's ever-growing needs for a better life." This puts much greater emphasis on the quality of how ordinary Chinese live.[29]

Here the "two centenary goals," in 2021 and 2049, are important once again.

The Party's goals for economic "rejuvenation" have been handed down from leader to leader, beginning with Mao's vision of surpassing the United States, on to Deng's program of using gradations of economic liberalization to free the nation's productivity, on into the first articulations of the "two centenary goals" under Jiang Zemin and Hu Jintao that laid out the long-term framework for China's ascendency.

Xi Jinping, as the current steward, explained the following to his country in 2017:

> After adopting the policy of reform and opening up, our Party laid out three strategic goals for achieving socialist modernization in China. The first two— ensuring that people's basic needs are met and that their lives are generally decent— have been accomplished ahead of time. Building on this, our Party then developed the vision that by the time we celebrate our centenary, we will have developed our society into a moderately prosperous one with a stronger economy, greater democracy, more advanced science and education, thriving culture, greater social harmony, and a better quality of life.[30]

That first centenary is in 2021, 100 years since the founding of the CCP. The second is in 2049:

> After this, with another 30 years of work, and by the time we celebrate the centenary of the People's Republic of China, we will have basically achieved modernization and turned China into a modern socialist country . . .
>
> We must show firm resolve in implementing the strategy for invigorating China through science and education, the strategy on developing a quality workforce, the innovation-driven development strategy, the rural vitalization strategy, the coordinated regional development strategy, the sustainable development strategy, and the military–civilian integration strategy.[31]

Xi adds that *the coming ten years* are a kind of fulcrum between now and 2049.

In Xi's own words, 2017 to 2027 "is the period in which the time frames of the two centenary goals converge."[32] As he explains, "In this period, not only must we finish building a moderately prosperous society in all respects and achieve the first centenary goal; we must also build on this achievement to embark on a new journey toward the second centenary goal of fully building a modern socialist country."[33]

The Party's "two-stage development plan" from 2020 to 2049 is "based on a comprehensive analysis of the international and domestic environments and the conditions for China's development." The plan's objectives demand stating. The "first stage"— from 2020 to 2035— has these goals:

- China's economic and technological strength has increased significantly. China has become a global leader in innovation.

- The rights of the people to participate and to develop as equals are adequately protected.

- The rule of law for the country, the government, and society is basically in place.

- Institutions in all fields are further improved; the modernization of China's system and capacity for governance is basically achieved.

- Social etiquette and civility are significantly enhanced. China's cultural soft power has grown much stronger; Chinese culture has greater appeal.

- People are leading more comfortable lives, and the size of the middle-income group has grown considerably. Disparities in urban–rural development, in development between regions, and in living standards are significantly reduced; equitable access to basic public services is basically ensured; and solid progress has been made toward prosperity for everyone.

- A modern social governance system has basically taken shape, and society is full of vitality, harmonious and orderly.

- There is a fundamental improvement in the environment; the goal of building a Beautiful China is basically attained.[34]

In the "second stage," from 2035 to 2049, China will build upon "having basically achieved modernization," and then achieve the following goals by 2049:

- New heights are reached in every dimension of material, political, cultural, and ethical, social, and ecological advancement.

- Modernization of China's system and capacity for governance is achieved.

- China has become a global leader in terms of composite national strength and international influence.

- Common prosperity for everyone is basically achieved.

- The Chinese people enjoy happier, safer, and healthier lives. The Chinese nation will become a proud and active member of the community of nations.[35]

The goals may sound vague. But let's focus on the detailed objectives, especially for technology, innovation, and natural resources, and we will see a picture that has already begun to appear.

CHINA'S AMBITIONS IN TECHNOLOGY AND INNOVATION

China's technological ambitions require the help of many non-Chinese entities.

China has, to a certain extent, set itself up to pull in talent and creativity. Building from the lure—the great mirage of China's colossal market—companies, researchers, scholars, and universities from around the world have been brought in to teach, transfer, or otherwise hand over their knowledge and experience, and to help China build its technological abilities.

George S. Yip and Bruce McKern explain in *China's Next Strategic Advantage: From Imitation to Innovation* that "Multi-national corporations already operating in China have had the benefit of experiencing this vast laboratory of innovation . . . Not to be present and actively innovating in China is to miss the opportunity of the century."[36]

However, the same companies tell a different tale themselves, especially when it comes to access to China's enormous market. The 2018 "Business Climate Survey Report" from the American Chamber of Commerce in China tells us this:

> [A]n astounding 75% of members still feel increasingly unwelcome, reflecting the persistence of perceptions among foreign-invested companies that they are not treated equally with their domestic competitors. When talking about context, it is also necessary to recognize that some sectors, such as consumer products, feel the heavy hand of government much less than those connected with the government's most distorting industrial policies, like those listed in the Made in China 2025 initiative.[37]

China's long-term strategy is not about granting foreign companies special access to their market. It's about building a system in which *Chinese companies* and innovation satisfy the vast internal market, while exporting around the world. But, for now, foreign companies are necessary helpers in making the leap.

The United States is noticing, and a shift is underway toward long-term strategic competition.

The evidence and perspectives brought up in a Congressional hearing, "China's Technological Rise: Challenges to US Innovation and Security," help us understand the situation overall:

> China has undertaken a comprehensive industrial strategy to advance domestic high-tech industry through nonmarket means. Massive state subsidies and zero-sum tactics degrade foreign competitiveness, and the systematic and widespread theft of intellectual property and forced transfers of technology destroys innovation and research investments. Today is World Intellectual Property Day, a fitting time for a reminder that protecting U.S. innovation must be an inviolable part of our national strategy toward China.

And:

> These predatory industrial policies are in full display in China's ongoing attempts to dominate critical high-technology supply chains such as semiconductor production. The economic stakes are high. The United States is the world's leader in semiconductors. The industry employs more Americans than the steel industry, and semiconductors are our fourth most valuable export.[38]

The next big business story from China will not be about a revolution in market access for foreign firms. It is much more likely to be about China's "national champions" going global, competing with these same foreign firms from whom they gained technology and knowhow.

Importantly, the massive theft of intellectual property from companies around the world is at the heart of China's "economic miracle." And it is even more important for the next steps that the country must take. Famously referred to as "the greatest transfer of wealth in history,"[39] the systematic industrial espionage campaign waged by the Chinese state has effectively turned American corporations into the research and development arms of the Chinese state and its corporations. China can then go on to apply this research and development on far larger economies of scale, harnessing the advantage that Chinese leaders have understood for generations— the size of the population.

A critically important fact forgotten by many outside observers is this: China's economy is still *state-led.*

Despite reforms and the role of private enterprise in China, the Communist Party retains control over most industries and many companies, including those at the very top of the Fortune Global 500 (FG 500), a list of the world's largest corporations by revenue.

The Party decides which industries matter and invests massive resources.

In essence, international corporations are in competition with a 12 trillion-dollar authoritarian super-architect with global geopolitical objectives. Whether it is pouring billions into robotics, biotechnology, and quantum computing, or snapping up strategic acquisitions such as deep-sea mining corporations and leading-edge aerospace composites companies, China's innovation and technology strategy is built on forced technology transfer, cybertheft, massive state-led capital investment, and global strategic acquisitions done by state-run corporations.

Cybertheft—the most widely known example of the interference of the Chinese state in global business—has ranged from theft of designs for advanced US fighter planes and gas distribution networks to "personal information from healthcare providers." The process has lasted years, with "almost daily raids on Silicon Valley firms, military contractors and other commercial targets."[40]

In 2016, Xi Jinping assured President Barack Obama that China would curb the theft of intellectual property from the United States. But the reality appears to be different. The *New York Times*, reviewing a widely cited report on Chinese cyber-espionage, explained that after this summit:

Chinese attacks have decreased in volume, but increased in sophistication. The result is that Chinese hackers are now acting
more like Russian hackers: They pick their targets more carefully, and cover their tracks.

We see a threat that is less voluminous but more focused,
calculated, and still successful in compromising corporate networks, the report said.[41]

Outbound mergers and acquisitions are another vital component of
China's industrial strategy.

Acquisitions from the seemingly obscure corners of the tech world have
reportedly led to breakthroughs not only in civilian industry, but also in
China's military-industrial base.

Europe, especially, has proven to be a fertile ground for technology acquisitions. One author brands it a technological Africa where China can
acquire the resources it needs, not for basic manufacturing, but for advanced technology— buying not cobalt and copper, but entire corporations that represent years', even decades', worth of knowledge, innovation,
and effort.[42]

The acquisition ten years ago of a British semiconductor company may
have facilitated a breakthrough on China's new aircraft carriers. Xi has
asked that China's next aircraft carrier be fitted with EMALS— Electromagnetic Aircraft Launch System— an advanced carrier system currently
only available to the United States Navy. Should China pull this off, it may
have been with the help of this fine British technology, as the British company, now majority-owned by a Chinese firm, has reportedly been producing key components that can be used for EMALS aircraft carriers.[43]

Analysts have expressed concern over China's purchase of robotics companies in Europe, which could result in potential military use, noting that
"the introduction of robotics to the battlefield will ultimately allow the
PLA to specialize in high-end warfare."[44] And German engineering has reportedly played a role in the buildup of the Chinese navy, with German
technology finding its way into Chinese attack submarines and frigates.[45]
Meanwhile, China's next-generation fighter jets are widely known to be
made from stolen plans from the United States.[46] Universities have also

joined the fun. Take Oxford's annual "Oxford China Lecture" in Beijing in 2017, with the subject "Quantum Technology: A New Era in Computing."[47] Technology theft, transfer, acquisition, and research applied to China's industrial base is building the military, which is meant to fight the United States and its allies.

As noted in Part Two, the Communist Party has also brought China's corporations and military together through the policy of "Civil Military Fusion." Here, China's private sector and military technology development combine, spanning a wide range of emerging technologies from artificial intelligence to robotics. As the Communist Party is removes the lines between civilian and military technology development under "Civil Military Fusion," it is all the more concerning as we have yet to understand the full consequences of technology transfers from the US and Europe to China.

3.6

CHINA GOES GLOBAL: STATE AND PRIVATE ENTERPRISE TAKE ON THE WORLD

Just as the branches of the Chinese military carry out China's military strategy, dozens of state-owned companies carry out China's economic ambitions at home and abroad. Massive Chinese private companies are an even newer feature on the world stage, and these also play a role in building the country's future.

China's new entrepreneurs are a special case. As Bruce Dickson and Jie Chen explain in *Allies of the State: China's Private Entrepreneurs and Democratic Change*, China's entrepreneurs are connected and widely loyal to the Chinese state and Communist Party.[48] State-owned enterprises can double as instruments of state influence and geopolitical strategy—think of the role of China's overseas engineering companies in the Indian Ocean Region. Entrepreneurs are essentially autonomous businesspeople, often with strong Party connections. But even the country's richest entrepreneurs must not fall afoul of the far more powerful Communist Party.[49]

The Party worked from a careful strategy of building up the role of private business in China without losing political control.

The idea is that China's "capitalists" would be "embedded" within the Communist Party: rather than pose a challenge to the Party's supremacy, the political embeddedness and political activism of China's capitalists now helps support Party rule.[50] The practice of creating "party cells" in the largest firms[51] has expanded recently to include the demand for a Party-appointed *board member* on major firms.[52] Aside from the occasional defector, China's billionaires and corporations know how to show the right support for the Party's rule, policies, ambitions, and national narratives.

As one example, Tencent—now one of the world's largest technology companies—released an illustrative video depicting the Chinese military destroying an American aircraft carrier group and American fighter planes before landing amphibious vehicles on islands and raising the Chinese flag over plumes of smoke and ruined bases.[53] Jack Ma, Chairman of the Alibaba Group—one of the world's top ten companies by market capitalization[54]—once maintained an air of independence on the world stage until emerging as a loyal member of the Chinese Communist Party in 2018.[55] Meanwhile, his firm pioneers facial recognition technologies that have drawn worldwide concern over Communist Party control of Chinese citizens.[56]

Wang Jianlin, founder of Wanda Group, connoisseur of movie studios, investor of billions into Hollywood, and one of China's richest men, is a former PLA officer and a member of the Standing Committee of the Chinese People's Political Consultative Conference.[57] A page from Mr. Wang's own website under "Chairman News" recounts a 2013 interview with Fortune magazine: "Wang also talks about his China dream. He believes power and influence in great nations derive from the power and influence of great companies. Wang thinks this is the moment when business can play the same role in China."[58]

Wang sees his role as a businessman as supporting China's national ascendency and power. Great companies, he believes, "raise the country up and make it a superpower."[59]

Here's a section from the original article, based on a week spent with Mr. Wang in 2013:

> Wang's goal? He says it's to lift Wanda into what he calls, speaking through an interpreter, "the super-world-class top tier of companies" and, not least, to lift up his country too. Power and influence in great nations like the U.S. and the U.K., Wang says (channeling Calvin Coolidge), derive from the power and influence of great companies: They "raise the country up and make it a superpower." Wang thinks this is the moment when business can play the same role in the People's Republic. To him, that's the essence of the Chinese dream: companies like his building wealth, spreading influence, and paving the way to Chinese dominance on the global stage.[60]

China's billionaires and major companies continue to push the political vision, either because they believe in it or because it's the cost of doing business. Either way, China's entrepreneurs, its state-owned enterprises, and most other forms of economic activity are all integrated into the business of making China rise.

The Party learned decades ago that thriving meant facilitating a private sector. What does this mean for Chinese "Communism"?

As someone once explained to me, China may not be Communist, but it is Leninist. This means that Party control of society to the maximum extent possible remains in force regardless of what is taking place economically. While absolute control is not necessary— though new technologies are emerging for uses that earlier totalitarian regimes could only dream of—the Chinese Communist Party has maintained for decades a delicate balance of reform with control, and an emphasis on loyalty, benefits, and, of course, punishments for those who stray from the course. In short, the Party can maintain control of the country and its people, while *encouraging and enabling* economic productivity in order to meet its larger goals.

The "great rejuvenation" *requires* entrepreneurs and the private sector.

The Communist Party cannot innovate alone.

For the outside world, the idea that greater wealth and material prosperity in China would lead to liberalization or outright political reform was the great hope of many foreign observers, especially in the United States, where this ambition on China's behalf has been a part of US–China policy for decades.[61] The Party maintains a delicate, determined, and thus far effective balance in granting Chinese citizens the freedom to prosper and build wealth, while not straying from the objectives of the State or from loyalty to the Party when needed. China's first diplomats were considered by the Politburo as the People's Liberation Army "in civilian clothes,"[62] tasked with carrying out the missions of the country. China's private sector may be seen in a similar light by the Communist Party. The "great rejuvenation" is principally an economic game, and China's entrepreneurs and businesspeople are, in many ways, its officers and soldiers.

The Chinese State-Owned Enterprise (SOE) is a far more obvious instrument of the country's global game. From massive natural resource deals to strategic acquisitions, the state plays a game of strategic economics, expanding its global influence while securing access to resources, building infrastructure for trade, and opening up foreign markets for Chinese goods. These behemoths, which include some of the largest companies on Earth, are largely concentrated in foundational sectors of the economy.

China's economic story can be told by its companies.

One measure of the "economic miracle" is simple: GDP. Another is the sheer number of companies that populate the Fortune Global 500. In 2016, there were 103 Chinese companies on the list, compared with 134 in the United States, 52 in Japan, 29 from France and 28 from Germany.[63] This picture, like many of the most interesting aspects of China's rise, has taken shape very quickly.

The largest Chinese companies on the FG 500 are in energy, finance, and construction. China's two top oil companies, Sinopec Group and China National Petroleum, were number three and four on the list in 2018, ahead of Royal Dutch Shell, BP, and ExxonMobil.[64] Similarly, the top four largest banks in the world by total assets are all Chinese: Industrial and Commercial Bank of China, China Construction Bank Corp., Agricultural Bank of China, and Bank of China. They outrank JP Morgan Chase, HSBC, Bank of America, and Wells Fargo, leading the latter by over 1 trillion dollars in total assets.[65]

And this is now. *China is just getting started.*

What is striking is the speed and complexity with which the picture is changing, and how many misconceptions may exist. Here is a Fortune article from 2015:

> Chinese companies are anything but global brands. They enjoy monopolies or oligopolies at home, but often struggle to expand their business outside of the protected borders of their home country. "Chinese companies that wish to go global are hindered because they lack adequate knowledge of consumers in target markets and experience in building leading brands," Boston Consulting Group partners wrote earlier this year. Size is no substitute for strength in international competition. Today, many of the Chinese brands that are most known around the world— including Alibaba, Tencent, Baidu and Xiaomi, none of which are state-owned— remain too small (in terms of revenue) to make the list.[66]

2015 may already be old news. China's firms will not be locked into the Chinese market incubator in perpetuity. This is China's next big story, particularly with the "Belt and Road." Firms that are already some of the largest in the world simply because they service a vast domestic market are finding their way into many new locales.

Aside from China's oil majors and banks, the FG 500 mostly includes big domestic companies like China Southern Power Grid, China Baowu Steel Group, Shaanxi Coal and Chemical Industry, and China Post Group, which have grown to enormous size building the infrastructure of a country that posted double-digit growth rates for thirty years. However, the list is also dotted with global actors like Huawei Investment and Holding, China Railway Engineering, China Railway Construction, China COSCO Shipping, and China Energy Engineering Group.

These tell a different story. Huawei, for example, which is regularly linked to the Chinese military and intelligence services, is already global.[67] Whether it is advertising advances in artificial intelligence in the Dubai airport terminals or employing foreign executives like John Browne, former CEO of British Petroleum, Huawei has broken into developed and developing markets around the world, while making use of global supply chains and even management opportunities.

To the consternation of some in Britain's national security establishment, Huawei has built pieces of the British telecommunications infrastructure. It has been blocked on national security grounds in Australia from a similar attempt to work on the Australian state grid.[68] Using Scarlett Johansson and other American movie stars as sales representatives, it sells smartphones from Britain to Sri Lanka. In short, it has emerged as a genuine global actor, leveraging its cheaper costs and excellent marketing campaigns to compete with existing multinationals for markets around the world. This, again, is just the beginning, and it is also perhaps one of the most visible examples as it targets international consumers.

What is less visible is just as important.

While policy-makers from America to Australia debate the future of the "rules-based order," Chinese companies are quietly capturing market share not only in developed nations, but *around the developing world*. Take China Energy Engineering Group (CEEG), for example.

This company joined the FG 500 in 2014, at number 465. Let's start with something boring— very boring, and very important. In the words of its prospectus, the company "mainly focuses on construction, engineering, research, survey, design and service, hydropower investment, construction and operation, real estate development." In 2014, CEEG had 40,000 overseas employees, with $34 billion in overseas projects throughout the "Belt and Road."[69] Today, the company's annual revenue stream is worth nearly double that of AECOM and triple that of Jacobs, America's two leading public engineering firms, both of which are on the US Fortune 500, but neither of which appear on the FG 500 alongside the Chinese firm.

CEEG started at the *bottom* of the FG 500. It has since climbed to number 333 in 2018.

There are over 100 other Chinese companies on the list, most of which are more like CEEG than dashing Huawei, which is exploring intercontinental undersea cable projects that link Asia and Africa, and selling mobile phones around the Indian Ocean with the help of ad campaigns featuring American movie stars.[70]

China's most visible competitive advantages at present are in infrastructure and engineering. And we barely even see them compete unless we are in these markets. Let's continue with CEEG as an example. Its overseas projects are not in the United States or Europe. They are in Africa, Central Asia, Southeast Asia, and Central and South America. This is where China's champions are competing right now. The Asian Development Bank estimates that Asia has roughly $26 trillion in infrastructure needs out to 2030.[71] In 2007, the list of the top ten global engineering companies was made up of companies from Europe and China. Today, the top five are all Chinese, and each are worth double or even triple their competitors. There are no American companies on the list.[72]

China is going global already. The process is thoroughly underway, and the year is only 2018. Our firms do not understand the real risks that they face and they are not ready to compete with what is likely to be coming, as momentum builds through the coordination of state capital, diplomacy, research and development, and planning in myriad sectors in which the firms of other nations act as individual corporations.

And China's companies are also primary actors in the country's global *strategic* footprint.

Take China Harbor Engineering Company, a subsidiary of China Communications Construction Company. It has just completed over 250 hectares of maritime land reclamation in Sri Lanka, a similar process to the island-building projects in the South China Sea. In fact, China Communications Construction Company is the same company that built the islands in the South China Sea which now house Chinese military infrastructure; the company is now carrying out state-sponsored maritime construction projects across the "Belt and Road."[73] In Sri Lanka, these Chinese State-Owned-Enterprises are building a new "port city" at the heart of the Indian Ocean.[74] The small South Asian nation is at the center of the "Belt and Road," where PLAN submarines have docked in Chinese-built ports, and China's state banks have lent enough money to the country to force the transfer of ownership of the entire port of Hambantota to China.

Sri Lanka is a microcosm of the entire process of Chinese economic planning, engineering, labor, financing, military operations, and diplomacy—diverse elements working together to transform a nation thousands of miles from the Chinese mainland into a place within China's sphere of influence.

And this is happening not just in Sri Lanka—and not just in the Indian Ocean, the geographical heart of China's strategic ambitions—it is a model repeated in regions all over the world.

While staying in Colombo in 2016, I went every night to watch the China Harbor Engineering Company work by floodlight around the clock. While Sri Lanka aims to position itself as a major transshipment hub in the Indian Ocean—and rightly so—it is Chinese companies that are building the infrastructure, and in the case of Hambantota, ultimately owning it.

As a friend in the Sri Lankan Foreign Ministry explained to me, "They are simply going to own our country." He raised his hand slowly from his chest up to his eyes when speaking of the debt. I went down to the port of Hambantota courtesy of the Sri Lankan Ministry of Ports and Shipping. It was a year before the completion of the deal for a 99-year lease. Chinese cranes sat idle in the port. There was no activity except for a roll-on/roll-off vessel unloading Hondas from Japan. My guide pointed me to berths in the port already designated for perpetual use by China. I got a ride to Hambantota from a man from Colombo who spent his life as a sailor, working on ships around the world. "I think that China is going to achieve its goals," he said to me. "What goals are those?" I asked. "To own the world," he replied. "They will do it. Look at Sri Lanka."

This is not my view, it is the view of someone whose country is already experiencing the ground-level realities of China's overseas activities.

And if what he says comes to pass, it will be through the quiet but effective work of companies like China Harbor Engineering Company, China Communications Construction Company, and China Energy Engineering Group, whose chairman tells us: "Energy China is willing to work with Chinese and foreign friends to pursue common development, share the achievements and create a bright future for all!"[75]

Less exciting, but *more essential* than most of what we hear.

Whether it is a state-owned enterprise, or a company led by a famous individual like Communist Party member Jack Ma, chairman of Alibaba, China's companies are now going global, filling in the ever-larger footprint of China in the world. It is not only a reality that we can witness from the outside, it is a guiding ethos at the heart of company strategies. Their executives and strategists understand how difficult this will be, but they understand that it is where their futures lie. Take this example from Alibaba's annual report in 2016:

> Our future revenue growth also depends on our ability to expand into new geographic regions, including our expansion into international markets, and grow our other businesses, including our cloud computing business and the businesses we have acquired or invested in and new business initiatives we may explore in the future. In particular, we face risks associated with expanding into sectors or geographies in which we have limited or no experience.[76]

So then, how do Chinese companies play the game? And how coordinated is it? Like China's military strategy, corporate strategy is naturally a game of consolidation and expansion. It is done through acquisitions. "We have acquired and invested in a large number and diverse range of businesses, technologies, services and products in recent years," Alibaba's annual report explains, and through innovation, in keeping with a fast-paced and rapidly changing technological environment:

Our business has become increasingly complex as its scale, diversity and geographic coverage, as well as that of our workforce, continue to grow. We have also significantly expanded our headcount, office facilities and infrastructure, and we anticipate that further expansion in certain areas and geographies will be required.[77]

The company's executives are keenly aware of the need to adapt and innovate in order to be globally competitive:

The Internet industry is characterized by rapidly changing technology, evolving industry standards, new mobile apps, protocols and technologies, new service and product introductions, new media and entertainment content— including user-generated content— and changing customer demands. Furthermore, our competitors are constantly developing innovations in Internet search, online marketing, communications, social networking, entertainment and other services, on both mobile devices and personal computers, to enhance users' online experience.[78]

The strategy of state-owned enterprises is similar. But it is often linked explicitly to the strategic programs of the Chinese state.

Sinopec, one of China's primary state-owned oil companies, is number three on the FG 500, ahead of every American or European oil company. A message from its chairman, Wang Yupu, in 2016, emphasizes the company's involvement in the "Belt and Road":

In our overseas operations, we were actively involved in expanding projects across the Belt and Road region and we continued to make progress in developing a number of major projects, such as the Yanbu refinery in Saudi Arabia, which commenced operations during the year.[79]

The difference between Sinopec and Alibaba is explicit state support: "We will take advantage of opportunities that arise from the government's support policies, including reforms in the oil and gas sector and in state-owned enterprises as well as the Belt and Road initiative, to enhance the quality and profitability of our business."[80]

But, like Alibaba, Sinopec emphasizes its focus on innovation: "We will continue to implement our strategy of development driven by innovation, improving mechanisms for technological innovation and fast-tracking key technical breakthroughs."[81]

Other major State-Owned-Enterprises are similar. The most interesting expression is in the China National Offshore Oil Company (CNOOC)'s definition of what it means to be a state-owned company in the new era of a global China: "Focusing on 'striving for survival, seeking development, promoting reform, and strengthening Party building,' the company conducted all its work and solidly promoted the construction of the first-class international energy company with Chinese characteristics."[82]

And CNOOC is open about its role in China's external expansion: "[The Company] conscientiously implemented the major national strategy of 'the Belt and Road Initiative'."[83]

Like the Chinese military, the Party's role is absolute: "[The Company] insisted on firm leadership of the Party on state-owned enterprises, and fully played the effect of the leading and political core of the Party."[84]

This is what the world is competing with. Not just companies, but the Chinese state.

China's expansion is global. Its military is moving outwards. Its companies are headed outward, too. Importantly, their corporate strategy ties into the grand strategy of the Chinese state. Take this humble line from CNOOC, which explains that one of their lubricant products "has made a great contribution to the construction of multiple projects of 'The Belt and Road Initiative'," and that another product "has been applied to several strategic projects of Russia, Pakistan and other countries."[85] CNOOC is also focused on science and technology:

> The Company vigorously implements "science and technology drive" strategy . . . the Company fully plays the motivation and leadership of scientific and technological innovation, strives to make technological breakthroughs, successively deepens the scientific . . . [and] implemented the 13th "Five-Year Scientific and Technological Plan."[86]

Just as the branches of the Chinese military carry out China's military strategy, it is the dozens of state-owned super-companies that carry out China's economic strategy around the world.

This is how it works today. We are just at the beginning of China's companies heading out into markets around the world, competing with and often replacing Western counterparts in the rankings of major global companies. This is how China is planning to complete the "great rejuvenation of the Chinese nation" and to "restore China's central position in the world."

So, what could this really look like in the future?

TOWARD 2049: CHINA'S VISION OF ECONOMIC POWER

A friend in Washington likes to say, when talking to policy-makers, "It isn't 1945 any more." What he means is that the US no longer has the economic power to make the rules.

After the Second World War, the United States made up an unprecedented portion of the global economy, and stood on an ascending economic and historical trajectory much like that of the British Empire, which had risen to economic and military supremacy over the prior century. America's power was economic first and military second. The ability to churn out military platforms and manpower during the Second World War outstripped Japan's military capacity, and, with the combined might of the USSR, that of Axis Germany.

China understands this well. As the same friend once told me, "China has learned more from history than we have ever even read." One of the most interesting examples is the twelve-episode television series in China called "The Rise of the Great Powers," which, impressively, was broadcast to the entire nation to show the path of rising powers.[87]

An old adage goes as follows: "Who has the gold makes the rules." What China's leaders have learned is that to have the gold is not enough.

As Mao explained, "Power grows out of the barrel of the gun." In other words, who has the gold *and the guns* makes the rules. And the gold will buy the guns. Hence, military and economic power grow together. This is not China's learning alone— all major powers were built on economic and military power. As Professor Qian Chengdan, academic advisor on the documentary referred to above, explains, "There are skeletons in the closet of all these great powers."[88]

So, China must build its economy. This has been a national priority since 1949. It is the centerpiece of the "great rejuvenation of the Chinese nation."

What would this actually look like? There have been projections on the table for years explaining that China would surpass the United States, become the world's largest economy at double or triple the gross domestic product of the United States.

Indeed, China is repositioning itself to be the centerpiece of the world economy, and eventually the leading economic power on earth. The geographical footprint is colossal, with interests in every region of the world. The intention to master future technologies and global markets is also explicit. And the interest in the next frontier— space— is profound.

China fulfilling its vision of victory means inhabiting a world where China is the global military and industrial leader, the leading space power and space-faring nation, mining and extracting resources from every part of the planet, in order to feed and provide material comforts for its population, all while exporting its advanced goods to every continent, and projecting military power to all corners of the Earth.

China would have the world's largest military budget, the world's most advanced and innovative technologies, the world's leading universities, and a global communications system that would project the country's message not only to its own people, but to all peoples around the world. China would entice other nations and actors through economic and material benefits, and coerce or eliminate opposition to its interests— as needed— through military power.

Economic power can rapidly provide military power. It is not enough, as it was in prior historical periods, for China to be the world's largest market, the dream of Marco Polo and the destination for Spanish silver from the "New World." In order to realize its "China Dream," the Party must build the economy, release but control the country's entrepreneurs, innovators, and state-owned enterprises, share the mission of finding new global markets, maximize technological prowess, and move forward to fulfill Mao's original dream of "surpassing" the United States. From that point on, it would be a world where, through the sheer weight of China's economy, the country could lead on every major technological and military frontier. In short, as many people living or working in China have heard from Chinese colleagues and citizens, "The twentieth century belonged to America. But the twenty-first century will belong to China."

China's planning can take us only so far. It is in the imaginative space of 2049 that China's dreams grow more impressive. And it is the basic requirement of 1.4 billion people over the coming decades that can guide us further on China's vision of victory.

The fulfillment of the national mission remains a priority of the Party, and of many in the country. Let's take a full excerpt from a *Xinhua* profile of Xi Jinping:

> Media and observers, at home and abroad, see Xi as the right man to lead China from being "better-off" into a great modern country.
>
> In 1949, Mao Zedong announced the founding of the People's Republic of China, marking the end to a century of humiliation at the hands of foreign aggressors.
>
> Deng Xiaoping, who put forward the reform and opening-up policy, then paved the way for the nation to become rich.
>
> The coming five years between the 19th and the 20th Party Congress is the period in which the timeframes of the Two Centenary Goals will converge, Xi said when presenting the new CPC central leadership to the press.[89]

"Not only must we deliver the first centenary goal, we must also embark on the journey toward the second," he said, promising to work diligently to "meet our duty, fulfill our mission and be worthy of CPC members' trust."[90]

Xinhua, the official Chinese news agency, has a description of 2049 that is derived from the Party leadership:

> By then, China will be a global leader in terms of composite national strength and international influence. Prosperity for everyone will be basically achieved, a prospect that the Chinese nation has been longing for since the Opium War (1840–1842).
>
> At this point, Xi is the unrivalled helmsman who will steer China toward this great dream.[91]

This is, as Xi and his colleagues explain, the Party's "historic mission," and the Party "will run a campaign on 'staying true to our founding mission'."[92]

As Xi himself explains, "The original aspiration and the mission of Chinese Communists is to seek happiness for the Chinese people and rejuvenation for the Chinese nation."[93]

This, again, is the heart of China's mission. And economic preeminence is at the heart of this vision. But with preeminence comes much responsibility, as we shall see in the following parts.

Members of the Chinese Communist Party gathered for the 19th Party Congress in Beijing, October 2017. Xi Jinping stands in the center. At the 19th Party Congress, Xi announced his vision of a "new era" for China, built on "the invincible force of more than 1.3 billion people." *AP Photo/Andy Wong*

Soldiers from China's People's Liberation Army train in front of the slogan: "Listen to the Party's Command." The Communist Party's Politburo controls the military through its Central Military Commission. *Reuters/Petar Kujundzic*

A student protester in Tiananmen Square, 1989. The Communist Party has attempted to remove the memory of its massacre of thousands of peaceful, pro-democracy protestors on June 4th, 1989. June 4th, 2019 marks the 30th anniversary of this event. *Stuart Franklin/Magnum Photos*

China was once an ally of the United States, in the Second World War, under the Nationalist Party. Defeated by the Communists in the Chinese Civil War, the Nationalists escaped to Taiwan, now a democracy. *University of North Texas Libraries.*

The "Goddess of Democracy" statue in Tiananmen Square Beijing. The Massacre of June 4, 1989 claimed the lives of thousands. *Reprinted with permission from Zhou Fengsuo, Tiananmen Student Leader in 1989.*

Chinese People's Liberation Army personnel attending the opening ceremony of China's new military base in Djibouti, 2017, on the Horn of Africa in the Western Indian Ocean. China's first overseas naval base is an important step in a strategy to "safeguard the security of China's overseas interests." *STR/AFP/Getty Images*

Chinese military police attending an oath-taking rally in Xinjiang in 2017. Getty Images notes that earlier that year, in the Hetian Prefecture of the Xinjiang Uighur Autonomous Region where this rally took place, local government departments purchased 2,768 police batons, 550 electric cattle prods, 1,367 pairs of handcuffs, and 2,792 cans of pepper spray. In the background is a statue of Mao Zedong shaking hands with a diminutive Uighur. *STR/AFP/Getty Images*

ئىناقلىق، مۇقىملىق ـ ئامەت، بۆلگۈنچىلىك، بۇزغۇنچىلىق ـ ئاپەت

和谐稳定是福 分裂破坏是祸

Paramilitary police in a truck in Xinjiang in 2014 on their way to an oath-taking rally. The banner reads "Harmony and stability are blessings, separation and discord are disasters." *Reuters/Stringer*

Xi Jinping presides over a military parade in Beijing marking the 70th anniversary of Japan's surrender in the Second World War, 2015. The parade showcased China's ground, air, and amphibious military equipment, including the Type 99A2 main battle tank, pictured, and the DF-21D anti-ship missile, also known as the "carrier killer." *AP Photo/Ng Han Guan*

In the Inner Mongolia Autonomous Region, soldiers from the People's Liberation Army march in a parade to mark the 90th anniversary of the founding of the PLA. A prior Chinese leader called Mongolia "a fortress essential for [China's] defense and security." *Cui Nan/China News Service/VCG via Getty Images*

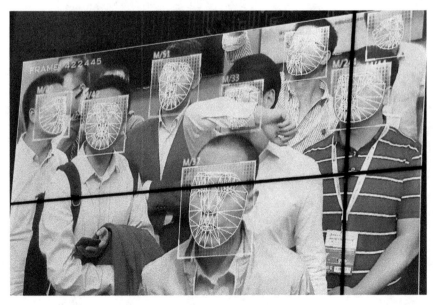

Facial recognition technology demonstration during the China Public Security Expo in Shenzhen, China in 2017. The Chinese Communist Party is building a high-tech surveillance state using Silicon Valley style emerging technologies from artificial intelligence to big data analytics and facial recognition systems. The new surveillance state is developed by China's corporations in partnership with Beijing. *Reuters/Bobby Yip*

A lone Uighur man looks on as a truck carrying paramilitary policemen travels by in Urumqi, capital of the Xinjiang Uighur Autonomous Region in 2014. Communist Party planners consider Xinjiang a "core area" of China's "Belt and Road Initiative." The banner reads "Willingness to spill blood for the people. Countering terrorism and fighting the enemies is part of the police spirit." *Reuters/Stringer*

Pakistani Prime Minister Imran Khan attends a welcome ceremony at the Great Hall of the People in Beijing in 2018. Infrastructure building in Pakistan is central to the "Belt and Road Initiative," improving China's economic and military access to the Indian Ocean and Arabian Sea. Like other "Belt and Road" countries, Sri Lanka and the Maldives, debt is mounting in Pakistan, and the country is seeking relief from other nations. *Reuters/Jason Lee*

Russian President Vladimir Putin toasts with Xi Jinping during their meeting in Moscow at the Grand Kremlin Palace on July 4, 2017. Russia and China maintain a "comprehensive strategic partnership of coordination" in their shared competition with the United States. *Mikhail Svetlov/Getty Images*

PART IV

国家利益不断拓展

THE CEASELESS EXPANSION OF NATIONAL INTERESTS

★ ★ ★ ★

CHINA'S GROWING GLOBAL REACH

Securing sustenance for all 1.3 billion people of China is, in itself, a huge accomplishment.[1]

—XINHUA NEWS AGENCY, NOVEMBER 2017

[B]acked by the invincible force of more than 1.3 billion people, we have an infinitely vast stage of our era, a historical heritage of unmatched depth, and incomparable resolve that enable us to forge ahead...[2]

—XI JINPING, 2017

CHINA'S ASCENDENCY IS A STORY OF AMBITION, BUT IT IS ALSO A story of *necessity*.

With the world's largest population, but insufficient natural resources, the ambitions of the country will be built on access to *every region of the globe*. And this is already happening.

From Africa to Latin America, from the Middle East to the Arctic regions, China is redefining the world map through what its military terms "the ceaseless expansion of national interests."[3]

China's global trade and resource quest is already leading to new international relationships that are changing the balance of power region by region. From a growing dependence on the Chinese market by oil-producing nations in the Middle East, to an emerging strategic competition between India and China in Asia's maritime regions, to growing influence in Africa and Latin America that has left American policy-makers behind, Chinese *global* investment, diplomacy, and military expansion are underway.

China, as we will see, is already far more than a regional power. What this looks like now, and what it will mean for China's relationships with the world's major regions— Africa, Latin America, the Middle East, and Europe— as well as for major actors— the United States, Russia, India, and Japan— must be explored in terms of China's own economic, military, and diplomatic strategies.

The foundation for a de facto Chinese victory is being laid across the world every day.

OVERVIEW: CHINA'S NEED FOR THE WORLD'S RESOURCES

hina's demand for oil, gas, meat, grain, minerals, protein, water, and other basic resources has grown enormously over the last thirty years and will increase in the coming decades.

For example, China is already the world's largest consumer of energy— 3.1 billion tons of oil equivalent (TOE) in 2017, and rising. This is nearly 1 billion TOE more than the United States, and more than the combined energy consumption of Germany, Japan, Britain, France, Canada, India, Brazil, and the whole of Africa.[4] British Petroleum estimates that, even as China's economy slows down, the country will consume over one-quarter of the world's energy by 2040.[5] Chinese demand for minerals has driven the global commodities cycle over recent decades, and led to expanded Chinese commercial activities in countries around the planet. Demand for agricultural products has led not only to massive export deals in the United States, Australia, Africa, and South America, but to large-scale purchases of land by China's government and companies. China has bought land around the planet to feed its population. Water is an important and potentially scarce resource in the future. China plays a dominant role in the waterways of Asia, especially in the Himalayas and Mekong region. Here, on major rivers originating on the Tibetan plateau, China is undertaking hydropower and damming projects on international waterways that are vital to countries around the region, with potentially shattering effects for smaller Asian nations.[6]

China's global quest for resources is a story that deserves to be revisited in the context of expanding global interests. The resource quest shows a kind of baseline that Chinese strategy and vision must attend to. Energy security, food security, resource and mineral security, and water security, like the mastery of advanced technologies and the creation of a powerful industrial base for civilian and military purposes, are all essential pieces of China's global strategy and activities. Moreover, Chinese interests are expanding around the world, and, therefore, as the Chinese military itself explains, these require military protection. In short, China's expanding resource interests provide an important blueprint for Chinese economic, diplomatic, and military expansion— the footprint for China's total global presence.

Importantly, China's expanding interests are going to change the strategic map of the world. Chinese economic interests currently exist in every continent and country. However, this is before China has achieved either of its "centenary goals." As resource interests grow in Africa, Central Asia, and Latin America, as energy interests grow in the Middle East, as Indian Ocean and Arctic trade routes grow in importance, we see the formation of a cohesive strategy intended to achieve a global China. We already have the beginnings of this in the "Belt and Road Initiative." This infrastructure-building initiative linking Europe, Africa, and the Eurasian supercontinent more tightly to China will improve Chinese energy and trade security, while building political influence in a multitude of countries.

The areas defined in the "Belt and Road," as well as those of the "First and Second Island Chains," will be the basic regions in which China intends to project military power, something we already see in the form of China's first overseas naval base in Djibouti, which complements its military island-building in the South China Sea. As China prepares to "fight and win wars" against major and minor foes in the future, it will largely be in this "Belt and Road" region that its military power counts. In Xi Jinping's words, the Chinese military must "solidly prepare for military struggle in all strategic directions."[7]

China's relationships with major powers will matter more and more as its global economic and military expansion grows. China's resource interests may remain largely in Africa, Latin America, Central Asia, Australia, and the Middle East. Its trading interests may continue to have most to do with developed markets in Europe and North America, with emerging markets around Eurasia, from Southeast to South Asia. But the political relationships that are likely to be most important to China in the coming decades are with the United States, Russia, Japan, India, and Europe, or what China thinks of as other "major powers."

As well as being the world's largest consumer of oil, China is the world's largest net importer, with the majority of its imports coming from the Middle East and Africa.[8] China's own domestic energy supplies are largely from its vast coal reserves.[9] It is the largest oil producer in East Asia, but the rapid increase in consumption over recent decades has led to a global quest for oil and gas. Imports from the Middle East (Saudi Arabia, Oman, Iraq, Iran, UAE, Kuwait), Africa (Angola, Republic of the Congo, South Sudan), South America (Venezuela, Colombia, Brazil), and Central Asia (Russia, Kazakhstan) are essential to China's sustained growth and economic rise.[10] This creates the need to protect the vast, global web of sea lanes bringing global energy to China, through a series of maritime choke points in the Indian Ocean and West Pacific Island Chains. China's "Belt and Road" strategy will link this vast geography through infrastructure and investment projects around Eurasia, Africa, and the Indian Ocean, and also other regions of the world.

It is to these regions, individually, that we now turn.

4.2

CHINA IN THE MIDDLE EAST

China understands the risks of energy dependence on and involvement in the Middle East, having learned from the experience of the United States.[11] It also fears dependence on overseas oil in general, thus leading to a strategy of massive investment in renewable energy sources at home, from solar power to electric vehicles. China's energy strategy involves diversification across a broad spiderweb of global suppliers, which in turn requires a military buildup in order to secure the choke points and sea lanes upon which its imports depend.[12] However, the Middle East remains important to its current "Belt and Road" and military strategy. The new base in Djibouti positions China militarily at the Western edge of the Indian Ocean, and military exercises with Pakistan and Iran help demonstrate China's presence in the Persian Gulf.[13]

"China's Arab Policy Paper," released in 2016, claims that "Friendship between China and Arab states dates back to ancient times. Over two thousand years ago, land and maritime Silk Roads already linked the Chinese and Arab nations." China has proposed jointly building the "Silk Road Economic Belt" and the "Twenty-First Century Maritime Silk Road" with Arab nations, as well as plans to "deepen China–Arab military cooperation and exchange," with emphasis on "cooperation on weapons, equipment and various specialized technologies," and joint military exercises.[14] In other words, despite real fears of excessive involvement in the Middle East, China is there to stay, and its presence will only grow stronger if all goes according to the Party's plans.

An author from China's Ministry of Foreign Affairs explains the centrality of the Middle East to the "Belt and Road":

As an energy-rich zone, [the Middle East] plays a decisive role in the position of international political and economic arena. In the process of building the "Belt and Road," [the] Chinese

government should pay close attention to the role of the Middle
East region. This region will also play its rightful role in security
coordination, economic cooperation, and cultural exchanges
under the "Belt and Road" framework, thus achieving the strategic docking and win-win cooperation between China and
Middle Eastern countries.[15]

The Middle East, in China's view, is a fulcrum of the "Belt and Road
Initiative." According to Wu Sike, former Special Envoy to the Middle East
from the PRC Ministry of Foreign Affairs, "The Middle East is the region
bringing together the land and maritime 'Silk Road'."[16]

Demand for Chinese finance, construction, and trade is evident
throughout the region. This ranges from invitations for Chinese help in
Syrian reconstruction efforts, to megaprojects in a variety of states.[17] As the
Brookings Institution succinctly explains, "By 2014, China had emerged as
the Middle East's dominant trading partner," importing not only oil, but
natural gas.[18] As the report explains, "the Middle East needs China as much
as China needs the Middle East."[19] The linkages between the region and
China go both ways, as China and Arab nations build infrastructure in one
another's countries. These range from Chinese-built projects in Iraq, to Qa-
tari terminals in Jiangsu, China.[20] China's military forces have already been
active in the region in security and protection roles, for example evacuating
35,000 Chinese nationals from Libya in 2011, carrying out antipiracy operations since 2008, and conducting naval visits to Saudi Arabia, the UAE,
Bahrain, Qatar, Kuwait, Oman, and Iran.[21] And this is now. As Chinese
strategy reveals, both through "Belt and Road" documents and specific
statements on the Middle East and Arab world, the Chinese presence, both
military and economic, will continue to expand.

CHINA IN AFRICA

hina's presence in Africa is about much more than energy. Chinese
workers, Chinese development banks, Chinese oil majors, State-Owned
Enterprises, and small-business owners have all joined a supersized
migration over the last twenty-five years. Chinese trade with Africa
has ballooned from $10.44 billion in 2000 to $127.97 in 2016.[22] China's
presence in Africa is visible in nearly every sub-Saharan country, and the
continent is already the main region where China's overseas military presence is taking shape.

China's ideological approach to the wider world is especially visible in
Africa. "China's Second Africa Policy Paper" uses the "community of shared
future" or "community of common destiny for mankind" concept, something we will explore further in Part Five. "China and Africa have always
belonged to a community of shared future," it says, and insists that "Over
the past five decades and more, they have always been good friends who
stand together through thick and thin, good partners who share weal and
woe, and good brothers who fully trust each other despite changes in the
international landscape."[23]

The policy paper, speaking broadly of the continent, notes the interactions of the "China Dream" and the "Africa Dream," envisioning a shared
future between China and Africa based on a "China-Africa strategic partnership featuring political equality and mutual trust," as well as "economic
win-win cooperation." The paper even places an intertwined China–Africa
vision within the context of China's goals to 2049:

> China is striving to achieve the "two centenary goals" and real-
> ize the Chinese dream of great national renewal . . . Africa is
> committed to accelerating its industrialization and moderniza-
> tion . . . Both the Chinese dream and the African dream aim to
> enable people to live a more prosperous and happier life. The

development strategies of China and Africa are highly compati-
ble.[24]

As China's trade and investment burgeons, its military presence on the
continent is also increasing. China's arms sales—especially small arms—
are increasing, which, as former US Ambassador David Shinn explains, are
"having an impact on African conflict zones," with their weapons "showing
up in places like Darfur, the Eastern Congo, Somalia," alongside Western
arms.[25] China deploys peacekeepers to the continent, alongside private security firms on its massive expanse of projects around the continent, and
has extensive exchange programs with African military officers, training
them in China's own military academies.[26]
    Chinese media and propaganda have begun to center on the idea that
"China and Africa need each other." And, as with the Middle East, the idea
that Africa is essential to China's "external strategies," and to the "great rejuvenation of the Chinese nation." As the Chinese news agency *Xinhua*
explains:

> China and Africa consider each other both as opportunities for
> development and as an important fulcrum of their external
> strategies. China's development needs Africa and Africa's devel-
> opment also needs China. In general African friends do not see
> China's development as a threat. The "Chinese Dream" for the
> Chinese nation is to achieve national rejuvenation and the "Af-
> rican dream" for African people is to achieve poverty reduction
> and development. Each can help the other.[27]

Xinhua broadcasts views from African officials that support these claims.
Former UN official Asha-Rose Migiro remarked upon the "immense appeal in Africa" of the "Chinese dream" because "it conjures a vision of collective achievement and espouses the same objectives that the continent is
striving to reach: poverty alleviation, economic growth, and attainment of
sustainable development." In her view, "a win-win partnership between
China and Africa could unleash the continent's economic potentials [sic]."[28]
    China's burgeoning presence in Africa—and the complexities that this
has produced—has, as Ambassador Shinn explains, begun to open ques-

tions about the core principles of Chinese foreign policy, especially the question of "noninterference" overseas. The reality is more complex, and includes a history of support for civil wars and revolutionary groups around the globe from Algeria to Vietnam in the first decades of the People's Republic of China. Beijing's actions in Africa in recent years demonstrate the ambiguities of "noninterference." As Shinn says, we can "split hairs on what is noninterference and what is not noninterference," but, owing to expanding interests (especially in oil), a growing community of overseas Chinese in Africa, and a lack of security in the region, China has taken actions in Sudan that it never would have considered taking ten years ago, owing to oil interests, personnel in the country, and the lack of security in the region.[29] The ambassador adds—in a note that will resonate with China watchers—that even Chinese scholars are using different terms to explain China's new overseas presence, such as "creative involvement" and "constructive intervention," and, as quoted from a Chinese scholar, "China is adopting a new approach which combines noninterference with conditional intervention."[30]

China's general public has also taken up the subject of expanding Chinese economic and military interests in Africa. *Wolf Warrior 2* is China's highest-grossing film ever. Set in an unnamed African country, it is the story of a Chinese special forces soldier fighting African rebels led by American mercenaries. By no coincidence, the film was released on the ninetieth anniversary of the founding of the People's Liberation Army. *Wolf Warrior 2* is revealing, as it plays to an idealized, violent image of China abroad. It depicts China's military protecting its people who have gone overseas, ending with a grand display of PLA hardware in the form of offshore missile strikes once Chinese citizens have found themselves besieged by African rebels and their American villain leader.

This film has been immensely popular in mainland China. As the lead actor says, "It was an explosion of patriotic feeling among all Chinese. The patriotic kindling in people's hearts has been dried as far as it can be, and I, Wu Jing, have taken a small match or spark and dropped it on, lighting up all of you."[31] Tellingly, the film was China's official submission to the 2018 Academy Awards for Best Foreign Language Film.

The film brings a vision of Chinese foreign policy, and even the role of the Chinese citizen, to the silver screen with moments including a Chinese ambassador talking down hostile rebels with the line "China and Africa are friends" and African soldiers showing their support for China, letting a convoy pass with the line, "Hold your fire, it's the Chinese."[32] In the climax, the protagonists find their way to a Chinese peacekeeping station in Africa, and the final shot is simply a Chinese passport filling the screen, with the words: "Citizens of the People's Republic of China: When you are in danger overseas, do not give up! Remember that behind you there is a strong and powerful fatherland!"

In keeping with China's growing military presence abroad and increasing military nationalism at home, the film's promotional tagline is "Those who offend our China must be executed even if they are far away"[33] (犯我中华者虽远必诛).

Africa is, in many ways, the giant petri dish for China's broader overseas presence: massive resource interests, government-to-government relations, a growing military presence, and a comprehensive propaganda message that includes, at the government level, "win-win cooperation" and "mutual respect," and, at the popular level, the annihilation of China's enemies as part of China's "great national rejuvenation."

On a trip to Kenya in 2018, I mentioned to a range of journalists in Nairobi that it occurred to me, as a former student of the history of empire, that Africa may become for China what India was for the British Empire. I expected them to tell me I was wrong or missing serious pieces of the picture. Instead, each of them told me it was an astute comparison.

The real relationship between China and Africa is, of course, far more complex than Chinese propaganda portrays. It ranges from the celebratory to the hostile. In Oxford, a Ghanaian academic said to me in poetic fashion, "If it weren't for the Chinese, we would not be able to have inexpensive clothing and electronics. My radio is Chinese and my batteries are Chinese. You see, because of the Chinese I have music." On the other hand, as the former chief economist of the African Development Bank told me, "I am tired of hearing about China in Africa. We have seen enough of what they can do. What I am interested in is, what can India do for Africa?" Resource deals in Africa are often controversial. Once the deal is done between Beijing and the host government, Chinese workers, engineers, project managers, and personnel are often brought in to build the infrastructure, extract the resources, and play their role in "feeding" China. In a conversation at the Mauritius Chamber of Commerce and Industry, a desk officer told me that large deals with the Chinese were eventually scrapped "when we learned that they wanted to bring in all their own workers and engineers." In other words, there was not much in it for the local economy.

However, the China–Africa relationship proceeds wrapped in heady rhetoric usually reserved for China's strategic partnerships and outright alliances, such as those with North Korea ("As close as lips and teeth") and Pakistan ("Higher than mountains, deeper than oceans, stronger than steel, sweeter than honey"). The Chinese government speaks of "Establishing and Developing Comprehensive Strategic and Cooperative China–Africa Partnership and Consolidating and Bolstering the Community of Shared Future between China and Africa."[34] When one reviews the detailed points of Chinese Africa strategy and policy, it is clear how central and comprehensive the continent is in China's global vision.

Some have called Africa "China's Second Continent."[35] As a resource and supply base, its importance is clear. And the comprehensive nature of Chinese initiatives in Africa as a whole deserve to be listed. Here are some examples:

- Deepening cooperation in international affairs
- Deepening economic and trade cooperation
- Helping boost Africa's industrialization
- Helping boost Africa's agricultural modernization
- Participating in Africa's infrastructure development across the board
- Strengthening China–Africa financial cooperation
- Promoting the facilitation of China–Africa trade and investment
- Bolstering resource and energy cooperation
- Expanding cooperation on the marine economy
- Continuing to increase development assistance to Africa
- Supporting Africa in strengthening its public health system and capacity-building

- Expanding cooperation in education and human resources development
- Stepping up science and technology cooperation and knowledge-sharing
- Enhancing cooperation on climate change and environmental protection
- Expanding tourism cooperation
- Broadening cooperation on press, radio, film, and television
- Encouraging exchanges between academia and think tanks
- Enhancing people-to-people exchanges[36]

In addition to economics and nation-building, on the continent on which China's first military base has appeared, and on which the "Wolf Warrior" of the Chinese popular imagination fights for Chinese interests abroad, the military and security component is explicit. Strategically, Africa sits at the center of the Eurasian-African-Indian Ocean supercontinental structure that China plans to build through its "Belt and Road." As Chinese investment and port-building activity increases, it is likely that other military bases will appear.

Chinese investment and infrastructure-building in East African nations— a critical strategic space in the Indian Ocean Region— regularly clocks in at nearly 20 percent of annual GDP or higher. Total Chinese investment and infrastructure-building in Mozambique from 2005 to 2016 is 83.4 percent of Mozambique's 2016 annual GDP, while investment in Ethiopia, where China is building infrastructure projects that link this Horn of Africa nation to the Indian Ocean, is 30.2 percent. Other East African nations have also taken on substantial levels of investment and infrastructure-building from the PRC. Total Chinese investment and infrastructure-building in Tanzania (19.6 percent), and Madagascar (17.2 percent) over the same period all clock in at nearly one-fifth of each nation's annual GDP.[37]

China's integration of African nations with one another is also of serious interest, for example through its Djibouti–Ethiopia rail corridor. In China's strategy this is meant to lead to improved security for natural resource flows back to China, while the sea lanes in the Indian Ocean are secured by an expanding Chinese navy. China's Africa policy paper explains that:

> China will further strengthen military exchanges and coopera-
> tion with African countries. It will deepen military-related tech-
> nological cooperation and carry out joint military training and
> exercises. China will scale up training of African military person-
> nel according to the needs of the African side, and innovate on
> the training methods. It will continue to help African countries
> enhance their capacity-building in national defense and peace-
> keeping to safeguard their own security and regional peace.[38]

China will also build up China–Africa "intelligence-sharing and capacity-building" and "support the efforts of African countries and regional
organizations in improving counter-terrorism capabilities and fighting terrorism."[39]

In other words, the military–security dimension to China's presence in
Africa is bound to increase, perhaps greatly over time. By 2049, a fully built
"Belt and Road" and Chinese Indo-Pacific strategic presence would have
Africa very much at its heart.

Meanwhile, regular Chinese citizens are doing their part as well. An
extended essay in the *New York Times Magazine* gives us two examples.

Harking almost to a sentiment in the early British Empire, we have
young men and even transplanted families striving to further their nation's
interests overseas. Take the story of a young man in his late twenties, working as an engineer in a Namibian uranium mine:

> In Beijing, where he worked before coming here, Teng lived
> under the gray blanket of coal-generated pollution that hangs
> over much of eastern China. Now he is working for the fu-
> ture— his own and his country's— under an endless African
> sky of cobalt blue. "I never imagined," he says, "I would end up
> halfway around the world" . . . He wants to see [the uranium
> mine] reach its full potential next year, fueling China's contin-
> ued rise. "This is an important thing for China," he says, "and I
> want to be a part of it."[40]

Or a couple that owns a restaurant called "Shanghai Nights," in Walvis Bay, Namibia:

> Inside, the lunch crowd was already gone, but six middle-aged Chinese men and women— including James Shen and his wife, Rose, the proprietors— crowded around a table peeling prawns and sucking heartily on the shells. Nobody spoke. Blaring from the flat-screen television on the wall was a special report on CCTV-4, a channel from China's state television broadcaster, breathlessly describing the powers of the People's Liberation Army. When a double row of explosions erupted in the sea, Rose exclaimed, "Wah, our China is so strong!"[41]

As for the soaring rhetoric of China–Africa relations, the story is not always so wonderful. It is often the story of friction between local labor and Chinese interests. As the secretary of a Namibian mine workers union explained of the relationship: "The Chinese will promise you heaven, but the implementation can be hell."[42]

China's rise in Africa is economic, military, and ideological, supported by many of its citizens. It is being accomplished with a measure of reciprocation, but China's growing presence also faces resistance from the host nations and their communities. The story has just begun. To satisfy its growth, China has already begun to build and buy and integrate all over Africa. Supporting the China of 2049 will be a story on a far larger scale.

CHINA IN LATIN AMERICA

China is also developing its resource base in Latin America. This stretches beyond Venezuelan, Colombian, and Brazilian oil and adds a new dimension to our picture: food.

As Dambisa Moyo explains in *Winner Take All: China's Race for Resources and What It Means for the World*, China has only 11 percent of the world's arable land, despite having the world's largest population. So, "China has embarked on aggressive land purchase and lease schemes well beyond its borders, particularly in fertile lands in Africa and South America."[43] China imports vast quantities of food and agricultural products from North America, but, as Dr. Moyo explains, "China neither wants to become beholden to America for its food sustenance, nor do Chinese leaders believe that they can meet food needs solely through imports. The Chinese are looking for land abroad on which to grow their crops, and here North America and the United States present problems, especially when it comes to land ownership and property rights."[44]

Over the last two decades, China has conducted a global campaign to secure farmland outside of China, spanning the planet from Argentina to Australia and New Zealand. A friend in the Australian defense community told me what China wants Australia to be: "a neutral farm and mine."

China targets "less developed regions," particularly in Africa and South America, as it can leverage advantageous property ownership regimes, such as leaseholds, in order to buy or hold foreign land on behalf of the Chinese state and Chinese people.[45] In short, many regions around the world will be used to feed the Chinese people.

Water is another key concern for China, and Latin America holds the world's largest water resources by a wide margin, nearly double that of Russia or the United States, with Brazil as the leading country.[46] Like energy demands, China's long-term water demands and *the need for arable land* will be critical, expected to well outpace the country's ability to supply itself. As

Dr. Moyo points out, "In 2030, China's water demand is expected to reach 216 trillion gallons, but its current supply amounts to just over 163 trillion"; that's a gap of 25 percent.[47] So, like China's energy demands, its demand for food and arable land is part of what the Chinese military calls the "ceaseless expansion of national interests."

China's agricultural companies are, like other state-owned enterprises, global operators. They often sign deals with nation states or provincial governments. In Argentina, the Beidahuang Group signed a deal giving the company "exclusive control over the supply of soybeans, corn, and other crops from an area of up to 320,000 hectares over twenty years"— though this deal failed.[48]

According to Elizabeth Economy, director of Asia Studies at the Council on Foreign Relations, Chinese companies prefer "to own land outright to ensure 'product safety, lower production costs, and better profits.' Where owning land outright is not possible, they invest in infrastructure and processing facilities; in the case of Brazil, this allows them to purchase soybeans directly from Brazilian farmers, circumventing multinational grain companies."[49]

In 2018, Chinese Foreign Minister Wang Yi formally invited Latin American and Caribbean nations to join the "Belt and Road" during a meeting between China and thirty-three nations of the Community of Latin American and Caribbean States (CELAC), a regional grouping which does not include Canada or the United States.[50] Increasing ties with Latin America and the Caribbean has been a clear priority under President Xi. Successive China–CELAC meetings have led to the "China–Latin American and Caribbean Countries Cooperation Plan (2015–2019)," which promises to "enhance collaboration in global economic, trade and financial institutions" while bolstering trade to $500 billion, and increasing reciprocal investment stock to $250 billion over ten years.[51]

It is clear that despite traditional American influence in the Western hemisphere, China's presence has grown massively, and that China's leaders see a bright future of engagement in the region. The US–China Economic Security and Review Commission, a Congressional commission, notes that through the use of the CELAC Forum, "China is able to push its foreign policy objectives and shape regional discussions without US or Canadian involvement," adding that "Chinese state policy banks have provided over $150 billion in loans to the region, exceeding the combined lending from the World Bank, the Inter-American Development Bank, and the CAF-Development Bank of Latin America." Chinese companies have also participated in ninety-one Latin American and Caribbean infrastructure projects.[52] Meanwhile, "China is expanding military-to-military exchanges, arms sales, and nontraditional military operations to strengthen its political capital and goodwill among LAC [Latin American and Caribbean] states, deepen its relationships with LAC military leaders, and position China strategically in the region."[53]

At a CELAC–China ministerial forum in Santiago, Chile, in January 2018, Alicia Bárcena, executive secretary of the United Nations Economic Commission for Latin America and the Caribbean, spoke favorably about the inclusion of Latin America in China's "Belt and Road":

Why is the Belt and Road important for our region?

First, because it will galvanize the economies of Asia and Europe, which will benefit Latin American and Caribbean exports.

Second, because the Belt and Road Initiative offers us a unique opportunity to bridge the great territorial gap that separates us, by means of better air, sea and especially digital connectivity to strengthen our ties in trade, investment, tourism and culture . . .

[W]e need to cooperate at the levels of industry, technology and innovation, on sustainable energy, electric transport and Industry 4.0. In connection with this, we propose holding the first CELAC–China Industrial Development Forum.[54]

In other words, China's global vision extends beyond even Eurasia and Africa, the core arenas of the "Belt and Road," and is meeting with enthusiasm *even in the Western hemisphere*.

From smaller nations to larger ones, Chinese initiatives have found a willing audience in South America. Ambassadors to China from Peru, Bolivia, and Ecuador have all expressed enthusiasm for the "Belt and Road."[55] In 2018, Chile formally "joined the Belt and Road,"[56] and, according to

Chinese state media, in a 2017 Beijing meeting Xi and Argentina's President Macri agreed that "the Belt and Road Initiative would be extended to Argentina and other Latin American countries."[57] Meanwhile, Xi called for "China–Mexico strategic synergy," while "commending close exchanges between the two countries' governments, legislative bodies and militaries."[58]

As with its strategy toward Africa, the Chinese government asserts a shared identity with developing nations. Calling Latin America "A Land Full of Vitality and Hope," Chinese strategy says that "the development of China cannot be possible without the development of other developing countries, including countries in Latin America and the Caribbean."[59] Official policy emphasizes trade, industrial investment and capacity cooperation, financial cooperation, energy and resources cooperation, infrastructure cooperation, manufacturing cooperation, agricultural cooperation, scientific and technological innovation, space cooperation, maritime cooperation, and economic and technical assistance, among other areas.

Importantly, China seeks greater financial integration with Latin America, including "cooperation between the central banks," expanded "cross-border local currency settlement," "RMB clearing arrangements," and "monetary cooperation." This involves "special loans for Chinese–Latin American infrastructure" and for the China–Latin American Production Capacity Cooperation Investment Fund.[60]

Agriculture is key:

> Efforts will be made to encourage enterprises on both sides to actively engage in agricultural trade, push for further exchanges and cooperation in agricultural science and technology, personnel training and other fields, deepen cooperation in livestock and poultry-breeding, forestry, fishery and aquaculture, and jointly promote food security. China will continue to set up and improve agricultural technology demonstration programs, promote the development and demonstration of modern agricultural technologies, and enhance agricultural technology innovation, agricultural production and processing capacity and international competitiveness on both sides.[61]

And so are energy and resources:

> China wishes to expand and deepen cooperation in the fields of
> energy and resources with Latin American and Caribbean coun-
> tries based on the principle of win-win cooperation and sustain-
> able development . . . China is ready to actively explore with
> Latin American and Caribbean countries the establishment of
> mechanisms for long-term supply of energy and resource prod-
> ucts and local currency pricing and settlement, to reduce the
> impact of external economic and financial risks.[62]

Additionally, in an ambition reminiscent of the industrial diplomacy of
the Soviet Union, China seeks to use its industrial capacity to increase technical knowledge-sharing in Latin America through "cooperation on technical consultation, construction and engineering, equipment manufacturing
and operation management in the fields of transportation, trade logistics,
storage facilities, information and communication technology, energy and
power, water conservancy, housing and urban construction."[63]

Finally, as the "Policy Paper on Latin America and the Caribbean" tells
us, China's military presence in the region will also increase via military and
defense exchanges:

> China will actively carry out military exchanges and coopera-
> tion with Latin American and Caribbean countries, increase
> friendly exchanges between defense and military leaders from
> the two sides, strengthen policy dialogue and set up working
> meeting mechanisms, conduct exchanges of visits between dele-
> gations and vessels, deepen professional exchanges in such fields
> as military training, personnel training and UN peacekeeping,
> expand pragmatic cooperation in humanitarian relief, count-
> er-terrorism and other non-traditional security fields, and en-
> hance cooperation in military trade and military technology.[64]

Chinese investment and trade in Latin America are bound to increase,
as the region is an essential component of China's overseas resource strategy.

Military cooperation is also in its early stages, especially with South America's two largest nations, Brazil and Argentina.[65] New arms deals with Argentina will involve the introduction of Chinese-made aircraft, and a space monitoring station is being built in Argentine Patagonia. It will be run by the Chinese military as part of China's "deep space network" designed to support future interplanetary missions.[66]

In Brazil, PLA officers have trained at the Brazilian military's elite jungle warfare school, and Brazilian officers attend China's National Defense University. China also competes for sales of advanced equipment to the Brazilian navy.[67] Regular trips to Beijing by Brazilian military leaders take place as part of the China–Brazil Defense Ministries Exchange and Cooperation Joint Commission. As reported by the PLA-sponsored "China Military" website, Brazil's secretary of strategy and international affairs in the Ministry of Defense recently explained during a 2016 visit to Beijing that "Brazil attaches great importance to developing state and military relations with China" and "hoped the two countries [would] further promote cooperation in defense and military affairs."[68]

China's leaders appear to see Brazil as its major partner in the Western Hemisphere. As Xi Jinping stated in September 2017, "China and Brazil have forged a mature and solid relationship as the largest developing countries respectively in the Eastern and Western Hemispheres and leading emerging economies."[69] According to Xinhua, the feeling is mutual. Brazilian President Michel Temer (2016–18) "said he is happy to visit China as his first overseas trip after taking office as president, adding that Brazil values its steadily improving comprehensive strategic partnership with China."[70]

Like Africa and the Middle East, Latin America forms an essential piece of China's global footprint based primarily on resource needs and other economic interests. And, as with China's economic interests everywhere, when China's "comprehensive national power" grows, its military footprint follows.

CHINA IN THE
ARCTIC AND ANTARCTIC

China also has polar policy objectives.

The "Belt and Road Initiative" is the organizing concept for China's global strategic footprint. It began with the Eurasian supercontinent and the Indian Ocean Region. Several years ago, at a conference held by the Oxford International Infrastructure Consortium, the director of one of China's official "Belt and Road" think tanks gave a speech to major pension funds and investors from around Europe. I was attending with a friend from the British Parliament who worked on Arctic and Antarctic issues in 2016. Understanding the importance that China placed on future Arctic shipping routes, we asked the speaker after the conference: "Does China think of the Arctic as part of Belt and Road?"

"We do not yet say so, but yes, the Arctic will be part of Belt and Road," he told us.

In 2017, Chinese strategists added the Arctic to the "Belt and Road." In the words of legal scholar Nengye Liu, "The signature foreign policy initiative of Chinese President Xi Jinping, the Belt and Road, is of unprecedented geographical and financial scope. Against this background, China has been showing strong interest in the resource-rich Arctic."[71] The author adds that "The Belt and Road Initiative could provide tools for China to achieve its Arctic policy objectives."[72]

In 2013, China won "observer status" on the Arctic Council—an international body composed of Arctic nations including Russia, Canada, the United States, and Denmark.[73] Nengye Liu writes of "China's growing Arctic interests" that "China now identifies itself as a 'near-Arctic State' and a major stakeholder in the Arctic."[74] Referencing statements by Chinese Foreign Minister Wang Yi, his explanation goes as follows:

The three main pillars of China's Arctic policy are respect, coop-eration, and "win-win" solutions. First, China respects the rights of the Arctic States and indigenous people as enshrined in international law. This means China recognizes the sovereignty, sovereign rights, and jurisdiction of Arctic States under the United Nations Convention on the Law of the Sea. In return, China would seek recognition of its own legitimate rights in the Arctic under international law. For example, China enjoys cer-tain freedoms in the high seas portions of the marine Arctic, such as freedom of navigation, overflight, research, and fishing. China has expressed its intention not to challenge the existing governance regime in the Arctic. Rather, China would prefer to be involved in shaping the development of Arctic governance to China's benefits.[75]

In other words, "China's legitimate rights in the Arctic" have largely to do with trade and maritime passage. Hence its importance in the "Belt and Road" project of Eurasian integration and, as in other parts of the world, as a source of natural resources. In Liu's summation: "The key objective of China's Arctic Policy is not to be left behind in the changing governance of the *resource-rich North Pole.*"[76]

China's government describes its Arctic interests as enduring and long-standing. In the words of China's Vice Foreign Minister, Zhang Ming, in 2018, "China started to turn its eyes to the Arctic as early as 90 years ago."[77] Zhang explained that "at present, China's activities in the Arctic mainly focus on scientific research."[78] But what of the future? The foreign ministry presumably sees potential for much deeper involvement in this region: "The Arctic enjoys great potential as a shipping route and with its rich resources." This includes "high seas and international seabed areas," where "non-Arctic countries have the rights to conduct scientific research, navigation and exploration in the Arctic region," and that the "interna-tional community must work together to protect and utilize the Arctic."[79]

In other words, China wants a seat at the table for what it calls the "uti-lization" of the Arctic.

China's State Council featured a report in June 2017 that sheds light on the strategic project of Arctic trade routes: "China has proposed three marine economic passages connecting Asia with Africa, Oceania, Europe and beyond in a bid to advance maritime cooperation under the Belt and Road Initiative."[80]

The Chinese government envisions three "blue economic passages":

> The China-Indian Ocean-Africa-Mediterranean Sea Blue Economic Passage
>> The China-Oceania-South Pacific Blue Economic Passage
>> [O]ne that will lead to Europe via the Arctic Ocean.[81]

Beijing's vision for the region focuses on sea lines of communication. The article featured by the State Council deserves to be quoted in full:

> China will strive to designate three "blue economic passages" — the China-Indian Ocean-Africa-Mediterranean Sea Blue Economic Passage; the China-Oceania-South Pacific Blue Economic Passage; and one that will lead to Europe via the Arctic Ocean.
>
> The China-Indian Ocean-Africa-Mediterranean Sea Blue Economic Passage will be based on coastal economic belts in China. It will link the China-Indochina Peninsula Economic Corridor and run westward from the South China Sea to the Indian Ocean, connecting the China-Pakistan Economic Corridor and the Bangladesh-China-India-Myanmar Economic Corridor, according to the document.
>
> The China-Oceania-South Pacific Blue Economic Passage is set to head south from the South China Sea into the Pacific Ocean.[82]

This is China's future footprint. The State Council and the Party envision a globally connected China with full access to the world's resources and integration of all the world's major sea routes under the "Belt and Road Initiative."

In September 2017, China's "Xue Long," or "Snow Dragon" (an icebreaker ship) completed a successful voyage through the Arctic Northwest Passage, which Xinhua announced would bring "a wealth of navigation experience" for Chinese ships headed to the Arctic in the future.[83]

China's emphasis on building relations with Arctic nations, including Finland, Denmark, and Norway, is evidenced through a series of high-level visits and through the establishment of the China–Nordic Research Center and China–Nordic Arctic Cooperation Symposium.[84] Chinese cooperation with Russia in the Arctic has also increased, especially after tightened sanctions passed in the wake of Putin's annexation of Crimea have limited the assistance of US and European oil companies to Russia.[85] Chinese engineers have begun work in the Russian Arctic on infrastructure projects ranging from energy extraction infrastructure to rail projects and a deep-water port; Russia and China also announced the establishment of a Russian-Chinese Polar Engineering and Research Center as a partnership between two universities, to focus on Arctic industrial development.[86]

In short, China views the Arctic as another major area in which it can find resources and build transportation links to achieve global reach. It affects this, as in other regions, through infrastructure and investment under the rubric of "win-win" diplomacy and government-to-government interactions, which its companies can follow.

China views the Arctic as an essential arena in its global strategy. Given a regional government model that is different from areas such as the Middle East, Latin America, and Africa, it must step more carefully for now, advocating on the one hand for "rights" and "interests" as a "near-Arctic" nation, and on the other for respecting existing governance regimes.

However, as Ann-Marie Brady, the leading expert on China's presence and ambitions in the Arctic and Antarctic, explains, the polar regions are now part of China's national narrative. A new Chinese film, approved by state censors, called *Antarctica 2049* was produced by Fang Li, CEO of a company which "supplies the technology used in China's deep sea mining, seabed bathymetrics, and polar marine exploration."[87]

Dr. Brady elaborates: "As China strengthens its polar capacities, the Chinese government is now incorporating the polar regions into its meta-narrative on national identity, national interests, and China's global rise as an economic and political power." Moreover, "China's expanded polar presence and expanded scientific program are explained to the Chinese public as being part of China's efforts to secure a share of polar resources in the future, which will help underwrite China's continued economic growth, as well as an indicator of China's improved comprehensive national strength."[88]

In other words, the poles are part of the "China Dream," both for economic purposes and for the power politics inherent in the "great rejuvenation of the Chinese nation." Meanwhile, "The Chinese government spares no effort to hide its designs on Antarctic mineral resources from possible foreign criticism, to the extent of even deliberately mistranslating a speech of its supreme leader." This was a speech by Xi Jinping which in Chinese read "to better understand, protect, and exploit the Antarctic," and appeared in English as "to better understand, protect, and *explore* the Antarctic." Like much of China's communications strategy, the most benign word-choices in translation are essential to Chinese communications. In the whole speech, Xi describes China as a "polar great power."

Like its access to the Middle East, Africa, and Latin America, and like its ambitions for "national rejuvenation," China's power, influence, and interests extend throughout the earth and into space, including in regions which most see not as China's own. The Arctic brings resources, diversified shipping routes, and prestige, all of which are essential to the "great rejuvenation." The messaging is of benignity, but the intended presence is clear, and part of what is already a global China.

THE INDO-PACIFIC: THE INDIAN OCEAN REGION AND SOUTH PACIFIC STATES

For centuries, the Indian Ocean has been the world's great maritime trading region. In the ancient world, it linked the Romans to India and China, the Persians and Greeks to South Asia, China to India, and Southeast Asia to Africa and the Middle East.[89] In the modern era, it has been a vital trade route between the Middle East and America, between China and Europe, and, with the rise of the container ship, one of the jugular veins of a globalized world.

When China's leaders talk of building a "Twenty-First-Century Maritime Silk Road" under the "Belt and Road Initiative," they are appealing in part to China's role as a focal point in ancient global commerce, epitomized by the ancient silk road trading routes to China. Xi famously commented in Kazakhstan in 2013: "As I stand here and look back at that episode of history, I could almost hear the camel bells echoing in the mountains and see the wisps of smoke rising from the desert."[90]

The new concept of a "Maritime Silk Road" is a modern sea route which spans the Indo-Pacific from the South China Sea, where China is building its military islands, through the Strait of Hormuz to the Middle East, and through the Suez Canal to Europe. The Indian Ocean Region must be understood as the guts of Asia's economy. Ninety percent of world trade travels by sea, and the Indian Ocean sea lanes are among the busiest in the world. They link Europe, the Middle East, Africa, and Asia to one another, and they link the Americas to the Middle East. The area is so vast and complex that it is split between three US military combatant commands in US global military planning: Central Command (CENTCOM) in the Middle

East and Persian Gulf, Africa Command (AFRICOM) in Africa and the Western Indian Ocean, and Indo-Pacific Command (INDO-PACOM) in the Pacific and Eastern Indian Oceans.[91]

China's initiatives in the Indian Ocean and Indo-Pacific are trade-based, but as Part Two explains, closely linked to Chinese military power. As a joint document between the Chinese Ministry of Foreign Affairs and Ministry of Commerce explains: "The 21st Century Maritime Silk Road is designed to go from China's coast to Europe through the South China Sea and the Indian Ocean in one route, and from China's coast through the South China Sea to the South Pacific in the other."[92] Hence the importance of Chinese island-building and military activities in the South China Sea—the fulcrum of their vision for the Indo-Pacific. China's own military regions are, at present, focused on the Chinese mainland, aside from the "Southern Theatre Command," which concentrates on the South China Sea. From here, the Chinese navy builds its presence within the "nine-dashed line" on its "blue national soil."

Toward what end? If there is one region which China truly depends on, it is the Indian Ocean Region. As a leading scholar in Sichuan explained to me years ago, China would depend on the region, and its resources, "for the next forty years," meaning up to at least 2049.

Chinese trade with Africa, the Middle East, and Europe, and with other parts of Asia, all depends upon Indian Ocean sea lanes. However, these trade flows must pass through a series of chokepoints before returning to China, especially the aforementioned Strait of Malacca. Hence what Hu Jintao termed China's "Malacca Dilemma," a problem which crystallizes the importance of diversifying energy and resource supply routes around the globe through the "Belt and Road."

The result is that China's naval presence in the Indian Ocean is growing. Chinese investment is also growing. As mentioned, China has invested approximately $600 billion in the Indian Ocean Region over the past ten years, more than any other region on Earth.[93]

The Chinese military is currently focused on the South China Sea, but China's island-building here is part of a much larger strategy. The Indo-Pacific is a region that combines two of the world's great oceans—the Indian and the Pacific—and the chokepoint-riddled jugular of world trade and global economics.[94] As explored in Part Two, China's long-term strategy envisions projecting military power throughout the entire maritime system, running from what they refer to as the "first and second island chains" in the West Pacific to the Strait of Hormuz in the Middle East at the Western edge of the Indian Ocean.

China is building up its strategic influence with the help of Russia and Pakistan. It has held naval exercises with Pakistan in the Indian Ocean, and is supplying Pakistan with diesel-electric submarines to counter China's rival, India. China has conducted naval exercises with Russia in the Mediterranean, South China Sea, East China Sea, and Sea of Japan.

Importantly, the Indian Ocean Region is home to numerous Chinese port-building projects. From Hambantota in Sri Lanka, to Myanmar, Malaysia, Pakistan, and East Africa, China is doing its best to retool the region in order to better suit its strategic interests. The *Nikkei Asian Review* reports that Chinese academics and business people have partnered with retired generals in Thailand to study the possibility of building a canal through Thailand's Isthmus of Kra.[95]

Importantly, Chinese ownership is often a feature of its port-building and infrastructure projects. For example, in Hambantota, at the heart of the Indian Ocean Region, for a comparatively cheap $1 billion-plus agreement, a Chinese company now owns an 80 percent stake in the port. As *Reuters* reports, this came soon after Sri Lanka's prime minister offered to swap equity in Sri Lankan infrastructure for debt owed to the Chinese.[96] Exploitation of developing countries heavily indebted to Chinese state financing is expanding China's grip on strategic locations in the Indian Ocean Region. Chinese debt financing sows the seeds, and, when the situation matures, Beijing is able to pluck ports and infrastructure like ripe fruit. This has produced concern in India, Japan, Australia, and the United States, as well, of course, as in nations which are increasingly indebted to China.

As the Indo-Pacific emerges as the world's most significant geopolitical region, the question looms: How much influence and control might China come to have in this region at the heart of its "Belt and Road" super-project?

While Chinese activities and influence are largely concentrated in the First and Second Island Chains and in the Indian Ocean, China's reach also extends to the South Pacific. This is clarified and codified in the three "blue economic passages," one of which is "China-Oceania-South Pacific, travelling southward from the South China Sea into the Pacific Ocean."[97]

China's presence in the South Pacific is long-standing. An academic observer wrote in 2008:

> Although many observers consider the South Pacific backward and remote, China's relations with the region have nonetheless developed rapidly since the late 1990s. Of the 14 nations that make up the Pacific Islands Forum (PIF) (excluding Australia and New Zealand), the eight that recognize the PRC (the Cook Islands, the Federated States of Micronesia, Fiji, Niue, Papua New Guinea, Samoa, Tonga, and Vanuatu) have seen their diplomatic, economic, and cultural relations with China intensify—with an increasing number of official visits and various financial assistance packages aimed at enhancing trade, building infra-structure, equipping government and military assets, and developing natural resources. This rising Chinese involvement in the South Pacific also comes at a time when the U.S. and European allies are decreasing aid and scaling back their presence.[98]

4.7

CHINA AND THE "MAJOR POWERS": THE UNITED STATES, RUSSIA, INDIA, JAPAN, AND EUROPE

Beijing is able to work effectively within regions where power is diffuse. However, one of the greatest challenges in completing China's ascending vision of victory will be outmaneuvering, coopting, or breaking the power of other major nations, especially the United States.

While Russia, India, and Japan each play important roles in their own regions — and will continue to do so in the future — China's core challenge is to siphon power away from America, the reigning superpower, without provoking a response that will derail China's activities and plans. Despite new actions on trade and commerce in 2018, US understanding of China's ascendancy remains chaotic and contradictory. "Engage but hedge" lives on as US national security sounds the alarm on China, but US business and finance works to make the most of the Chinese market. In foreign policy and academic circles, American discourse paints polarizing categories about those who are "hawks" and those who are "doves," even as the actions, objectives, and strategies of the Chinese Communist Party are on vivid display in Asia and around the world.

Beijing adds to this confusion in America and elsewhere in the world through its own brand of interference operations, directed against democratic countries. In contrast to Russia's attempts to sow political discord in America's 2016 elections, Chinese influence operations present a positive, sanitized image of China to nations around the world. This is meant to distort a country's discourse on China and to constrain action against Beijing. In the words of a 2018 report from a group of leading American

China experts, Beijing's influence operations target "think tanks, universities, and media [as well as] state, local, and national government institutions." In doing so "China seeks to promote views sympathetic to the Chinese Government, policies, society, and culture; suppress alternative views; and co-opt key American players to support China's foreign policy goals and economic interests."[99]

However, the challenges for China should not be underestimated when it comes to strategic competition with the United States.

The United States retains enormous advantages in terms of economic and military power, a global alliance system, and leadership in the innumerable institutions built under the Pax Americana. The US lacks, however, at present, the strategic focus of a rising nation like China. Thus, the Chinese Communist Party is able to work around the edges of American power, building its own global presence. China's leaders prepare for military confrontation with America and its allies[100] while also working to complete an economic ascendency of such proportions that the US may ultimately— if this strategy is successful— find itself outmaneuvered and ultimately surpassed and replaced in each realm in which power is built.

China is likely to press ahead with attempts to outmaneuver US alliances and partnerships, gradually peeling countries away from an American order and into China's economic orbit through trade, investment, and commercial incentives that America can't or won't provide. The integration of Europe into the "Belt and Road," for example, is paramount to Chinese strategy; the weakening of US–European ties across the Atlantic, driven by deeper European economic integration with China, would be a cornerstone of Chinese long-term strategic victory. Splitting the US alliance system in Asia is commonly understood to be one of Beijing's long-term objectives, especially when it comes to the relationship between the United States and Japan— this is a relationship that Party strategists and leaders see as hostile to Chinese power in Asia. In the words of one of the Communist Party's senior ideologists, speaking to former US National Security Advisor Zbigniew Brzezinski in 2013:

> China today is neither the Qing regime, nor Germany in World War I nor Japan in World War II. It definitely will not work to go back to the old way of checking China by supporting Japan.

> In a word, encirclement of China is destined to fail. They must recognize and acknowledge the existence of a New East.[101]

In the long term, with the breaking of the US presence in Asia and the integration of Europe and other major continents into the "Belt and Road," China would be free to consolidate its power in an intercontinental system in which America plays a weakened role. This would, at worst, convert the US into an isolated, island continent, detached from a colossal geographical system, one where China sits at its center as the dominant military and economic power.

What role would the United States and other major powers take in a China-led world? What would it mean for the de facto end of American preeminence in global affairs?

While China insists that its rise can be a "win-win," and much American discourse focuses on the fear of war with China, the reality is that China's rise is in fact an open challenge to the United States. China shows some comfort and effectiveness in formulating its relations to entire regions, especially when engagement is based on beneficial trade flows and resource acquisition. However, China has, in its modern history, shown a far greater discomfort in its relations with major nation states. Its military conflicts with India, Russia, and the United States during the founding decades of the People's Republic of China attest to this. All such wars or conflicts were considered to be defensive struggles waged in China's interest. China's leaders did not hesitate to use military force when they felt that they had been pressed too far, meaning that vital interests were at stake, or that China's position in its region was threatened and the country had to make a stand.

What has changed dramatically since China's wars of the twentieth century is both the scope of China's global interests and its military capabilities. In short, China's "region" is in fact evolving into a *global playing field*. In the 1950s, as mentioned, there were four key strategic regions that mattered as China built its national industry, consolidated its borders, and took the first steps on its journey as the "New China": the Himalayas (Tibet), the Korean peninsula, Taiwan, and Southeast Asia. China fought wars in each of these arenas, all considered vital to the reconstruction of China's geopolitical position—pure sovereignty and territorial integrity itself—following the "Century of Humiliation."

China's assistance to fellow Communist states, North Korea and Vietnam, was not simply an act of Cold War camaraderie: these actions resulted from calculated assessments of Chinese national interests and security, in a period in which "territorial integrity" was felt to be at risk, and "sovereignty" was seen as a fragile and hard-won thing. These were not yet the operations of a major military power, but those of an agrarian, preindustrial society. Nonetheless, China's leaders were able to muster massive quantities of manpower and the experience of nearly constant warfare in their own region, from the Second World War to the Chinese Civil War, as well as a powerful sense of national purpose at a leadership level. China, throughout the twentieth century, deployed these assets against perceived enemies and adversaries all along their frontiers.

The China of today has changed. China is no longer concerned only with its traditional strategic geography. It is now a global actor, building a multi-regional military, with an intercontinental vision of its "legitimate rights and interests." China's leaders tell their military that they must "improve their combat capability and readiness for war,"[102] and their people that the Central Military Commission "should lead the armed forces to be ready to fight and win wars, and to undertake the missions and tasks of the new era."[103] One of the most important questions for other countries is simple: What kind of wars is China planning to fight?

The use of paramilitary power to compel smaller nations to bend to China's will is substantial. In the South China Sea, China's "gray zone" paramilitary operations are directed against Southeast Asian nations who have rival claims to China's "blue national soil."[104]

But major powers must also beware. China's military, above all, is designed for conflict with the United States.[105] It is also designed to deter and defeat India, and, if necessary, Russia, though Russia–China relations are currently at a high point. In the twentieth century, China fought wars in or conducted military operations against nearly every nation on its periphery: Korea, India, Russia, Japan, Taiwan, and Vietnam, and against the United States and United Nations in Korea, in addition to waging a bloody civil war. In the twenty-first century, its strategic space has expanded beyond the imagination of China's original leaders.

Despite "win-win" rhetoric in English, Chinese language discourse is not always so peaceful, especially at a popular level. Recall Mao's inflammatory speeches on the ability of hundreds of millions of Chinese people to absorb a nuclear war with any adversary, and consider the lines below which played across Chinese national media in 2013. They originated in the Communist Party-run *Global Times* and were syndicated across numerous outlets online as China's national media reported on new nuclear submarine-launched ballistic missiles (SLBMs). The paper called China's SLBMs "the national weapon," the development of which is "an important event in the history of US–China relations":

> Because the Midwestern states of the United States are sparsely populated, in order to improve the killing effect, the nuclear killing of US soft targets should concentrate on major cities on the West Coast, such as Seattle, Los Angeles, San Francisco and San Diego . . .
>
> If the Dongfeng 31A is launched over the North Pole, it can easily destroy a series of large cities on the East Coast and in New England, such as Ann Arbor, Philadelphia, New York, Boston, Portland, Baltimore, and Norfolk. The population of these cities accounts for one-eighth of the total population of the United States.[106]

More recently, in December 2018, at the Military Industry List summit in Shenzhen, China, Rear Admiral Luo Yuan (retired), deputy head of the PLA Academy of Military Sciences, explained that China could sink two US aircraft carriers. As reported in the *Navy Times*: "'What the United States fears most is taking casualties,' the admiral said, before adding that such an attack on two of the U.S. Navy's steel behemoths would claim upwards of 10,000 lives."[107] Luo also described the "Five National Foundations" of the United States (五大立国之本): the military, the US dollar, talent, voting, and the cultivation of enemies (树敌);[108] he explained that China should "use its strength to attack the enemy's shortcomings. Attack wherever the enemy is afraid of being hit. Wherever the enemy is weak . . ."[109] Despite coverage in multiple countries, neither Admiral Luo's statements nor the conference in Shenzhen found their way into the most prominent American news outlets.

Will China make accommodations with major nations like Russia and India? What will its relationship be with Europe, which is both a major market and a base for important technological harvests for the PRC, and whose military power, while significant, is mostly far away? And what about Japan, the arch-enemy in China's popular culture, but also a substantial military power and close ally of the United States? And what about the United States itself? These are among the most important questions in the coming years of China's rise to global power.

Concern among major nations is already visible. India is worried about Chinese influence in the Indian Ocean Region and military activity in the Himalayas. Russia, which despite its "comprehensive strategic partnership" with China and Xi Jinping's assessment that Russia–China relations are "now the best ever,"[110] may also be playing a long-term losing geopolitical game with the PRC. Russia's stalling economy is now only 15 percent of China's GDP. As it loses its military edge over China, it also cedes influence in Central Asia, and potentially even in the Arctic over the long run. As a Russian scholar remarked recently in Washington, Russia is concerned, ultimately, about an Asia dominated by China. I asked her why, then, was Russia helping China to build its military capabilities? She replied that Russia *had to sell something to someone*.

Europe provides a fascinating case. Burdened with regional concerns at present, from immigration, to terrorism, to the question of Russia itself, policy-makers often see China as a welcome source of relief to otherwise troubling economic circumstances. The *China Daily* in Europe, for example, studiously avoids military and security issues in Asia, instead using its columns to invite European companies to come and surf the wave of Chinese mergers and acquisitions, while also throwing in that— unlike the European colonial powers— China intends to rise peacefully. This is a convenient message for the moment. However, as US–China problems increase, European nations may find it difficult to remain bystanders to a shifting strategic balance that is dangerous to their American military partner and defender. The problem of China's ascendency will be all the more urgent for Europe as programs like Made in China 2025 threaten to damage European competitiveness—a fact that European businesses and governments are increasingly aware of.

In short, it is a brave new world for countries small and large as China's rise continues, as its ambitions increase, and its sheer global weight is felt more and more. From major regions to major nation states, China's global impact is already more profound than anything else seen since the end of the USSR, and perhaps rivals the rise of the United States itself. It is built not only on ambition, but on *sheer necessity* wedded to a vision of global proportions. Resource interests, food security, water, protein, fishing rights, maritime trade routes, mining interests — all of which span the planet — are the baseline interests for China's 1 billion-plus people.

What this new world will mean for China in an ideological sense — the power and the glory, the responsibility, and the message to humanity that will live with China's rise in a world marked by its "comprehensive national power"— is the subject of Part Five.

PART V

人类命运共同体

A COMMUNITY OF COMMON DESTINY FOR MANKIND

★ ★ ★ ★ ★

CHINA'S VISION FOR THE NEW WORLD ORDER

Thousands of years ago, China envisaged a world where people live in perfect harmony and are as dear to one another as family. Today, President Xi Jinping has given the world a new name—a community of common destiny.[1]

"XI'S WORLD VISION," XINHUA NEWS AGENCY, 2017

It is a global vision and the undertaking of a major leader, combining China's own development with that of the whole world, transcending traditional Western schools of thought on international relations based on the zero-sum game and power politics.[2]

"XI AND HIS ERA," XINHUA NEWS AGENCY, 2017

WHAT WOULD IT MEAN FOR CHINA TO RULE THE WORLD?

The answer has been in front of us all along. It has been in front of us as we read the Chinese Communist Party's statements, observe their strategies and actions, and come to understand *the intentions* behind China's ascendency in this century.

It is simple: China's rise, in the minds of its leaders and many of its people, is *not a rise, but a restoration.*

It is a restoration, simply put, of the *power and prosperity* enjoyed by the Chinese Empire.

It is the restoration, as the Communist Party sees it, of *an entire world defined by China's supremacy.*

Most importantly, both as a political culture and as a civilization, China has plenty of experience ruling a world system. It is from the earlier time of supremacy that much of the character of current-day Chinese political thought and action derives.

Prior to the "Century of Humiliation," which began in 1840, the emperors and bureaucrats of Imperial China dominated not the whole world, but *their known world.*[3] That is, prior to the rise of European empires, and long before what we know today as globalization, China's rulers dominated East Asia, establishing a system with China at the center and in which the smaller states around China's borders were vassal states. China's rulers had a detailed system of governance, passed down over centuries, for both internal and external rule, and for the maintenance of this imperial system. All of this was broken apart in the "Century of Humiliation." Since that fateful time, China's leaders have worked to restore Chinese power on the world stage.

Today, the Chinese Communist Party's strategy is intended to deliver the creation of a new world system with China at its center — and the de facto end of an American-led world.

In an effort to appeal to the world beyond China, China's leaders brand their global vision "A Community of Common Destiny for Mankind."

CHINA'S VISION
FOR WORLD ORDER

n order to understand this vision, we must turn first to ancient China. The most important thing to understand about the imperial Chinese order is that it was built on a hierarchy, both inside and outside China's borders.

One of the great American China scholars, John K. Fairbank, observed in 1968: "the Chinese world order was a set of ideas and practices developed and perpetuated by the rulers of China over many centuries."[4]

Let us look at what he says, and then let us think about what this means today as we begin to see the striking similarities between the Communist Party's practices and those of China's imperial past.

China's imperial system involved a series of vassal states organized in terms of their *proximity to Chinese power* in a "graded and concentric hierarchy" which defined China's external relations. Fairbank identifies three geographical zones. The first, the "Sinic Zone," was made up of tributary states close in distance and in culture, some of which had even been directly ruled at times by China. These included Korea and Vietnam, and pieces of what is today the "First Island Chain" in the Pacific. The second was an "Inner Asian Zone," comprised of "tributary states and tribes" neither ethnically nor culturally Chinese. The third was the "Outer Zone," regions inhabited by those classified in the Chinese language as *waiyi* 外夷, or "outer barbarians."[5] In Chinese, the character *yi* 夷 has many meanings. It describes "non-Han people," and some translate it as "barbarians."[6] It can also mean "to destroy or exterminate."[7]

The places inhabited by the "outer barbarians" were farther away, at the edges of the world then known to China, and included parts of Southeast Asia, South Asia, and Europe.[8] Within this mix of zones, China itself was known as the "Middle Kingdom," the geographical center of the world, and the center of world power. China's system, and its approach to the world, was, as Fairbank writes, marked by a "concept of Sinocentricism and an assumption of Chinese superiority." Additionally, China's foreign relations were meant to express the values that underpinned political order inside of China.[9]

Harmonization of the internal and external political order was essential to the Chinese system, both for practical and ideological purposes. In practical terms, pacification of outer regions was important to internal stability because "when the barbarians were not submissive abroad, rebels might more easily arise within."[10] In ideological terms, adherence to careful ritual and custom enabled the power of the Chinese state, with the Emperor at its center. The system was built upon "ideological orthodoxy" and compliance with "correct teachings." Indoctrination in particular texts "promoted harmony between rulers and ruled" and, in doing so, perpetuated China's social order.[11]

The Chinese system was markedly different from that of Western Europe, where (at least for the big players) international relations was a game of relatively equal states that led to a diplomatic tradition that aspired to a balance of power.[12] Incidentally, this is the tradition that Henry Kissinger both studied and practiced as a scholar and a statesman.[13] In contrast, the Chinese world order was *not an order made of states of equal power*. It was an order that derived from Chinese supremacy. Because of its sheer wealth and size, China was the "natural center" of the East Asian world.[14] The European tradition, emanating from a competition among relatively equal, sovereign states, and the tradition of statecraft it created, has carried on into the twenty-first century as the basis for order in an American-led world, something known to many as the international rules-based order. Fairbank noted fifty years ago that China's troubles in adapting to an international order comprised of nation states in the twentieth century were partly a result of the country's traditional views of a China-centric world order.[15]

It is this international rules-based order led by the United States that today's leaders in China consider a constraint on Chinese power, *one they seek to end*.

Moreover, as Fairbank explains, the classical Chinese order was not exactly "international." In contrast to Europe's case of competing equal states, *there were no states that were equal to China's size and power*. The Chinese conception of world order was very different from one derived from competing states. According to Fairbank, the Chinese system with its tributary states could not actually be called international "because the participants in it did not use concepts corresponding to Western ideas of nation, or sovereignty, or quality of states each having equal sovereignty."[16]

Instead, the world order rested upon a principle of *"superordination–subordination."*[17]

This was a world in which China's power was the center, the sun around which the rest revolved.

The administrative structure had three groups: "clan vassals," "inner vassals," and "external vassals." Here, the harmonization of internal and external order becomes clearer: China's rulers expected "ideological commitment" not only from China's own elite, but from the rulers of *states outside of China*. Moreover, in the Chinese definition of world order, the influence, the wisdom, and the virtue of the Chinese Emperor extended not only throughout the whole of China "but continued outward beyond the borders of China to all mankind and gave them order and peace . . . as parts of a concentric hierarchy."[18]

Importantly, as Chinese power expanded, the "exterior vassals" of today became the "interior vassals" of tomorrow.[19]

Additionally, rulers outside of China "participated in the Chinese world order by observing the appropriate forms and ceremonies" in their interactions with the Chinese Emperor, all of which constituted the tribute system. Foreign rulers received a "noble rank" in the imperial hierarchy. They performed the ceremonies of the Chinese court, including the "kowtow," or placing one's head on the floor before the emperor in an expression of obedience, and were allowed the "privileges of trade."[20]

Before 1840, China's rulers had three primary methods for dealing with "foreign areas": military or administrative control; attraction via culture, ideology, or religion; and manipulation through "material interest" or diplomatic means.[21]

Through these methods the Chinese imperial system influenced the known world from Central Asia, Tibet, and Vietnam (military control), to Portugal and Britain (manipulation through material interest).[22]

To give an example from distant Britain, let us look at a description of the ill-fated Macartney mission of 1793, Britain's first diplomatic mission to China, controversial for its role in Western, Chinese, and global narratives of history. Historian Pankaj Mishra describes the British delegation reaching the Middle Kingdom at the height of its grandeur, and a doomed meeting point between East and West. It deserves to be read in full:

> The Chinese emperor, then a fit eighty-year-old, graciously asked after King George's health and offered Macartney some rice wine during a "sumptuous" banquet, which struck the Englishman as possessing a "calm dignity, that sober pomp of Asiatic greatness, which European refinements have not yet attained."
>
> The British delegation was treated with bland courtesy for a few more days before being abruptly ushered out of the country with a reply from the Celestial Emperor that stated unequivocally that he had "never valued ingenious articles" and had not "the slightest need of England's manufactures." It was right that "men of the Western Ocean" should admire and want to study the culture of his empire. But he could not countenance an English ambassador who spoke and dressed so differently fitting into the "Empire's ceremonial system." And, the emperor added, it would be good if the English king could *simply act in conformity with our wishes by strengthening your loyalty and swearing perpetual obedience.*
>
> The letter had been drafted well before Lord Macartney arrived in Beijing. The condescending tone reflected the Chinese elite's exalted sense of their country's pre-eminence.[23]

Leading scholars observe that a similar vision of China's superiority marked Beijing's relations with other states even in the early period of Communist rule. For example, while supporting Vietnamese leaders at the height of ideological alignment in the Cold War, "Chinese leaders were disappointed and angry when their Vietnamese comrades deviated from the Chinese line."[24] This is demonstrated clearly by China's anger over the North Vietnamese decision to launch their 1968 Tet Offensive over Chinese objections.[25]

While history does not repeat itself, its realities are a guide. In a world where China is supreme, we may ultimately see the erosion of the Westphalian world order, one maintained by the US and its allies since the end of the Second World War, and its replacement with a system built on Chinese supremacy. China's classical world order casts China as the arbiter of "order and peace" for "all under heaven." And today, Xi Jinping speaks of building a counter to the American-led system: "The Community of Common Destiny for Mankind." Global institutions, from investment banks to consultancies to economic forums, are eager to see and to participate in the continued rise of Chinese economic power. However, these institutions do not understand the consequences of the Communist Party's vision of dominance in world affairs.

A GLOBAL "MIDDLE KINGDOM"

C hina's rulers today have a vision that is geographically and materially grander than anything their forebears could have imagined.

This vision is first and foremost about the integration of Europe, Africa, and Asia as an economic system, with China at its center. Let's look at the "Belt and Road" once more, this time in the words of a book appropriately titled *The Belt and Road Initiative: What Will China Offer the World in Its Rise?* This work, "Recommended by the Bureau of Theory of the Publicity Department of the Central Committee of the CPC, and the Cadre Education Bureau of the Organization Department of the Central Committee of the CPC," insists that "The Belt and Road Initiative will reconstruct the geopolitical and geoeconomic maps of the world, and help Chinese enterprises go global, marking China's transformation from a regional civilization to a global one."[26] This global strategic initiative into which Chinese economic power will expand "covers 65 countries in Central Asia, ASEAN (the Association of Southeast Asian Nations), South Asia, Central and Eastern Europe, West Asia and North Africa," an area with 4.4 billion people "and an economic capacity of US$21 trillion, accounting for 63 percent and 29 percent of the world's total, respectively."[27]

China's senior policy-makers acknowledge in no uncertain terms that this "Belt and Road" is the geographical foundation for their "Community of Common Destiny for Mankind," also known as the "Community of Shared Future." They also tell us "China intends to turn into practice the vision for common development and a 'community of shared future' through the Belt and Road Initiative."[28]

While the desired geographical scope of China's influence is clear, what is the nature of the "Community of Common Destiny for Mankind"?

As Fairbank explains of Imperial China, internal and external order were "so closely related" that "one could not long survive without the other."[29] As in the past, it is likely that the practices inside China today, the technological advancements, concepts of governance such as "social stability" and "harmony," and mechanisms of what the Communist Party calls "social management," could extend eventually outside of China, if not in full, then at least in part, should the world find itself with China as the unrivaled center of power. China could seek to exert its influence throughout the world, as in a prior China-centered order, through practices of "control," "attraction," and "manipulation."

What are China's internal control practices? How is China actually ruled?

To begin with, the Chinese Communist Party maintains an authoritarian model that aspires to a vision of comprehensive "social management." It is a concept which, while aided by recent technological innovations under Xi Jinping, in fact goes back decades to the heart of the Communist Party ethos, and arguably even further back, with roots in the political philosophies of ancient China.

According to China security scholar Samantha Hoffman, the concept of "social management" dates to the "first discussions of law and social order" at the founding of the People's Republic of China in 1949. It returned in new expressions over the decades, particularly as Chinese political thought came under the influence of systems-engineering concepts. The 1984 report *On the New Technological Revolution* advocated the use of "systems engineering" and "complex systems thinking" in the "social domain," that is, as a method for social control.[30] The 1984 report states that "Leaps and bounds in science and technology [since the 1940s have] influenced or given rise to transformations in the way social management agencies work. The theory and practice, perspective and method of systems engineering were born, and developed from these changes." The report states that "only if we fully grasp [the concepts of] information, data, systems analysis, and decision modeling, can we truly possess 'foresight and sagacity,' and generate the courage and a bold vision consistent with the flow of history."[31]

From these conceptual roots, and with the anticipation of the importance of "data systems analysis, and decision modeling," the Communist Party envisioned an idea of pure control. In short, not only through technology, but also through *design and innovation* the Communist Party would come to rule China effectively—and utterly. In the words of a scholar of Chinese law: "the political project has consistently been . . . collectivist in nature. It focuses on a future to be achieved, rather than a present to be governed, it elevates the nation and its interests over the concerns of the individual, who is expected to perform continuous sacrifice in furtherance of national goals."[32]

From the totalitarianism of Mao Zedong to the rule of Deng Xiaoping, Jiang Zemin, Hu Jintao, and Xi Jinping, we have arrived at authoritarianism for the twenty-first century. This authoritarian vision, like Chinese concepts of "war control" in the military domain, is a vision of society as a machine that can be controlled by the Communist Party.

This "collectivist" vision is married to the idea of absolute loyalty to the Chinese Communist Party. In pursuit of the "two centenary goals" it intends to reach in 2021 and 2049, and in pursuit of the absolute goal of "the great rejuvenation of the Chinese nation," Party theorists explain that Xi Jinping's goals reflect "the common aspiration of every Chinese" and that the Party must "unite all Chinese forces."[33] They add that "The future and destiny of every individual are closely bound up with those of the nation."[34] Xi Jinping himself adds that "patriotism is the core of the Chinese national spirit."[35]

In other words, the Party forges unity within the nation in order to work toward the common objectives defined by the Chinese Communist Party. The Party maintains this unity to the best of its ability through methods which are, for now, specific to China. In order to "enhance cohesion," the Party uses history as a rallying point that places the Chinese people against the outside world, invaders, foreigners, Japan, and the West, and the perpetrators of the "Century of Humiliation," an abyss from which the Party can deliver the Chinese people to achieve the "great rejuvenation of the Chinese nation."[36]

In order to improve systems of "social management," the Party maintains a rigorous surveillance state. It utilizes emerging technologies such as artificial intelligence, big data analysis, and facial recognition systems to test and implement specialized programs, such as the "Social Credit Score" system. While this system is still in its infancy, it envisions the creation of "a system of rewards and punishments on the basis of blacklists and redlists," in which "miscreants are blocked from specific activities," and then sorted "into categories on the basis of probabilistic computations."[37]

China legal scholar Rogier Creemers notes that the Chinese Communist Party has achieved "unprecedented" penetration of Chinese society in comparison to prior periods of Chinese rule, whether by China's emperors or during the republic prior to the PRC.[38] He explains that "Successive ideological campaigns implanted the imagery of the Party and its leaders at the centre of daily life" and that "within its first decade of rule, the Party managed to . . . eliminate external threats to its regime," establishing the position of power which it has held for decades.[39]

Samantha Hoffman reveals that: "The CCP has clearly explained that it sees innovating social management as its blueprint for maintaining power." Moreover, "advances, particularly through application of technology, can enable the CCP's ideal form of authoritarianism, which integrates cooperation and coercion."[40]

Thus, the Communist Party's security state works to fulfill its broader philosophical goals of harmony, stability, and social control through the development and implementation of new technology to achieve old authoritarian goals. This ranges from monitoring, surveillance, and data-sharing to the nascent Social Credit System.[41] All of this helps the state security system achieve objectives such as "A pre-emptive management of threat at the source" and "Pre-empting challenges to the Party's control via creation of a system, in which every member of society has the responsibility to participate in their own management."[42]

If these are the systems envisioned and increasingly employed inside China, what would this mean for world order?

Like the Chinese empire of the past, today's Chinese national security state envisions a kind of seamless flow from Chinese internal power to China's foreign relations.

An article in the Communist Party journal, *Quishi*, or *Seeking Truth*, "A New Chapter in National Security Guided by General Secretary Xi Jinping's Overall National Security Concept," brands the "Community of Common Destiny for Mankind" part of China's *national security concept*, one that will produce "far-reaching international influence."[43] The article adds that:

> The overall national security concept emphasizes the promotion of international security, the realization of self-security and common security, jointly building the Community of Common Destiny for Mankind. This concept of security discards old

ideas of a zero-sum game, absolute security, alliance theory, etc., establishing on an international level an inclusive security concept which embodies the Chinese manner, reveals the Chinese mind and spirit, and manifests Chinese wisdom.[44]

It states that "The overall national security concept advocates the construction of the community of common destiny for mankind which is widely inclusive and produce far-reaching international influence."[45] In other words, the "Community of Common Destiny for Mankind" is not only an economic concept, but also *a security concept*. It is a concept of international order built around China's "comprehensive national power," "far-reaching international influence," and growing military power.

It is a concept of order built on, in Xi Jinping's words, "peace and development."[46]

Peace and development with China at the center.

The construction of not only global Chinese interests but also of *global Chinese power* is likely to result in a world in which China's form of governance becomes more and more relevant to the outside world. China would be recognized not only for its mechanisms and technical innovations, but for the philosophy of social order in which Chinese leaders and many Chinese people take great pride: the concept of "harmony" and "stability" under Communist Party rule.

As Fairbank explains, speaking of a world that existed well before the advent of artificial intelligence, big data, and the possibilities unleashed by the high-tech surveillance state, the Chinese order was held together not only by the mechanisms of its tributary system and internal bureaucracy, but also by a *philosophy of social order*, a hierarchy with an important "ideological component" in which "proper ceremonial forms" were meant to regulate the interaction between an authority and their beholder."[47] These rituals—the Confucian *li* 礼—were complemented by a "system of regulation and punishment by criminal law,"—*fa* 法—"the available and necessary means of control."[48]

This was ancient and medieval China, the great civilizational system in which China's current leaders and many of its people take immense pride. Its customs and traditions are of a different time, but their influence is clear. Is it true that, today, the guiding philosophy in the Chinese system is the harmonization of society with alternating mechanisms of ritual and control? Add to this version of systems theory the Communist Party's machine theory of social life and the aspiration for comprehensive "social management," and we begin to see a vision that is not only enabled by high technology, but rooted in deeper cultural origins.

As in many societies, law is the key to political philosophy. But as Dr. Creemers explains, in China the "*law is not a method of limiting the power of the state, but empowering and channeling it.*"[49] The Chinese Constitution enshrines the power and rights of the state over the freedom and rights of the individual while delineating a citizen's obligations. Article 51, for example, points out that citizens "exercising their freedoms and rights may not infringe upon the interests of the State, of society or of the collective, or upon the lawful freedoms and rights of other citizens." Article 52 says citizens have the duty "to safeguard the unification of the country and the unity of all its nationalities." Article 53 states they must "observe labor discipline and public order and respect social ethics," while Article 54 adds to their duties safeguarding "the security, honor and interests of the motherland."[50]

How many in the world's democracies would wish their lives to be dictated by such a system?

In today's China, absolute rule is manifest in the supremacy of the Communist Party. Consider the promotion in no uncertain terms of the doctrine of the "three supremes" by both Hu Jintao and the president of the Supreme People's Court, Wang Shengjun, even before the ascendancy of Xi Jinping to unprecedented power within the Party system: "In enforcing the law, judges should take into account first the supremacy of the Party's undertaking, second the supremacy of the popular interest, and only third the supremacy of the law."[51]

The Chinese Communist Party's innovation in the broader Chinese political tradition is the replacement of the emperor with Xi Jinping and the imperial bureaucracy with the Chinese Communist Party.

These are China's ideas and methods today, all of which are currently being deployed for the sake of "rejuvenation" and ascendency. What might the methods of government be in a world with China at its center? Is this indeed, the "destiny for mankind"?

The Chinese national security state and the Chinese philosophy of governance are deeply intertwined. Consider this from China's National Intelligence Law:

> Any organization and citizen shall, in accordance with the law, support, provide assistance, and cooperate in national intelligence work, and guard the secrecy of any national intelligence work that they are aware of. The state shall protect individuals and organizations that support, cooperate with, and collaborate in national intelligence work.[52]

In other words, any, each, and every individual and entity is beholden to the Chinese state and Chinese Communist Party. Every corporation and citizen must cooperate with the Communist Party to accomplish its global mission of providing security and building power for the Chinese State and the Communist Party.

In the National Security Law of the People's Republic of China, "national security" is defined as "a status in which the regime, sovereignty, unity, territorial integrity, welfare of the people, sustainable economic and social development, and other major interests are relatively not faced with any danger and not threatened internally or externally."[53] The law advocates the promotion of "international security" in order to "maintain national security in all fields." The requirement of *any* entity beholden to the Chinese state is thus to be used by the Communist Party for global economic and military expansion.[54] This is why companies such as Huawei should not be allowed to operate inside the United States or other democratic nations.

Importantly, just as the Communist Party sees itself in fundamental conflict with the United States and "the West" in terms of geopolitics and history, it also explicitly sees itself in conflict with the West *in terms of values.*

China's leaders and officials are honest about their dislike of and discomfort with an American-led world and American values. As chair of the National People's Congress Foreign Affairs Committee Madame Fu Ying put it in *The Financial Times* in 2016, "The U.S. world order is a suit that no longer fits." She added, "The western-centered world order dominated by the U.S. has made great contributions to human progress and economic growth. But those contributions lie in the past."[55] Party ideologists maintain that "The world order, dominated by the West for the past three hundred years is now on the decline."[56]

Madame Fu Ying also insists that "After emerging victorious at the end of the Cold War, the United States crowned itself as the world leader and has tried to extend the Western order to the new world order . . . Politically, it seeks to transform non-Western countries to a Western political system and a set of values with evangelical zeal."[57]

The Chinese Communist Party has its solution to the problem of an American-led "rules-based international order": they call it "The Community of Common Destiny for Mankind."

The link between internal and external security is clear as Party ideologists confront what they see as the danger of "Western values" not only in the international arena, *but also at home in China.*

China's active campaign against "Western values" targets Chinese schools and universities above all, as well as Chinese students overseas, in order to preserve the Communist Party's view of the past, present, and future among China's citizens.

Beijing's Minister of Education, Yuan Guiren, stated in 2015 that universities must "by no means allow teaching materials that disseminate Western values in our classrooms."[58] He added that "Any views that attack or defame the leadership of the party or smear socialism must never be allowed to appear in our universities."[59] An internal document circulated in 2013—"Communiqué on the Current State of the Ideological Sphere"— explained that "management of the ideological battlefield has been strengthened, stimulating ideological unity and cohesion of forces,"[60] while denoting seven dangerous values the Party intended to crack down upon:

1. Propagating Western constitutionalist democracy

2. Propagating "universal values" ("Western liberties, democracy, and human rights")

3. Propagating civil society, attempting to deconstruct the social basis for Party rule

4. Propagating neoliberalism, attempting to change our country's basic economic system

5. Propagating Western news views, challenging our country's principle that the Party manages the media and its press and publications management system

6. Propagating historical nihilism, attempting to deny the history of the Chinese Communist Party and the history of the New China

7. Challenging Reform and Opening.[61]

For decades, one of the key tenets of America's China policy was the assumption that China would "liberalize" or "democratize" as it grew rich, following the path of small East Asian nations such as South Korea and Taiwan. This assumption ignored two important things: China's sense of history and destiny, and the Party's dedicated will to prevent any such outcome from happening.

The 2013 Communiqué tells us more. On liberalization and democratization, here is what the Communist Party thinks of that:

> The danger of propagating Western constitutionalist democracy lies in setting the Party's leadership against the implementation of the Constitution and the law, denying Party leadership with Western constitutionalist democracy and abolishing the people's democracy, essentially, this aims to deny our country's Constitution and the system and principles determined in it, realize a change of banners in the end, and bring the Western political system and model to China.[62]

The Communist Party also sees "propagating Western constitutionalist democracy" as an attempt "to distort the Chinese Dream of national rejuvenation, saying that 'constitutionalist democracy is the only way out,' and 'China should follow the global trend of constitutionalism'."[63]

As for "propagating universal values" such as human rights, this is characterized as "attempting to shake the ideological and theoretical basis for Party rule." The document explains that:

Some people propagate the political objective of "universal values," aiming to make Western values transcend time and space, transcend countries, and transcend the common values of the classes of humankind, they believe that Western liberties, democracy and human rights are universal and eternal . . .

Under the situation that Western countries have held economic, military and scientific superiority for a long time, these arguments are strongly misleading and duplicitous, their objective lies in confusing fundamental differences between Western value views and the values that we propose, and in the end to replace the Socialist core value system with Western values.[64]

Consider also these words from Zhou Qiang, Chief Justice and President of the Supreme People's Court of China:

[China's courts] must firmly resist the Western idea of "constitutional democracy," "separation of powers" and "judicial independence." These are erroneous Western notions that threaten the leadership of the ruling Communist Party and defame the Chinese Socialist path on the rule of law. We have to raise our flag and show our sword to struggle against such thoughts. We must not fall into the trap of Western thoughts and judicial independence.[65]

Think of this another way: the Chinese Communist Party sees the conflict with "the West" as existential. Its political and social system is directly threatened by "Western" ideas. What the Party has created has immense value for China's leaders, and they refuse to let it go. China liberalizing in a Western manner places the Communist Party on what Sun Tzu called "death ground."[66] Its very survival is at stake. Communist Party leaders— in their view— have no choice but to resist the West's rules and ideas. China's system must remain restrictive in order to survive. Moreover, as Sun Tzu says, "the clever combatant imposes his will on the enemy, but does not allow the enemy's will to be imposed on him."[67]

The Communiqué of 2013 is unequivocal about the view of the "West" as a threat to Party rule: "Western anti-China forces and domestic 'dissidents' also incessantly carry out infiltration activities in our country's ideological area and challenge our mainstream ideology," including "demands for political reform, human rights, the release of 'political criminals'." It adds that "the position of Western anti-China forces pressuring us to change will not change, and they will point the spearhead of Westernization . . . In response we can absolutely not relax our vigilance, and certainly not lower our guard."[68]

Again, it is the Chinese Communist Party that reigns supreme. The law is a conduit for Party rule and power. Ideology exists for the sake of "unification of thought."[69] The people are an "invincible force" to be used for achieving the Party's goals, and the Party is the only possible "vanguard" of the people. Chief among these goals are the "great rejuvenation of the Chinese nation," the construction of the "Belt and Road," and the building of "The Community of Common Destiny for Mankind." Thus, the people are being used by the Party.

Are other nations being used by the Chinese Communist Party as well? Who will be the "foreign nobles" and tributaries in the twenty-first century? Will other nations enable the Chinese Communist Party to achieve its goals and facilitate China's ascendancy? How does the Communist Party deal with other nations now? How will other nations be dealt with in the future?

"INTERIOR VASSALS" AND "EXTERIOR VASSALS" IN THE "COMMUNITY OF COMMON DESTINY FOR MANKIND"

As we gaze across the concentric circles of Chinese rule, from Beijing and the mainland itself, to the "Special Administrative Region" of Hong Kong, to the "Autonomous Regions" of Tibet and Xinjiang, we see variations of the original Chinese imperial hierarchy.

During the time of the Chinese Empire, while Hong Kong was barely more than a fishing village, Xinjiang and Tibet were autonomous places—entire civilizations that were conquered and incorporated into the Chinese imperial system. Today, they fall within the borders of the People's Republic of China. They are key examples when it comes to the Communist Party's principles of "sovereignty and territorial integrity." The Chinese military is tasked to defend China's control of these and other places at all costs. The Communist Party security state has also employed experimental tactics in these regions for advanced control and "management" of the local population.

As Fairbank reminds us, the "exterior vassals" of one period become the "interior vassals" of another.

Let us turn to Hong Kong, famous in world news for its student and popular uprisings as the Communist Party takes control of its political process. In 2017, speaking on the twentieth anniversary of the British handover of this territory to the People's Republic of China, Xi declared that "The people of Hong Kong, now masters of their own house, run their local affairs within the purview of autonomy of the HKSAR [Hong Kong Special

Administrative Region]. *The people of Hong Kong enjoy more extensive democratic rights and freedoms than at any other time in its history.*[70] In addition to the subversive use of the idea of democratic rights and freedoms, Xi presents the Communist Party as liberators. That is, the people of Hong Kong are "now masters of their own house."

This is also the rhetoric that the Communist Party applies to the starker examples of Xinjiang and Tibet, which we shall turn to in a moment.

As for the character of Communist Party rule in Hong Kong, another statement from Xi's speech is also instructive: "Any attempt to endanger China's sovereignty and security, challenge the power of the central government and the authority of the Basic Law of the HKSAR, or use Hong Kong to carry out infiltration and sabotage activities against the mainland is an act that crosses the red line, and is absolutely impermissible."[71]

Such is the nature of the reintegration of this territory with the "motherland" and the Communist Party security state. Moreover, in alignment with the standard "patriotic education" programs on the mainland, Xi explains that Hong Kong "needs to enhance education and raise public awareness of the history and culture of the Chinese nation," adding a need to "step up patriotic education of the young people."[72] As mentioned earlier, "patriotic education," including the use and control of history, is one of the core methods by which the Communist Party "manages" its population. This involves combating "Historical nihilism," or "attempting to deny the history of the Chinese Communist Party and the history of the New China."

The story of Tibet is well known. Let us turn to Xinjiang, which in Chinese means "New Frontier." Its story has only garnered broad international attention since 2018, as revelations of Communist Party concentration camps holding as many as 1 million people have come to the attention of the world. This predominantly Muslim desert province was an important destination on the ancient Silk Road, an area repeatedly conquered and reconquered by competing steppe empires that defined the geopolitics of the ancient and medieval Central Asian world.[73] The Qing Dynasty reconquered Xinjiang in the late nineteenth century; it eventually passed into the hands of the Chinese Communist Party.

Xinjiang is China's largest province. It is larger than Alaska and more than double the size of France. But in a country where the population of individual provinces can be as high as that of other nations, it is among the least populated, with about 23 million inhabitants,[74] about the same as Florida or Australia. Today in Xinjiang, China's leaders have built a surveillance system known as "grid-style social management." This "segments urban communities into geometric zones so that security staff can systematically observe all activities with the aid of new technologies. The system relies on big data analytics, connecting a network of CCTV cameras with police databases to achieve enhanced, even automated surveillance."[75] Xinjiang's Party administrators have advertised over 90,000 new security-related positions as they seek to implement and innovate the practices that have been used in the pacification of Tibet.[76] The Communist Party Secretary, Chen Quanguo, has implemented a strategy of "paying generous salaries to thousands of impoverished Uighurs [the local population] to get them to monitor their own people."[77]

Even more troubling is that a network of concentration camps has emerged in Xinjiang as one of many means of controlling the Uighur population. The United Nations has estimated that up to 1 million Uighur have been sent to these camps, roughly 10 percent of the adult Uighur population in the province.[78] Reports of torture and death in the camps continue to appear in the press.[79] Broadly speaking, in Xinjiang the Communist Party has forced residents to "install spyware on their phones allowing authorities to monitor their activity online."[80] China's state-run media has explained that this is "a phase that Xinjiang has to go through in rebuilding peace and prosperity."[81] A leading Communist Party official told the United Nations that "Xinjiang citizens, including the Uighurs, enjoy equal freedom and rights."[82] On a different note, speaking of the "reeducation camps," a Communist Party official stated that "You can't uproot all the weeds hidden among the crops in the field one by one—you need to spray chemicals to kill them all. Reeducating these people is like spraying chemicals on the crops. That is why it is a general reeducation, not limited to a few people."[83]

The *Wall Street Journal* reports that study tours have been organized as "Law-enforcement agencies from across China have been eager students of Xinjiang, with officials from as far afield as Shanghai and Hong Kong organizing study tours . . . Police officials from across the country travel to Xinjiang for 90-day exchanges to train local officers while trading ideas and tactics."[84] The *Journal*'s Beijing-based reporter explains that the region is "serving as a laboratory for China's authoritarian leadership as it tries to control people and extinguish threats to its rule."[85] Meanwhile, Uighurs can face "stiff punishment for not adhering to Beijing's narrative about how China's central government's policies are benefitting the region and its ethnic minorities."[86]

Chinese leaders have long considered control of Xinjiang and Tibet essential to the security of the Chinese heartland.[87] But why is the control of Xinjiang so important today?

Because Xinjiang, in the eyes of the Communist Party, is one of China's primary *gateways to the outside world.* Consider this: in a text titled *Pivot Cities on the Belt and Road*, which outlines and ranks numerous cities both in and outside China for their importance and potential value to the strategic vision of the "Belt and Road," Xinjiang is described as "*The core area of the Belt and Road.*"[88] It is "the northwest gateway for China," and "enjoys a superior location, abundant resources, and a complete industrial infrastructure."[89] Moreover, "Xinjiang is designated as the core area of the Silk Road Economic Belt in the Belt and Road planning. Urumqi, as the capital of Xinjiang, is located at the center of the Eurasian Land Bridge, strategic in linking up the three oceans (the Pacific, West Atlantic and North Indian Ocean) and the four global economic regions (Northeast Asia, Southeast Asia, Central Asia and West Europe)."[90]

It is a passageway to the Indian Ocean through the China–Pakistan Economic Corridor, and a foundation for access to South Asia, allowing China to go "westward to the sea."[91]

It is also a passageway to Europe: "A number of China's westward international freight railways, i.e. the Chongqing-Xinjiang-Europe Railway, Wuhan-Xinjiang-Europe Railway, Zhengzhou-Xinjiang-Europe Railway, Xi'an-Xinjiang-Europe Railway, and Yiwu-Xinjiang-Europe Railway, leave the country through the Xinjiang land port."[92]

Control of Xinjiang was once about China as a regional power. Today, control of Xinjiang is also about China *as a global power.*

And thus, the concentration camps of Xinjiang are, in fact, *the concentration camps of China's "Belt and Road."*

China's strategists and geographers envision the integration and eventual control of a vast intercontinental landmass through the "Belt and Road", through the tools of economic, diplomatic, and military power. As described in Part Two, control of Xinjiang and Tibet is similar to views of control of the South China Sea, where the expanding Chinese navy and marine corps are tasked to "safeguard national territorial sovereignty and maritime rights and interests, and maintain security and stability along China's periphery."[93]

If Xinjiang is the most extreme known example of what control looks like on the ground inside China's "Autonomous Regions" in the "core area of the Belt and Road," a place where once-independent civilizations, conquered and integrated into China over the centuries, are now under careful Party rule, what will Chinese power look like across the rest of the "Belt and Road" if China's ascendency is complete? What is the eventual fate of the rest of the "Community of Common Destiny for Mankind," in the world the Communist Party aspires to, the world of 2049?

Let's understand one thing clearly: "The Community of Common Destiny" includes not just a vision of an end-state, but also a diplomatic strategy for the attraction and coercion of other states. Just as China's rulers use a variety of methods and concepts for internal control, they have also developed methods and concepts in order to achieve external aims. Some are visible now, well before a Chinese world order has taken shape in reality.

Though China's leaders speak on a regular basis of the need to "prepare to fight and win wars," engaging in what has been called "The most ambitious military modernization in the world," Xi also speaks frequently of peace and peaceful coexistence. What does this mean? Under the framework of "The Community of Common Destiny," Xi explains that "China pursues an independent foreign policy of peace, and is ready to enhance friendship and cooperation with all other countries on the basis of the Five Principles of Peaceful Coexistence."[94]

The Five Principles of Peaceful Coexistence actually have a bloody history and should be viewed as important elements of Chinese diplomatic strategy. They include:

1. Mutual respect for territorial integrity

2. Mutual nonaggression

3. Mutual noninterference in internal affairs

4. Equality and mutual benefit

5. Peaceful coexistence.

The Five Principles are seen by Chinese leaders as a cornerstone of Chinese foreign policy. They were created with India in 1954, and announced to the world as a new way of conducting international relations. India's then Prime Minister, Jawaharlal Nehru, praised them, stating that "If these principles can be recognized in a much wider sphere in Asia, then the risk of war could be reduced, and the possibility of cooperation could be enlarged among Asian countries."

The "Principles" proved meaningless in the disputes between India and China. Less than a decade after Nehru praised them, war came indeed, as India hit the hard reality of Chinese interests. The framework was not practical. It was essentially used to justify each party's claims against the other, before, during, and after military conflict. Today, Chinese leaders and diplomats continue to advance the "Five Principles" as a "new" way forward in the world. And it is also China's right, apparently, to determine what is to be "mutually respected."

Meanwhile, as is evidenced from Chinese Communist Party archives, China's use of peace rhetoric, in a manner similar to that of the former USSR, had everything to do with the advancement of its geopolitical interests.[95] The Chinese Communist Party used peace rhetoric to oppose US military alliances, the American presence in Asia, and even to categorize different nations according to their receptivity to Chinese interests. Consider Premier Zhou Enlai's major diplomatic mission to Bandung in 1955, where the Chinese Foreign Ministry categorized countries as "Peace and Neutral Countries," "Close to peace and neutral countries," "Anti-peace and neutral countries," and "Anti-peace and anti-neutral countries," adding in a secret diplomatic notice that "We should select some key countries from each category" and "solve some specific issues."[96]

When China–India relations broke apart ahead of the Border War of 1962, China justified its military action to nations around the world in terms of its peaceful intentions. But here is the view of the situation from the Indian Ministry of Foreign Affairs:

> It is obvious, in retrospect, that the Chinese government had from the beginning no intention of abiding by the terms of the 1954 Agreement but had used the Agreement as a temporary expedient for tiding over the immediate problems facing them

in Tibet. The Government of India, on the other hand, made important sacrifices and gave up considerable rights and interests which they had acquired in Tibet from the past in the hope that relations between China and India would thereafter be based on the Five Principles of Peaceful Co-existence and develop in co-operation and harmony to the mutual benefit of both countries and strengthen peace and stability in this region of Asia. These hopes have foundered.[97]

Today, China offers similar peace-and-prosperity rhetoric not only in Asia, but also "for mankind."

The Communist Party also offers a "new" approach, tailored for the United States, called the "New Model for Great Power Relations," a kind of superpower variation on the Five Principles of Peaceful Coexistence. Xi Jinping summarized it so:

1. No conflict or confrontation, through emphasizing dialogue and treating each other's strategic intentions objectively

2. Mutual respect, including for each other's core interests and major concerns

3. Mutually beneficial cooperation, by abandoning the zero-sum game mentality and advancing areas of mutual interest.[98]

In short, as in the case of its relations with India before the 1962 war, the Communist Party seeks American acquiescence to a vague definition of respect for "core interests and major concerns," which undoubtedly would only become, as the Five Principles did for India, a diplomatic cudgel with which to beat the United States in any international arena once true conflicts did arise. In the case of India, the collapse in relations was arguably made worse for their having ceded this diplomatic ground and thus allowing China to propagate a message in global forums that India was breaking the Principles— vague as they are— *to which it had agreed.*

American leaders, beginning with the Obama Administration, have wisely rejected China's "New Model of Great Power Relations."

The subversion, appropriation, and manipulation of concepts, speech, and slogans by the Chinese Communist Party should be no surprise. While China's economic prosperity confuses America's ability to understand "Communism," propaganda is still one of the core competencies of a Communist or Leninist state.

In order to delve further into the "Community of Common Destiny," let us look at a policy paper providing further definition to Communist Party initiatives in Asia. As the State Council explains, "China will shoulder greater responsibility for regional and global security." The policy paper, "China's Policies on Asia-Pacific Security Cooperation," explains that "China is working to construct a community of shared future for countries along the Lancang–Mekong River and between China and the Association of Southeast Asian Nations (ASEAN), as well as in Asia and the Asia-Pacific area as a whole."[99]

The paper lists a range of security forums that China has already built or been instrumental in building, from the Shanghai Cooperation Organization, a regional military bloc built in partnership with Russia, to the China–ASEAN Ministerial Dialogue on Law Enforcement and Security Cooperation, and the Conference on Interaction and Confidence-Building Measures in Asia. The document explains that China will build a "new model of international relations" in the region:

> China remains committed to the principles of amity, sincerity, mutual benefit and inclusiveness in conducting neighborhood diplomacy and the goal of maintaining and promoting stability and prosperity in the Asia-Pacific region. China stands ready to work with all countries in the region to pursue mutually beneficial cooperation and steadily advance security dialogues and cooperation in the Asia-Pacific region, and the building of a new model of international relations so as to create a brighter future for this region.[100]

The State Council also takes a shot at the US alliance system in Asia, which, as referenced in the views of Mao Zedong, has long been anathema to China's vision of the Asia-Pacific:

Old security concepts based on the Cold War mentality, zero-sum game, and stress on force are outdated, given the dynamic development of regional integration. In the new circumstances, all countries should keep up with the times, strengthen solidarity and cooperation with openness and inclusiveness, make security vision innovations, work to improve regional security systems and explore a new path for Asian security.[101]

In short, China proposes a "new model of international relations," with the advent of Chinese-led regional security groupings, the breakdown of the US alliance system, China-led economic integration through the "Belt and Road," and new Chinese financial institutions, all built on "the principles of amity, sincerity, mutual benefit and inclusiveness."

What does this "new model of international relations" look like in practice?

Two examples are key. I say this because in the past, these tenets— "sovereignty and territorial integrity"— have been China's reason for interstate war.

The first example is an insistence that "China has indisputable sovereignty over the Nansha Islands and their adjacent waters."[102] The second example is the statement that "The Diaoyu Islands are an integral part of China's territory. China's sovereignty over the Diaoyu Islands has a sufficient historical and legal basis."[103]

In the context of these two examples, the document refers to China's commitment "to resolving disputes peacefully through negotiation and consultation" in the case of the South China Sea, and to "communication and consensus on crisis management and control" in the East China Sea, including that "China is willing to properly manage the situation and resolve related issues through continued dialogue and consultation" with Japan.

In reality, even a cursory understanding of the events of recent years gives the lie to these statements. China's actions in both the South and East China Sea are known to the world as acts of economic coercion, legal warfare, "gray zone" operations, paramilitary harassment of smaller neighbors, violations and outright rejection of international law, and other means of "might makes right." All of which, from the point of view of the Chinese

Communist Party and People's Liberation Army, are eminently justifiable, given China's "indisputable sovereignty," the "integral" nature of these territories to China, the history of "national humiliation," and the objectives of the "great rejuvenation of the Chinese nation." The discourse on the South and East China Sea is exhaustive and need not be recounted here; readers are familiar with the situation.[104]

I will include only this statement from a newspaper-seller in Shanghai whom I met amidst my hundreds upon hundreds of conversations with Chinese citizens about international relations: "Why are all these small countries bullying us? How can Vietnam, Philippines, all these small countries try to stand up to China? It is because of America!" In other words, America's presence in the region is empowering smaller countries to stand up for themselves against China.

While China's diplomacy speaks of "amity" and "sincerity," what prevails is Chinese power.

China's use of economic and military coercion to pursue its interests has already spread beyond Xinjiang, Tibet, and Taiwan—China's traditional "core interests." Instances of economic and military coercion abound inside the West Pacific: Filipino banana exports rotting on the docks because of the South China Sea dispute, the ban of rare earth mineral exports to Japan over disputes related to the East China Sea, boycotting Chinese tourism to South Korea over the deployment of US missile defense systems. China's authorities have shown that they are unafraid to use their trading relationships with other nations as leverage in forcing others to accept the Chinese interest. They are quite willing to coerce other nations that have insufficient power over China.

The reality of Chinese power and coercion is visible already: take the example of the Philippines. Chinese paramilitary vessels harass Filipino merchant vessels in the South China Sea while the Chinese government builds militarized islands, deploys advanced weapons systems, and on top of this causes economic pain by halting agricultural imports from a nation which has China as its top export market—and the entire Asia-Pacific region now has China as its top trading partner. When China finally did resume banana imports in late 2016, Filipino Agriculture Secretary Emmanuel Piñol said that: "We very much appreciate the action of the Chinese government, as this will relieve our banana farmers from the serious problem

during the suspension considering that China is a huge market for our banana industry."[105]

Is this the vision of harmony that China has in mind?

Acquiescence to China, including its military interests, which in the
case of the South China Sea have been rejected by the international court
system, in return for continued access to Chinese markets and the enjoy-
ment of Beijing's good graces.

While it may have come as an unwelcome surprise from the perspective
of many American policy-makers that China would choose to become
more "assertive" in its region rather than integrating into an American-led
world, the reality is that these practices are authentic to Communist Party
foreign policy vision and practice, a policy resting on the use of "comprehensive national power." They are also consistent with the deeper traditions
of Chinese statecraft within its region. In Asia, at the time of Imperial
Chinese rule, world order was "not organized by a division of territories
among sovereigns of equal status, but rather by the subordination of all
local authorities to the central and awe-inspiring power of the emperor."[106]

What more can we learn from the classical Chinese principle of governance in a cohesive world system, that of "superordination–subordination?"[107]

We can see this hierarchical idea shining through in the reality of China's diplomatic conduct and in occasional accidental statements. China's
Foreign Minister, Yang Jiechi, stated in a meeting with ASEAN leaders in
2010: "China is a big country, and other countries are small countries—
and that's just a fact."[108]

While examples abound in Asia, what else can we learn from around the
world, and from around the regions of "Belt and Road"? After all, as China's
state-run news agency makes clear, Xi Jinping's concept of the "Community
of Common Destiny" is about "China's approach to *global governance*."[109]

We can understand what it would be like for Japan or Vietnam to live
within a world defined by China's supremacy—both nations are already in
regular crisis over China's growing power and are eager for America to remain
powerful in the region. What would it be like for other nations that have not
had the historical experience of Chinese supremacy? What would it be like,
for example, for New Zealand to live within the world of 2049? I asked this
question in conversation with a friend who is a leading scholar on Chinese
governance. "If you were a shepherd in New Zealand," he said, "You might

not know the difference. But if you were the Prime Minister of New Zealand, it would be a very different world indeed." He added that, if you were a dairy farmer in New Zealand, you might find your quality of life dropping without knowing why, if your Prime Minister did not adhere to the wishes of Beijing, and China then imported fewer of your dairy products.

China's approaches of control, attraction, and manipulation are visible across the world already. While America has begun to face the question of election interference by a different foreign power, Australia is famously on the front lines of China's threats of interference in democratic nations. Consider the following threat to Australia's Labor Party leadership from the head of China's Central Public Security Comprehensive Management System, Meng Jianzhu: "According to *The Australian*, [he] warned the Labor leadership about the electoral consequences of failing to endorse a bilateral extradition treaty: 'Mr Meng [sic] said it would be a shame if Chinese government representatives had to tell the Chinese community in Australia that Labor did not support the relationship between Australia and China'."[110]

As the ambassador of a small European nation told me in Beijing: "The Chinese do not want us to work together as the European Union. They want to isolate us, one by one." The same is true of ASEAN in Southeast Asia, of the hated US alliance system in the West Pacific, and of other forums where China sees its interests being threatened. Here, as Chinese political scientist Yan Xuetong phrases it, "ancient Chinese thought" really does meet "modern Chinese power."[111]

In the United States, China's instruments of influence have even applied pressure at a *state rather than national level*. In 2009, North Carolina State University canceled a speech by the Dalai Lama. The local Confucius Institute at North Carolina State, one of many Communist Party-funded Chinese-language institutes that appear on college campuses around America and around the world, allegedly attempted to prevent the Dalai Lama from speaking— and succeeded. The University's Provost offered the following comments to the press: "I don't want to say we didn't think about whether there were implications. Of course you do. China is a major trading partner of North Carolina."[112]

As reported by *The Nation*, the director of the Confucius Institute at this university told the provost that the Dalai Lama's visit would derail the "strong relationships we were developing in China."[113]

For the United States, this kind of threat is often directed at companies, which, lacking the backing of focused American strategic power, are threatened and cajoled by the Chinese state into compliance with what seem like small concessions, but in reality represent far more important principles. In addition to forced technology transfer, cyber- and human espionage, and predatory joint ventures, the Chinese state has forced companies to apologize for what it sees as a misrepresentation of China's interests on matters of great geopolitical importance.

For example, the US clothing company, Gap, was forced to apologize to China for marketing a t-shirt with a map of China on it— a shirt that was not being sold in China— that failed to include China's claims to the South China Sea, to Taiwan, and to Himalayan territories that the Chinese state disputes with India. Gap issued the following apologies according to the *Washington Post*: "Gap Inc. respects the sovereignty and territorial integrity of China . . . As a responsible company, Gap Inc. strictly follows Chinese rules and laws."[114]

And so, American companies are forced to obey Beijing's line on matters such as the South China Sea, which are actually of great geopolitical importance in Asia and which matter immensely for the future of American power in Asia. The motive is, of course, "material interest," and the method is coercion. China has taken this approach with American companies in the travel, hospitality, and other industries. European companies have been affected as well. Daimler-Benz was forced in 2018 to apologize for quoting the Dalai Lama on its Instagram account. The post showed a Mercedes-Benz on a beach with the following quotation: "Look at the situation from all angles, and you will become more open."[115] After drawing the ire of Chinese citizens on the internet for quoting the Dalai Lama, Daimler-Benz issued the following apology: "We will promptly take steps to deepen our understanding of Chinese culture and values, our international staff included, to help standardize our actions to ensure this sort of issue doesn't happen again."[116]

A WORLD TRANSFORMED: A DAY IN THE LIFE OF CHINESE POWER

During my last year living in China, I rented a room in a beautiful old *hutong*, the system of alleyways and courtyard homes that still remain from dynastic China. I lived in Beijing near the Yonghegong Lama Temple. From my window I could see the gold exchange where families and investors would trade *Renminbi* for precious metal, and dozens of small houses where bottle collectors would store what they had gathered around the city before taking it to recycling plants to sell. On my daily walk, I would pass an elementary school where children gathered in the yard each day. Among the scrolling characters visible from outside the gates, were two of the most important ones that China's system teaches its young people: 富强 *Fu qiang.*[117]

Wealth and *Power.*

Up the concrete staircases to my building, amidst spray-painted telephone numbers for electronics and appliance repairs, were red and gold paper signs with another character, 福 "fu," for "happiness."

Among my favorite images of modern China is one taken in an unnamed city, where two elegant young women wearing fashionable clothing walk along a city street, one of them carrying a white umbrella for the sun. Behind them are bright glass buildings and orderly traffic barriers that those who have lived in China are familiar with. But something stands out in this scene of quiet and elegant modernity. It is the gigantic poster hanging on the building that the two women are walking in front of. On it, dozens of soldiers are screaming with their mouths wide open, holding their bayonets high in front of the red flag of the Chinese military. The sign reads, 有血性 "Have blood" or "Have courage."

China's offerings on a future world order have less to do with a vision for a future of humanity than they do with a vision for the rectification of wrongs perceived by China in its narrative of "national resurrection."

For all to be right with the world, an old system would have to be done away with and a new one put in place, with China, as its leaders now tell us, "moving closer to center stage," restoring China to the *central position in the power structure of the world.* Not as a state among states, but as the epicenter of a global system of power, wealth, and influence.

This is consistent with the vision of the founders of the People's Republic of China. A leading historian of China notes: "Mao and his comrades made it clear that one of the primary missions of the 'new China' was to destroy the 'old' world in which China had been a humiliated member during modern times."[118] Another agrees: "When he devoted his life to revolution, Mao aimed at transforming not only the old China but also the old world order . . . Just as the old international order had helped cause China's suffering and humiliation, so too would the creation of a new order contribute to the rebirth of a strong and prosperous China."[119]

China's leaders— and many of its people— still revere Mao Zedong. But this vision is not the Communist Party's alone. It is the vision at the heart of China's restoration— a cause to which numerous Chinese citizens and patriots have devoted their lives— and of which the Communist Party is only one expression.[120]

Today, when Xi Jinping emphasizes the duties of the young, the dedication of China's younger generations to the "great historic mission" is also at the heart of "China's restoration." It is not only about the Party, but also about China's people and its future generations. As Xi explains:

> A nation will prosper only when its young people thrive; a country will be full of hope and have a great tomorrow only when its younger generations have ideals, ability, and a strong sense of responsibility. The Chinese Dream is a dream about history, the present, and the future. It is a dream of our generation, but even more so, a dream of the younger generations. The Chinese Dream of national rejuvenation will be realized ultimately through the endeavors of young people, generation by generation.[121]

And China's youth reciprocate. As scholar Zheng Wang asks in *Never Forget National Humiliation: Historic Memory in Chinese Politics and Foreign Relations*: "But *why* is this young generation in China, many of whom attended elite schools in the United States or Europe, so patriotic and nationalistic? . . . China's opening up and the international community's engagement with China in the last thirty years seems to have resulted in a new generation of anti-West patriots."[122]

This author's own encounters with this point of view are extensive and innumerable. I will relate only two examples. The first was a moment that reflected a scene very much like the portrait above of the two young women walking in front of the painting of screaming soldiers. I was living in Beijing in 2014, when Russia was in the process of annexing Crimea in the Ukraine. I had a Chinese conversation partner, a young woman who liked to wear fashionable clothing and was an active internet user. She told me how she admired what Putin was doing in Crimea because, she said, when this land belongs to Russia, it must take what belongs to Russia, as China must do in the South China Sea. She then began to tell me about how she looked forward to a trip to Paris that year so that she could go shopping. The two ideas, in her mind, had no apparent contradiction. Paris for shopping. Crimea and the South China Sea for armed annexation.

The second story involves a Beijing bar party with a mix of expatriates and students, Chinese and foreign. I spoke with a young Chinese woman who had received her master's degree from Cambridge University and told me, in regard to China, that "This would be a good year for us to go to war with India because America is too distracted to do anything about it." An American friend of hers was sitting at a nearby table, texting with a young man who was a member of the Chinese Communist Party. "He is going to be very powerful someday," the Chinese girl said. The American girl appeared to be emotionally distressed. She and the young Chinese man were apparently considering a romantic relationship. "But I don't think I can be with someone who hates America so much," she said.

To be sure, China has many voices. When I asked a friend in Beijing, for example, "What is the China Dream?" He paused and then said, "China Dream. There is none." Then, touching his heart, he said, "My dream. My dream is to go to America." Numerous other discourses, dreams, and aspirations live within the country, including those of many who hope to get out.[123] But the reality is a political structure where the Communist Party, its goals, and its vision retain absolute authority, and its methods evolve according to the imagination and pragmatism of the Communist Party. As a friend in Shanghai explained to me, "We are all in the net in China. It is just a question of whether they want to catch us."

The state-sponsored narrative that fills China's schools, universities, television, newspapers, and radio— and therefore Chinese society— is about China's rise to power, the rectification of its "humiliation," and "the great rejuvenation of the Chinese nation." It is both a vision of world order and a view of a world restored. A world in which China's preeminence is achieved and recognized, and China is unconstrained. A world, in short, with China at its center.

Many sources, from the US National Intelligence Council to the *Economist* magazine and World Economic Forum, glibly forecast a world in which China will be the leading economy by the 2030s. This is only a decade away. Most Western timeframes have to do with short-term elections, rapid-fire news-bites, and short-term corporate earnings cycles, so even ten years from now can sound very far away. But the 2030s is a time when most reading this today will still be alive. The time frame that the Communist Party is working toward—toward the epochal shift, the historic turning point, of 2049—is a time in which many who are living now will still be alive, or at least their children and grandchildren will still be living. The world that China aspires to bring about is one that will affect us all.

China's vision of victory is nothing short of a sea-change in the global balance of power. History, for China's leaders, is made up of massive epochal cycles, of the rise and fall of empires and entire civilizations. Mao Zedong was famous for quoting innumerable lessons from the history of ancient China, and today's leaders have studied the rise and fall of nation states as important knowledge for governance and leadership, and today's leaders have studied the rise and fall of nation states as important knowledge for governance and leadership. And China's leaders, famous for their general backgrounds in engineering, are detailed and meticulous planners, something demonstrated by the evidence assembled throughout this book. Their worldview is not built on chance and reaction, but on planning and control.

China's national narrative has been constructed in order to unify the nation and give China's people a sense of purpose under the Party's rule, and China's leaders are investing heavily in instruments of social control in order to guide the Chinese people along the path toward "national rejuvenation" and prevent any disruption in the system they are building.

What is it like to live in a society built on internet policing, active detentions, and the suppression of human rights campaigns considered subversive by the Chinese state, a society that envisions massive use of artificial intelligence and facial recognition technologies for state control and the infamous "social credit score" that aims to track data on individuals, giving them a "score" according to measures relevant to the state?

Consider this backlash against a young Chinese woman named Yang Shuping, who was asked to give the valedictory speech at the University of Maryland in 2017: Ms. Yang stated that "I have learned [that] the right to freely express oneself is sacred in America . . . My voice matters. Your voice matters. Our voices matter." Discussing LA riots in the 1990s, she explained that "I was shocked, I never thought such topics could be discussed openly . . . I have always had a burning desire to tell these kinds of stories, but I was convinced that only authorities owned the narrative, only authorities could define the truth."[124]

Ms. Yang also criticized air pollution in China— something Chinese citizens criticize every day— and spoke of "another kind of fresh air for which I will be forever grateful— the fresh air of free speech."[125]

The backlash which ensued from Chinese citizens at home and abroad made newspapers around the planet. In what is known in China as a "human flesh search," Chinese citizens picked through the internet looking for details of Ms. Yang's life and of her family which could be used to threaten and attack her. Online shaming went into full force, coming from innumerable directions, on the one hand enabled by Chinese state media, and on the other from thousands of private citizens at home and even abroad. Take, for example, these Facebook comments to Ms. Yang from "Marcus Ren" and "Shirley Liu": "As a Chinese if you don't like and respect your own country then get out of our country please. We don't need any trash in China. Respect to your motherland or otherwise get out of China alright? Shuping Yang you're full of lies and you have made our Chinese students ashamed #Proud of China."[126]

Here are several other examples: "[Yang] is a big liar and she is so over for thinking and talking about my country. I am so proud of become a Chinese person in the world. [sic] I don't think 'fresh air' will be important things in people's life," and "Technically she is the shame of Kunming [her hometown] the most beautiful place in China. B*tch," and "I believe that Chinese students will not choose [University of Maryland] from now on! As to Shuping Yang, get the fuck out of China ASAP!"[127] And "China does not need a traitor like you. Just stay in the U.S. and breathe your fresh air."[128]

Here is another post, translated from Chinese:

> What if you turned off the comments? You think you are so smart huh? The air in America is sweet? Why don't you just say that even feces in America are sweet too? Are your parents back at home aware of your talks about your motherland? Don't you feel a tinge of shame? I'm so fucking proud of being Chinese. I lived and studied in Beijing. There may be smog there, but I fucking love with a passion the very land you mocked! You don't

think Kunming is deserving of its name—the city of everlasting spring? Such an ugly person should do more studying and go out less, you're a fool and an eyesore when you do. You must be a phony torch-bearer of socialism. Oh, wait! You're! Not! Worth it! I am so ashamed of you! (I intentionally wrote this in Chinese).[129]

The Communist Party-affiliated Chinese Student and Scholar Association (CSSA) made an official video calling her remarks false, and a former CSSA president explained that "Insulting the motherland to grab attention is intolerable. The university's support for such slandering speech is not only ill-considered, but also raises suspicion about other motives."[130]

Ms. Yang soon made a public apology:

The speech was only to share my own experience abroad and did not have any intention of denying or belittling my country and home town. I deeply apologise and sincerely hope everyone can understand, have learned my lesson for the future . . . I deeply love my country and my home town, I feel extremely proud of my country's prosperous development and I hope in the future to use my time abroad to promote Chinese culture, contributing positively for my country.[131]

And so, the young woman returned to the fold of China's national narrative, promising to use her time abroad to "promote Chinese culture."

What is important is that incidents such as these are *not reserved for Chinese citizens alone.*

When the Chinese government coerces companies, countries, individuals, and institutions, it invokes both Chinese law and, most interestingly, *the Chinese people.* Following an incident where American companies listed Taiwan and Tibet as separate countries on their websites, an article appeared in the *China Daily* titled "No flouting of China's core interests will be tolerated." The government-run outlet stated that "Foreign companies should be aware that Chinese people are particularly sensitive to the status of Tibet, Hong Kong, Macao, and Taiwan, which are all parts of China," adding that "They should have known that they would provoke a strong reaction from Chinese people."[132]

It is here that the Communist Party internal security state and the external methods of Chinese rhetoric and power begin to synergize in ways that are especially unique to Chinese power.

The Party often refers rhetorically to "one billion Chinese people" in its diplomacy and foreign interactions. As Mao made clear at the founding of the PRC, the core idea of the Chinese revolution is that "The Chinese people have stood up." As the Chinese Foreign Ministry explained to India just months ahead of war in 1962: "to wish that Chinese troops would withdraw from their own territory is impossible. That would be against the will of 650 million Chinese. No force in the world could oblige us to do something of this kind."[133]

The Communist Party phrases its interests in terms of *the size* of its people, both when making threats and also when defining the future. This brings us to a statement by Xi Jinping, possibly one of the most important statements by any Chinese leader in recent decades. Addressing the nation at the Nineteenth Party Congress in 2017, Xi described China and its *national momentum* as follows: "Rooted in a land of more than 9.6 million square kilometers, nourished by a nation's culture of more than 5,000 years, and backed by the invincible force of more than 1.3 billion people, we have an infinitely vast stage of our era, a historical heritage of unmatched depth, and incomparable resolve that enable us to forge ahead..."[134]

Just as Mao invoked the ability of "the Chinese people" to absorb nuclear war with China's adversaries, and thus China would prevail, Xi Jinping considers the people to be an "invincible force" by which the Party's goals will be realized.

This view of the utility of human beings is perhaps China's driving force under the rule of the Chinese Communist Party— it is not a vision of institutions or international laws so much as a will to power, and a view of a population forged by the Party into "an invincible force." One defined by 1 billion people rising from "humiliation" to "resurrection."

The coercive force of Chinese economic and military power has already been expressed to foreigners in terms of this sense of national will.

The phrase "hurting the feelings of the Chinese people" is used regularly in official Chinese correspondence with foreign nations. In 1987, with the United States, when the US House of Representatives passed a bill condemning human rights abuses in Tibet when the Dalai Lama visited the

United States.[135] In 1989, with Norway, when the Dalai Lama received the Nobel Prize. In the 1990s, with the United States and France, when they sold arms to Taiwan. In 1994, with Japan, for assisting the Taiwanese in attending the Asian Games. In 1994, with Britain, for allowing Taiwanese authorities to attend Second World War memorial events in Hong Kong. In 1995, with Nicaragua, over Taiwan's status in the United Nations. In the 1990s, with nations as diverse as Germany, South Africa, and Guatemala on issues pertaining to Tibet and Taiwan. Throughout the 2000s, with Japan for "historical issues between China and Japan." Throughout the 2000s, with the European Parliament, the United States, France, Britain, "Western Forces," and "Western Media" over Tibet.[136]

In 2016, Swedish human rights activist Peter Dahlin was arrested in Beijing. He spent three weeks in a "black prison," one of China's "covert interrogation centers," before making a televised confession. "I have caused harm to the Chinese government," he said. "I have hurt the feelings of the Chinese people."[137]

According to the *Guardian*, China's state media portrayed Dahlin as an agent of "western anti-China forces" working to undermine the Communist Party; his arrest and confession meant that the Communist Party had "smashed an illegal organization that sponsored activities jeopardizing China's national security."[138]

The Chinese state, and, in the state's telling, "the Chinese people," tend to respond most severely to human rights issues, questions of "interference in China's internal affairs," and challenges to China's "sovereignty and territorial integrity." However, these are early days. The use of China's coercive power is not new and will not be limited in the future to issues such as Tibet and Taiwan or internal security. It is reported, for example, that China's state-sponsored Confucius Institutes, which, as mentioned, populate university campuses across the United States and the world, also forbid discussion of China's military buildup.[139]

In the case of the country's twentieth-century wars, China was willing to use military force soon after the Communist Party had determined that its interests were challenged by an opposing nation. The difference, of course, in the twenty-first century, is that China's interests are no longer limited to its border areas and periphery: they already span its region, and increasingly the globe.

The world is visibly living during a period of Chinese expansion: eco-nomic, military, and ideological. What is unique about China is its sense of proportion and its sense of righteous *restoration*. While the British claimed in their heyday that "the sun never sets on the British Empire," and while the United States was sometimes guided by a concept of "Manifest Des-tiny," what was different was that the former was driven by a sense of con-quest, and the latter a sense of a frontier, each charting out a world that its primary actors had never seen before. China's expansion is driven above all by a sense of *restoration*: the restoration of a world in which China's power was uncontested, and in which China's place is, as the nation's name in Chinese, the "Middle Kingdom," implies, *at the center of the world*.

Through China's numerous strategic plans, from Made in China 2025, which would put the country at the top of global industry, to the "Belt and Road," which defines the enormous geographical space across which Chi-nese trading and resource interests lie, to military plans from land, sea, air, cyber, space, and frontier technologies, which are built to "safeguard the security of China's overseas interests," the rise of China reminds us of some-thing both very new and very old indeed: the age of empire is not over. And a new age of competition has begun.

One of China's greatest challenges is how to communicate its intentions to a world that may not ultimately tolerate a change of this magnitude. Chi-nese leaders have inherited a Marxist sense of historical destiny—the view that the arc of history bent toward their victory was a core tenet of Commu-nist leaders around the world. However, China is playing a harder game—to rewrite the world according to its interests. Achieving this depends upon divisions amongst its neighbors and in other bodies around the globe.

But China must also provide a message to the world of a Chinese rise that is at once beneficial to all and also inevitable, which it does through its numerous speeches and official channels, such as the *China Daily*. Mean-while, China's Communist Party has, at its core, an ideology which the Party, in its own words, considers opposed to the "West" and its "universal values," such as human rights, freedom of speech and assembly, and other basic institutions often taken for granted in democratic, rights-based soci-eties. China must play this game both internally and externally. While eco-nomic interests may be the origin of a nation's expansion, and military power then follows, messaging may be the most subtle stage of empire because it must explain, justify, and advocate for an expanded presence to all parties whom this presence concerns.

Xi Jinping has, like his military, demanded "absolute loyalty" from China's media, explaining that "The nation's media outlets are essential to political stability."[140] As the *Guardian* points out, this requirement has been present since the founding of the PRC. In the words of Mao Zedong, "Revolution relies on pens and guns." As Xi explained to media workers in China:

> The media run by the party and the government are the propaganda fronts and must have the party as their family name [sic] . . . All the work by the party's media must reflect the party's will, safeguard the party's authority, and safeguard the party's unity. They must love the party, protect the party, and closely align themselves with the party leadership in thought, politics and action.[141]

Prominent China media watchers, including Bill Bishop and David Bandurski, agree that Xi has achieved his objectives in the media domain. China's "revolution" and "restoration" are not simply meant for the Chinese people— they will affect all of us. China's message of a benign and inevitable rise has— with no exaggeration— now reached nearly the entire planet.

China Central Television (CCTV) is the Chinese Communist Party's primary English-language and foreign-language media outlet. In a 2013 report for the Center for International Media Assistance, Anne Nelson explains that China "has set its sights on the global information system," citing a decade-long effort that some date to the 2001 announcement of Xu Chaungchu that Chinese state media would be "going out" into the world: "This effort has been designed to enhance China's image and convey its perspective to the world, taking advantage of the disruptions affecting Western state broadcasters and Western media markets in general."[142]

CCTV is "supplemented by an international service, boasting three major global offices in Beijing, Washington, and Nairobi, and more than 70 additional international bureaus." Importantly, "CCTV's biggest impact may be in regions where China is directing its international investments. The Nairobi operations complement extensive investments in African infrastructure, many of them in communications; China is also pursuing critical investment in Latin America and Southeast Asia." Moreover, according to Nelson, "CCTV's Washington bureau illustrates its ability to hire world-class international journalists and to allow them to do their jobs, as long as their reporting does not cross party lines. CCTV effectively reports to the Chinese Communist Party (via the state broadcasting agency), and the party will determine both its initiatives and its no-go areas for the foreseeable future."[143]

Ms. Nelson explains that "In an era when Voice of America and BBC World Service budgets are battered by funding cutbacks and partisan politics, China is playing the long game. CCTV's content is defined by the same ideological directives and limitations that govern the country's university debates, feature films, and microblogs."[144]

Additionally, the Communist Party's Confucius Institutes have taken root in most countries, promoting a Party line on a range of issues important to the PRC. Communist Party funding also finds its way into think tanks and universities promoting "friends of China," while attempting to isolate other voices on China's global rise. Finally, Chinese companies and entrepreneurs have begun a substantial relationship with Hollywood, which is driven largely by the appeal of the Chinese domestic box office. While China has begun to take a larger role onscreen in Hollywood films, often in a heroic supporting role, as in *The Martian, Independence Day: Resurgence,* and *Arrival,* a more important shift may be taking place in Hollywood: self-censorship. A friend who writes naval thrillers, one of which is headed to the big screen with an all-star cast, recently told me he was thinking about writing his next script on China, Pakistan, and India, but "in Hollywood, now China can never be the bad guy." This is a profound propaganda coup for a nation that is a source of military and economic coercion directed against many democratic nations. We should understand that one of the most crucial operations for China's leadership is to control the message, not only at home, but also abroad.

As an article in the *Washington Post* covering a planned investment by the Chinese Communist Party in a multi-story television complex in Washington, DC, explained:

China watchers see an even larger aim in China's multimillion-dollar investment in Washington: capturing the attention and perhaps the hearts and minds of viewers throughout the United States and the Western Hemisphere. China's ambition, they say, is to use news reporting and cultural programming to advance its "soft power," or cultural influence, making it commensurate with the nation's growing economic might.[145]

In other words, the Party is using state-controlled media to build influence outside of China's borders, and has "poured billions of dollars into the international expansion of government-controlled news sources such as CCTV and Xinhua."[146] And just as Chinese companies have employed celebrities like Scarlett Johansson to promote their message in global markets, the Chinese state has hired American and international journalists from NBC, Bloomberg TV, Fox News, and others to promote China's message to the world.[147]

In short, China's rise is one of history's greatest examples of the "whole-of-government approach." From economics, finance, diplomacy, media, communications, military power, intelligence, and education, China has deployed every tool of its "comprehensive national power" in order to achieve its rise, and to expand its influence and presence beyond its borders and into the wider world. In doing so, China's leaders assure us all that we are on course to reach the "great rejuvenation of the Chinese nation," that is, their vision of victory in 2049.

2049: CHINA'S VISION
OF A NEW WORLD ORDER

W hat would it really look like for China to achieve its goals? What is China's message to the world as it pursues its path to power? Is it a vision, as Chinese leaders say, of "harmony" amidst China's "comprehensive national power"? What role will other nations play in a system built after the "great rejuvenation of the Chinese nation" and the completion of the Communist Party's "historic mission"?

One thing is clear: China's ascendency would mean the de facto end of an American-led international order. Returning to my friend's comment: "It is not 1945 any more" — or, in other words, it is not the time in which the US had the largest share of global GDP, underwrote global security, and built many of the world's institutions in America's democratic, rights-based image. That world would all come to an end. China's leaders aim to bring about the end of the American-led order, as successive generations of Communist Party leaders have desired for decades.

2049 will be China's 1945. In other words, it will be the time when China has the overwhelming share of global GDP, underwrites global security, and is able to create a world order according to its principles and national objectives.

China's leaders have a road ahead that is long and hard. Most people do not think about, plan for, or envision a world thirty years into the future. However, the comprehensiveness of the thinking, vision, and planning of China's leaders and Chinese society is breathtaking. China's vision and actions span virtually every realm of human activity from military planning in advanced space systems and artificial intelligence, to industry, agriculture, and manufacturing, to communications and diplomatic operations in every nation, region, and continent on Earth. This Chinese approach is a way of looking at the world that many are not accustomed to. While the

United States has great global reach, it works to maintain rather than build its global power. Moreover, American planning is not nearly as comprehensive as Chinese global strategy.

While this book is not concerned with the *likelihood* of China meeting its objectives, the book is meant to create awareness of Chinese strategy and ambitions and to have the reader take China's quest seriously. It aims to bring us behind the curtain in order to see the reality of China's global strategic activity and to understand the totality of Chinese planning and thinking insofar as it is accessible to the public. China's vision of victory is visible because of China's need to communicate, manage, and guide its mammoth operation.

What China's leaders and people must accomplish in order to fulfill "the great rejuvenation of the Chinese nation" is evident every day. China's ascendency has already shaken the global military balance, strained the strength of American and democratic institutions, and enriched and enraptured people around the Earth. However, in the minds of China's leaders, the ascendency is just beginning. Despite decreasing economic growth rates, China's ambitions are increasing. Its growth can only be maintained through *"going out"* or *"going global."*

The Communist Party's objective— the objective of *one hundred years of national effort*— is China's preeminence. This is a vision of a world in which China's "comprehensive national power" is second to none and unconstrained. A Chinese world order, phrased in the kind and humble terms of "peace and stability," but built on the reality of Chinese economic, military, and ideological power. It would mean a world where China has no rival and no peer, and in which China's "restoration" is at last complete.

In short, nothing less than a "Chinese century." And maybe even more.

CONCLUSION

Either we live by accident and die by accident,
or we live by plan and die by plan.

THORNTON WILDER,
The Bridge of San Luis Rey

I wrote this book during my first year back in America. I was born in America, grew up in America, went to school in America, and, after college, lived and traveled abroad for over ten years. This is how I came to see the world and how I came to understand the great challenge that China poses, not only in Asia, but also in many other regions, and to many other peoples and nations.

I lived most recently in the United Kingdom, where I spent a good amount of time at Winston Churchill's childhood home, which is close to Oxford, where I studied China and India during my doctoral years. Churchill said, and it applies to what we are talking about in this book: "The British nation is unique in this respect: they are the only people who like to be told how bad things are, who like to be told the worst."

This book— *China's Vision of Victory*—is in many ways a book about how bad things are becoming, and how much worse they might become.

It is a book about what is happening as we do little to confront these realities. America may not like to be told how bad things are. America, like any good rebellion, is built on hope.

This is also a book about why we should care about what is happening in the world, and what, if we do care, we can do about it.

Many people have accepted China's rise as inevitable, as an irreversible turn in history, as the fulfillment of what has to happen, in some kind of natural course of things. Just as headlines cry out "How the West lost China," another set of headlines has cried out something else, for years now. Books have been written with titles such as these: *When China Rules the World: The End of the Western World and the Birth of a New Global Order, Easternization: Asia's Rise and America's Decline, from Obama to Trump and Beyond*, and *Destined for War: Can America and China Escape the Thucydides Trap?*

A discourse has also arisen about the idea of an inevitable decline of the United States, and an inevitable rise of China. It is not only many in China who have come to believe in their rightful rise to supremacy. Many in America and around the world have come to believe in this inevitability as well.

Like my friend in Washington who told me "It is not 1945 anymore," there are countless people who propose ways in which the United States can accede to China's new order, and countless others who have given themselves one justification or another for abandoning a world they insist must fade away. Whether it is the financier in New York who tells me that this is just the course of things, and resistance would be "like the British Empire going to war to save its colonies," or an article in *Foreign Policy*, one written by authors from a range of nationalities, titled "It Is Time for America to Consider Accommodation with China." The article goes on to state:

> If America wants to perpetuate the old order, it will have to accept a very serious contest with China, and this is what some people now advocate. But while America remains very strong, China is more formidable in many ways than any previous adversary, and its strength will most likely grow faster than America's over coming decades. The costs and risks of escalating rivalry could be very high, and Americans cannot assume that China is any less determined to change the regional order than America is to preserve it. It is time to ask whether preserving primacy in Asia is worth the price.[1]

Graham Allison has captured the most recent round of big-picture thinking on China, with his book *Destined for War*, which argues that China and America must do all they can to avoid a war as China rises to power. Allison diagnoses the problem as follows: "China's emergence as the number one power in Asia— and its aspiration to be number one in the world— reflects not just the imperative of economic growth, but also a supremacist world view bound up in Chinese identity."[2]

Allison proposes the following approach: that the United States "should consider all strategic options, 'even the ugly ones,' which would include accommodating China's ambitions without sacrificing America's 'vital interests'."[3]

Professor Allison goes on to explain that "Accommodation is not a bad word. Opponents seek to conflate it with appeasement. But the two are not synonymous in the realm of strategy. Accommodation is a serious effort to adapt to a new balance of power by adjusting relations with a serious competitor— in effect, making the best of unfavorable trends without resorting to military means." He adds that "I don't believe the U.S. has a vital interest in every island in the South China Sea", or that the US should defend "every claim made by the Philippines or Vietnam. It does not even require defending the Philippines."[4]

Allison's book has earned the high praise of numerous current-day sages and experts. Henry Kissinger said the "Thucydides Trap identifies a cardinal challenge to world order . . . I can only hope that the US–China relationship becomes the fifth case to resolve itself peacefully rather than the thirteenth to result in war." Walter Isaacson asked, "Can the US avoid confrontation with China? That is the geopolitical question of our age."

The problem with Allison's work is that he is more concerned with avoiding his Thucydides Trap than *avoiding Chinese victory.*

The question rests on a straw man: accede to China, accommodate China, or go to war. What kind of choice is this for free nations? This is "accommodation" on pain of violence— something akin to the set of choices facing a victim during a burglary.

Professor Allison makes this argument despite rightly diagnosing China's aspirations for power and its desire, as he puts it, "to be number one" not only in Asia, but in the world.

There is another way.

I was studying the Chinese Civil War at Oxford.

My mentor was teaching me to understand how historians write about history, how they explain, in short, *what happened*— what they take as *inevitable*, and what they believe *could have changed*. In the late 1940s, as the Chinese Communist Party swept through the central plains of China, destroying Nationalist armies and finally winning the war, nearly every account considered this outcome virtually inevitable. The corruption, decay, exhaustion, in short, the *decline*, of the Nationalists opened a path to victory for Mao Zedong and his forces, despite millions of casualties on both sides. As these historians explained it, the path to victory was open, much as China sees its path to supremacy today.

Like these historians, today's Chinese leaders see their nation's rise to supremacy as inevitable. The path is open.

Only one book stood out among many histories.

One book, *Decisive Encounters*, stated that in fact it was the Nationalists, not the Communists, who held the superior position. They had better forces, control of all but a handful of provinces, the support of both superpowers, and the extensive experience of military operations in the Second World War. However, the decisions and errors that they made led to their defeat, and to a turning point in history.[5]

We need to *recognize* that in fact the United States is in a far stronger position overall than China.

The US economy is *still much larger* than China's, at $20.5 trillion versus $13.5 trillion respectively. The United States, not China, is able to project military power globally, and has armed forces that have been tested in nearly every geographical and operational domain on Earth. In terms of geography, the United States enjoys open access to two great oceans, a boon in the history of American power, while China must work every day to secure the geographical spaces that are vital to its security along its "Belt and Road." In terms of education and technology, it is in the United States, not China, where China's best engineers and innovators have received their training for decades, and where Chinese state-backed companies and initiatives seek to harvest innovation and technology through business acquisitions or outright cybertheft. The United States can feed itself and fuel itself. China cannot. The list of America's advantages goes on and on. This contrast is the state of an existing power versus a rising power.

However, this situation is changing rapidly, and the window for American opportunity is closing.

I believe that this contest for preeminence is not a contest for the year 2049—a year by which this contest will be over—but rather, it is a contest for the year 2030.

In roughly a decade, America will reach a turning point if we do not *plan* and act. A transformation will begin to take shape from a world that remains largely American-led—democratic and based upon the rights and values that we and our allies hold to be essential to life—to a world that begins to transition toward Chinese power and toward China's vision of victory.

Napoleon Bonaparte said, "China is a sleeping giant. Let her sleep, for when she wakes she will move the world." But the question is not "Will China sleep?" The question is "Will America sleep?"

America can still prevail in this contest for global leadership.

First, we must realize that this contest is fundamentally about economic power. Unlike the USSR, a superpower which never achieved the economic heft of the United States, a failure which contributed to its collapse, China's entire strategy for achieving supremacy is based on a rising economy. China's strategy is based on an ability to achieve, through its "invincible force of 1.3 billion people," an economic, technological, and, eventually, military capacity unlike that of any other nation.

Second, we must gather and build the power of our alliances, friendships, and commitments around the world, in other words, the world that has been built from our own victories and values. I would like to make one fundamental proposition here: a contest between China and America will be a close-run thing. However, a contest between China and *the democratic world* will be impossible for China. America must remain engaged in global leadership, with a focus on the world's democracies.

The United States and other democratic powers must strengthen our connectivity, and economic, military, technological, educational, and innovation potential, in ways which enable us to build ourselves and build each other, while *closing China off* from access to the things that pave its way to power. This effort will take leadership in all levels of society. It will take a deep and detailed focus on strategies that will allow democracies to come together to maintain, build, and grow our own "comprehensive power."

Third, the military balance is in our favor, and it must remain so. The United States and its allies hold an edge, albeit a waning one, in the military balance with China and other authoritarian nations, including Russia. However, as a senior member of the US government explained to a closed forum which I attended, America's "unipolar" moment, that is the moment of uncontested supremacy after the Cold War, was the "nightmare" scenario for Russia, China, and other authoritarian powers. Every day since then, they have gone to school on us, and done their best to learn how to defeat the United States and counter the advantages that we enjoy. They have now made rapid gains against us.

The military balance is the arena in which we enjoy the greatest advantages at present. However, these advantages are rapidly eroding as China builds its own technological capacities, often through the unintended help of US companies, financiers, and educational institutions, as well as those of US treaty allies.

Additionally, it should be recognized that China is basically correct in its age-old dictum about wealth and power: 富国强兵. This means, "A rich country, a strong military." It is the essence of China's rise, and it may even be the essence of history. From Adam Smith's *Wealth of Nations*, to Paul Kennedy's *Rise and Fall of Great Powers*, it is visible that a country's wealth is its foundation for rise or fall, for good or ill.

In short, our contest with China for global leadership will be *a contest of prosperity*. It is a contest that America must win. Winning this contest may also be our only way to avoid either war or China's victory.

When I was teaching the Space Race to undergraduates in England, I realized that I could either call my class "The Space Race and the Cold War" or "The Space Race and the Origins of the Space Age." It was this contest for space, carefully designed, and beautifully executed, that both laid part of the foundation for an American victory over the Soviet Union, and also brought about extraordinary advances in technology and exploration. John Glenn, America's first astronaut to orbit Earth, went to the heavens on an Atlas-6 rocket, a type used for nuclear missiles. The same technology that was capable of destroying an adversary's nation also took us to the stars. The same global contest that began the end of a totalitarian empire set the stage for a new era in human progress: the use and exploration of the cosmos.

We must take charge. We must *design* this new contest. We must bend it to our advantage.

Rather than fearing the cost of competition or the trials of standing against another nation's thirst for supremacy, let us build our competitive power on the strengths of our own system, the unity of our alliances, and the maximum potential for wealth and strength in *a free and rights-based world*.

Something else must be said now about China's vision of victory.

While it has become clear that expecting China to "liberalize" as it got rich was a fantasy of the West, there is another side of China's Communist

Party that was ignored by the world throughout all these years of China's growing wealth and its military buildup. That is the human cost in China. Human rights have generally been relegated to the world of NGOs, activists, individual journalists, and the occasional politician. They have largely been abandoned in the Western conversation on China when it comes to diplomatic engagement, trade, business, and, in short, the question of "accommodation" itself.

The human cost is an important side to the story. A tidy phrase, "human rights," has come to stand in for a problem that has been at the core of Communist Party rule for decades, including during the years of China's "economic miracle." Perhaps this problem is too easily dismissed by those in awe of China, and those who are eager to benefit from China's ascendancy.

However, the problem of human rights in China becomes all the more important, as the story of China today is no longer only about what happens inside China. We now face the prospect of Chinese power that extends well beyond its borders, and, if the Communist Party achieves its goals, power that would exist without equal, without peer on Earth. The very heart of China's vision of victory is a form of "comprehensive national power" that extends across all geographies, economic sectors, and military domains necessary to secure China's "return" to supremacy over other nations.

Something must be understood now as truth and fact: the death toll exacted by the Chinese Communist Party since its victory in 1949 is among the highest exacted by any organization in human history. Most of the massive human costs in China occurred under the rule of Mao Zedong. But many of the Communist Party's most ruthless practices remain. Perhaps it is because these deaths have all been Chinese, Uighur, Tibetan, or others under the Communist Party's dominions that the world has largely looked away. Perhaps the world will continue to do so, favoring trade and commerce over the question of the human costs in China, just as we have done over the past thirty years of China's rise.

What does it mean to live within a system that considers the concept of "human rights" to be an instrument of foreign subversion?

The Communist Party spends roughly as much on its internal security as it does on its entire military. This involves substantial investments in mass surveillance, "black jails," secret detention facilities, censorship, plainclothes police, and paramilitary forces. Freedom of assembly, freedom of the press, freedom of religion, freedom of speech, and academic freedom are but a few of the important casualties of China's authoritarian system. The use of torture and forced confessions is common practice. The more grotesque features of China's system of repression include a countrywide system of gulags, or "reeducation through labor" camps, and harvesting the organs of China's political prisoners.

These practices are as much a part of the "plan" as an expanded and modernized military, advanced technologies, and a growing economy. But none of these practices have really been used outside of China.

China's activity in Asia and around the globe exists in a world in which America is still the sole superpower. It is a world in which China's vision of victory has not yet been achieved, but merely projected, planned, and *imagined*. The Communist Party's vision has not yet been accomplished. In fact, it never needs to happen, if America finds the will to compete and win.

What China has been able to accomplish economically and geopolitically is profound. China has taken a treaty port on a 99-year lease in Sri Lanka. It has built up artificial islands in the South China Sea. It has achieved what the new Commander of US Pacific Command calls "the most ambitious military modernization in the world." China has achieved all of this in the shadow of and limited by a world that is still defined by overwhelming American power. However, as a leading historian put it to me, "The way the Chinese look at it is, why shouldn't they have a go? The British had their turn. America had its turn. Now it's ours."

A friend in the State Department once explained to me that Chinese strategy is "a mystery, not a secret," meaning that Chinese leaders themselves do not know what they want, and that their strategy is always evolving. The mystery is that we do not know, and they themselves might not know, just what they will do with the power that they seek should they attain it. While Chinese leaders, as this book has shown, are careful planners, long-term strategists, and have a very clear vision in mind, there remains an element of truth to what my friend at State once said. That is this: the Chinese vision of victory is about a world in which China's power is limited not by any other state or superpower, but only by the Chinese Communist Party's imagination. For the Communist Party, coming to global preeminence is not an end in itself: it is also a beginning. What the Communist

Party or its successors could do with this power is why America should be concerned and why America must prevail.

As Xi Jinping explained in his 19ᵗʰ Party Congress speech, China's "rejuvenation" is based on the "invincible force of more than 1.3 billion people." China's leaders have stated that we are now in "a new era," and that "we have an infinitely vast stage for our new era, a historical heritage of unmatched depth, and incomparable resolve . . . to forge ahead..." In other words, Chinese strategy is the application of an "invincible force" to an "infinite stage." It is the triumph of both China's will and China's system, in short, over the world as a whole.

The world waited for decades for China to "liberalize" as its economy grew. Perhaps it would be foolish to wait again for its system to change, *as its power grows*. From the perspective of the Chinese Communist Party, the practices and repressions of China's system have not held China back— they have enabled it. The past thirty years and more are proof.

Henry Kissinger, the father of modern US–China relations, once called America "the modern world's decisive articulation of the human quest for freedom, and an indispensable geopolitical force for the vindication of humane values."

When we note the building of a massive DNA bank for millions of Uighurs in Xinjiang, the use of advanced facial recognition and mass surveillance, the disappearance of political prisoners, or simply the torture of a young Tibetan woman by pressing needles into her fingertips, we must ask ourselves this question as we choose our course as a nation in this generation.

We must ask ourselves now, as we make our choices, as we decide whether or not the future will be American-led, democratic, rights-based, or otherwise. As we see the planning, the events, and the realities behind the ascending Chinese vision of victory, let us ask just one more question:

What kind of force is China?

AFTERWORD

An American response to China has begun. From courageous testimonies in the U.S. Congress, to the work of numerous thinkers and specialists, to action on trade, defense, and economic security, we are reaching a turning point in how our country sees its relationship with China.

America has begun to understand the intentions and ambitions of China's ruling Communist Party. However, our understanding of this challenge cannot be confined to government and specialists alone. It is critical that across every sphere of American power, across all of what makes our democracy successful when we must do great things, we must wake up soon, and we must wake up fast.

Our military, our businesses and companies, our financial engines, our universities, our media, our political parties, our people, we all must understand the objectives of this adversary, so that we may unlock the creative power and potential of the United States and apply it to this great challenge.

The answer to the dangers posed by China's ambitions is simple: we must work to rebuild our own unity, strength, and prosperity. The unity of America is a force too great for any challenger. And we must focus, above all, on building our economic power.

We must focus on building the economic power not only of America, but also of the democratic world.

We must recognize that China's ascendency is not America's problem alone. Not at all. It is a problem that the world as a whole must grapple with. What the future looks like is a choice that free and democratic countries must make together. However, American leadership will be essential to securing the future of the free and democratic world. We must work with our friends and allies to harness our strengths, build our prosperity, prepare our resistance, and respond to China's Vision of Victory.

May this great task bring out the best in all of us. Our work has just begun.

ACKNOWLEDGMENTS

With thanks to the many, many people who made this book possible. With thanks to all whose efforts have come before and who have worked to illuminate this challenge. And with thanks to those who work every day to help our country succeed in this campaign.

With great effort, we will prevail.

ABOUT THE AUTHOR

DR. JONATHAN D.T. WARD has been studying the rise of China for more than a decade.
From travels with truck caravans in Tibet and
across the South China Sea by cargo ship in his
early twenties, to accessing Communist Party
archives that have now been closed to the world
while a PhD candidate at Oxford, to consulting
for the U.S. Department of Defense and For-

tune 500 companies, Dr. Ward has brought the experience of a traveler, the
discipline of a scholar, and the insight of a strategy consultant to one of the
biggest challenges of our time: what does China want, how will it try to get
it, and what should America do?

Dr. Ward is the Founder of Atlas Organization, a Washington DC and
New York based consultancy focused on the rise of India and China, and
on US-China global competition. He is a frequently invited speaker for
government, industry, think tank, expert, and public audiences in the
United States, Europe, and Asia. Dr. Ward has briefed a wide range of audiences from the US Defense Intelligence Agency to the Strategy Division
of the US Navy Staff, the Wall Street Journal, leading American corporations, and the UK Ministry of Defence.

Dr. Ward is represented by London Speaker Bureau as a keynote on
Global Trends. He is a member of the 2018 Next Generation National Security Leaders Fellowship program at the Center for a New American Secu-

rity in Washington DC, a Research Associate at the University of Oxford's Changing Character of War Programme, and a former visiting scholar at the University of Oxford China Centre. He speaks Russian, Chinese, Spanish, and Arabic, and spent ten years overseas in China, India, Russia, Latin America, Southeast Asia, Europe, and the Middle East before returning to the United States to found Atlas Organization. A US citizen, Dr. Ward studied philosophy, Russian, and Chinese at Columbia University as an undergraduate. He earned his M.St. in Global and Imperial History and his PhD in China-India relations at the University of Oxford.

NOTES

Introduction

1. Greg Ip, "Once an Optimist on US–China Relations, Henry Paulson Delivers a Sobering Message," Wall Street Journal, 2018, https://www.wsj.com/articles/once-an-optimist-on-u-s-china-relations-henry-paulson-delivers-a-sobering-message-1541548800 (accessed January 28, 2019).

2. Xi Jinping, "Secure a Decisive Victory in Building a Moderately Prosperous Society in All Respects and Strive for the Great Success of Socialism with Chinese Characteristics for a New Era," Delivered at the 19th Party Congress of the Communist Party of China, Xinhua, 2017, http://www.xinhuanet.com/english/special/2017-11/03/c_136725942.htm (accessed December 8, 2018).

3. "Commentary: Milestone congress points to new era for China, the world," Xinhua, 2017, http://www.xinhuanet.com/english/2017-10/24/c_136702090.htm (accessed January 28, 2019).

4. "China Develops Youth Credit System for Building High-Trust Society," Xinhua, 2018, http://www.xinhuanet.com/english/2018-05/10/c_137170145.htm (accessed January 9, 2019).

5. "China's Government Has Ordered a Million Citizens to Occupy Uighur Homes," Chinafile, 2018, http://www.chinafile.com/reporting-opinion/postcard/million-citizens-occupy-uighur-homes-xinjiang (accessed January 9, 2019).

6. "Milestone congress," Xinhua.

Part I: The Great Rejuvenation of the Chinese Nation

1. "The Road to Rejuvenation: Full text of China's Party Approved History," China Change, 2011, https://chinachange.org/2012/05/11/the-road-to rejuvenation-the-full-text-of-chinas-party approved-history/ (accessed December 8, 2018).

2. Ibid.

3. "Chasing the Chinese Dream," The Economist, 2013, https://www.economist.com/briefing/2013/05/04/chasing-the-chinese-dream, 2013 (accessed January 9, 2019).

4. Xi Jinping, "Speech at 'Road to Rejuvenation'," *China Copyright and Media,* 2012, Rogier Creemers trans., https://chinacopyrightandmedia.wordpress.com/2012/11/29/speech-at -the-road-to-rejuvenation/ (accessed December 8, 2018).

5. Ibid.

6. Chen Jian, *Mao's China and the Cold War* (Chapel Hill and London, 2001), 7.

7. Frank Dikotter, *The Tragedy of Liberation: A History of the Chinese Revolution 1945–1957* (New York, 2013).

8. "Chinese Professor Sacked after Criticizing Mao Online," *Reuters,* 2017, https://www .reuters.com/article/us-china-mao-idUSKBN14U0EG (accessed December 13, 2018).

9. "Chinese Official Fired after Calling Mao Zedong 'A Devil'," *South China Morning Post,* 2017, https://www.scmp.com/news/china/policies-politics/article/2062728/chinese-official -fired-after-calling-mao-zedong-devil (accessed December 13, 2018).

10. Alexander V. Pantsov and Steven I. Levine, *Mao: The Real Story* (New York and London, 2012), 42.

11. Ibid., 46.

12. Ibid., 68–84, 98–99.

13. *Selected Works of Mao Tse-tung* (London, 1954), Vol. III, 107.

14. Ibid., Vol. IV, 241.

15. 毛泽东西藏工作文选, (北京, 2008) *Mao Zedong's Tibetan Work* (Beijing, 2008), 12.

16. 西藏工作献选编, (北京, 2005) *Selected Documents from Tibetan Work* (Beijing, 2005), 52.

17. 中华人民共和国对外关系文件集 (1962) 第九集, (世界知识出版社编辑, 北京), 44. *Collected Documents on the Foreign Relations of the People's Republic of China* (1962), Collection No. 9 (World Knowledge Publishing House, Beijing), 44. Hereafter: *ZDWGX 1962.*

18. *Selected Works of Mao Tsetung*, Vol. V (Peking, 1977), 18.

19. Ibid., 18.

20. Chen, *Mao's China*, 7.

21. Qiang Zhai, *China and the Vietnam Wars, 1950–1975* (Chapel Hill and London, 2000), 4.

22. Sam van Schaik, *Tibet: A History* (New Haven, 2011).

23. Ibid., 214.

24. Pantsov and Levine, *Mao*, 445.

25. Sergey Radchenko, *Two Suns in the Heavens: The Sino-Soviet Struggle for Supremacy, 1962–1967* (Stanford and Washington DC, 2009), 146.

26. Peter Van Ness, *Revolution and Chinese Foreign Policy: Peking's Support for Wars of National Liberation* (London, 1970), 14.

27. 外交部开放档案馆，北京，中华人民共和国 105-01455-02, 27.4.1961第一亚洲司：《印度目前的内外动向》27.4.1961, 7. Foreign Ministry Public Archive, Beijing, PRC (hereafter FMA) First Asian Department: "India's current internal and external trends," April 27, 1961, 7. Author's travels in China; these archives are now closed.

28. 毛泽东年谱 1949–1976 (北京, 2013), *A Chronological Record of Mao Zedong 1949–1976* (Beijing, 2013), Vol. III, 555. Hereafter, *Record of Mao Zedong.*

29. *Record of Mao Zedong,* Vol. V, 163.

30. Qiang Zhai, *China and the Vietnam Wars,* 4.

31. After Mao's death there was a short succession period in which Hua Guofeng emerged as Chairman of the Communist Party. He was soon overshadowed by the far more consequential Deng Xiaoping.

32. Ezra F. Vogel, *Deng Xiaoping and the Transformation of China* (Cambridge and London, 2011), 15–45.

33. Ibid., 2.

34. Alexander V. Pantsov and Steven I. Levine, *Deng Xiaoping: A Revolutionary Life* (New York, 2015), 3.

35. Ibid., 262.

36. Vogel, *Deng Xiaoping,* 697.

37. *China Foreign Policy and Government Guide,* International Business Publications (Washington DC, 2007), 96.

38. Ibid.

39. Ibid.

40. Ibid.

41. Deng Xiaoping, "Building a Socialism with a Specifically Chinese Character," *The People's Daily, 1984,* http://en.people.cn/dengxp/vol3/text/c1220.html (accessed January 11, 2019).

42. *Selected Works of Deng Xiaoping,* Vol. III (Beijing, 1984).

43. Robert S. Ross, "The 1995–1996 Taiwan Strait Crisis: Coercion, Credibility, and the Use of Force," *International Security,* Vol. 25, No. 2 (2000), 87–123.

44. Ibid.

45. Vogel, *Deng Xiaoping,* 551.

46. Ibid., 551–52.

47. See Michael Pillsbury, *The Hundred-Year Marathon: China's Secret Strategy to Replace America as the Global Superpower* (New York, 2015).

48. Vogel, 662–63.

49. See Peter Hays Gries, *China's New Nationalism* (Berkeley and London, 2004) and Zheng Wang, *Never Forget National Humiliation: Historical Memory in Chinese Politics and Foreign Relations* (New York, 2012).

50. Xu Jian, "Rethinking China's Period of Strategic Opportunity," *China Institute of International Studies, 2014,* http://www.ciis.org.cn/english/2014-05/28/content_6942258.htm (accessed December 8, 2018).

51. Jiang Zemin, "Hold High the Great Banner of Deng Xiaoping Theory for an All-Round Advancement of the Cause of Building Socialism with Chinese Characteristics into the 21st

Century," *Beijing Review*, 1997, http://www.bjreview.com.cn/document/txt/2011-03/25/content_363499.htm (accessed January 12, 2019).

52. Ibid.

53. Ibid.

54. Ibid.

55. Ibid.

56. John Tkacik, Joseph Fewsmith, and Maryanne Kivlehan, "Who's Hu? Assessing China's Heir Apparent, Hu Jintao," *Heritage Foundation, 2002,* https://web.archive.org/web/20100615195945/http://heritage.org/Research/Lecture/Whos-Hu#pgfId=1010167 (accessed December 8, 2018).

57. Ibid.

58. "TV Docu Stimulates More Open Attitude to History, China, the World," *People's Daily Online, 2006,* http://en.people.cn/200611/26/eng20061126_325264.html (accessed December 8, 2018).

59. See Zheng Bijian, *Economic Globalization and China's Future* (Beijing, 2018), 100–02, for Chinese Communist Party discourse on a "multipolar world." See also John J. Mearsheimer, "Structural Realism," in Tim Dunne, Milja Kurki, and Steve Smith, eds., *International Relations Theories: Discipline and Diversity* (Oxford, 2006), 71–88, and Fareed Zakaria, *The Post-American World* (Norton, 2008), for American discourse on the subject.

60. "Firmly March on the Path of Socialism with Chinese Characteristics and Strive to Complete the Building of a Moderately Prosperous Society in All Respects. Report to the Eighteenth National Congress of the Communist Party on November 8, 2012," *Embassy of the People's Republic of China in the United States, 2012,* http://www.china-embassy.org/eng/zt/18th_CPC_National_Congress_Eng/t992917.htm (accessed December 8, 2018).

61. "A Few Questions for Susan Shirk," *OUPblog, 2007,* https://blog.oup.com/2007/04/susan_shirk/ (accessed March 2, 2019).

62. "Xi Stresses Joint Battle Command for Military Reform," Ministry of National Defense of the PRC, 2016, http://eng.mod.gov.cn/DefenseNews/2016-04/20/content_4650177.htm (accessed January 12, 2019).

63. Xi Jinping, "Road to Rejuvenation."

64. Xi Jinping, "Decisive Victory"

65. Ibid.

66. Ibid.

67. Zhang Dongmiao, "China Needs a Strong Military More Than Ever: Xi," *Xinhua, 2017,* http://www.xinhuanet.com/english/2017-07/30/c_136484692.htm (accessed December 8, 2018).

68. Xi, "Decisive Victory."

69. Ibid.

70. Ibid.

71. Ibid.

72. Ibid.

73. *Quotations from Mao Tse Tung* (Peking, 1966).

74. Xi, "Decisive Victory."

75. "Xi Says Beijing Ready to Fight 'Bloody Battle'," *Taipei Times, 2018* http://www.taipeitimes.com/News/front/archives/2018/03/21/2003689713 (accessed January 12, 2019).

76. Xi, "Decisive Victory."

77. Zhou Bo, "Protect the Period of Strategic Opportunity," *China Daily*, 2017, http://usa.chinadaily.com.cn/epaper/2017-08/17/content_30737436.htm (accessed December 8, 2018).

78. Xi, "Decisive Victory."

79. "China's 19th Party Congress: Implications for China and the United States," Wilson Center, 2017.

80. 中国建成一流军队是要超越美军?国防如此回应, "Is China Building a First-Class Military in Order to Surpass the US Military? The Defense Ministry Responds," *Sina Military*, 2017, http://mil.news.sina.com.cn/china/2017-10-26/doc-ifynfvar4261352.shtml (accessed January 12, 2019).

81. Ibid.

82. Xi, "Decisive Victory."

83. "Xi Stresses Joint Battle."

84. 中华人民共和国对外关系文件集 (1962) 第九集, (世界知识出版社编辑, 北京), 44.

85. Xi Jinping, "Build up Our National Defense and Armed Forces," in Xi Jinping, *The Governance of China*, Vol. I (Beijing, 2014), 237.

86. Ibid., 238.

87. Xi Jinping, "Build Strong National Defense and Powerful Military Forces," in *Governance of China*, 240.

88. *Selected Works of Mao Tsetung, Vol. V* (Peking, 1977), 18.

89. *Record of Conversation Following Pakistani Ambassador to the PRC Raza's Presentation of Credentials to Liu Shaoqi's FMA 105-01801-02*, January 9, 1962, Foreign Ministry Archives, Cold War International History Project Digital Archive (CWIHPDA).

90. Ibid.

91. *Notes, Memoranda and Letters Exchanged and Agreements Signed between the Governments of India and China: White Paper*, Vol. VI (New Delhi, 1960), 197–200. Hereafter, White Paper.

92. Xi, "Build Strong National Defense," 241.

93. Xi, "Decisive Victory."

Part II: Blue National Soil

1. 毛泽东年谱 1949-1976, *Record of Mao Zedong*, Vol. 3, February 2, 1959, 595.

2. James Griffiths, "China Ready to Fight 'Bloody Battle' against Enemies, Xi Says in Speech," *CNN*, 2018, https://www.cnn.com/2018/03/19/asia/china-xi-jinping-speech-npc-intl/index.html (accessed January 12, 2019).

3. Admiral Philip Davidson, "Advance Policy Questions for Admiral Philip Davidson, USN Expected Nominee for Commander, U.S. Pacific Command," *Senate Armed Services Committee,* 2018.

4. First and Second Island Chain, US Department of Defense.

5. Relief location map of Indian Ocean, Uwe Dedering.

6. U.S. Central Intelligence Agency, Perry Casteñada Map Collection.

7. Map of the Spratly Islands in the South China Sea, U.S. Department of State.

8. Selected Chinese Territorial Claims, U.S. Department of Defense.

9. Topographic Map of the World, Pacific Ocean Center, DEMIS Mapserver.

10. "Columbus sets sail," *History,* https://www.history.com/this-day-in-history/columbus-sets -sail (accessed March 3, 2019).

11. "President Xi Jinping Delivers Important Speech and Proposes to Build a Silk Road Economic Belt with Central Asian Countries," *Ministry of Foreign Affairs of PRC, 2013,* https://www.fmprc.gov.cn/mfa_eng/topics_665678/xjpfwzysiesgjtfhshzzfh_665686/t107 6334.shtml (accessed January 20, 2019).

12. Jiafeng Chen, "Camel Bells and Smoky Deserts," *Harvard Political Review, 2016,* http:// harvardpolitics.com/world/camel-bells-and-smoky-deserts/ (accessed December 13, 2018).

13. Jamil Anderlini and Lucy Hornby, "China Overtakes US as World's Largest Goods Trader," *The Financial Times,* January 2014, https://www.ft.com/content/7c2dbd70-79a6 -11e3-b381-00144feabdc0 (accessed January 20, 2019).

14. *The Science of Military Strategy 2013 Edition* (Beijing, 2013), 209, cited in Michael McDevitt, "Becoming a Great 'Maritime Power,' A Chinese Dream," CNA (June 2016), 10.

15. McDevitt, "A Chinese Dream," iii–xiii and 1–21.

16. Xu Sheng, "Follow the Path of Maritime Power with Chinese Characteristics," *Qiushi Online,* http://www.qstheory.cn/ 2013 cited in ibid., 8.

17. State Council, "China's Military Strategy (full text)," 2015, http://english.gov.cn/archive/ white_paper/2015/05/27/content_281475115610833.htm (accessed January 12, 2018).

18. Vogel, *Deng Xiaoping, 551–52.*

19. Daniel Hartnett, "The Father of the Modern Chinese Navy – Liu Huaqing," *Center for International Maritime Security,* 2014, http://cimsec.org/father-modern-chinese-navy-liu -huaqing/13291#_ftn10 (accessed January 12, 2019).

20. Jonathan Ward, "Sino–Indian Competition in the Maritime Domain," *Jamestown Foundation China Brief, Vol. 17, No. 1* (2017).

21. "Full Text: Vision for Maritime Cooperation under the Belt and Road Initiative," *Xinhua,* 2017, http://www.xinhuanet.com/english/2017-06/20/c_136380414.htm (accessed December 11, 2018).

22. See McDevitt, "A Chinese Dream," on the expansion of China's maritime power.

23. David Scott, "U.S. Strategy in the Pacific—Geopolitical Positioning for the Twenty First Century," *Geopolitics,* Vol. 17, No. 3 (2012), 607.

24. Bernard Cole, "Reflections on China's Maritime Strategy: Island Chains and the Classics," Conference Paper, US Naval War College, 2014, cited in Patrick M. Cronin, Mira Rapp-Hooper, Harry Krejsa, et al., "Beyond the San-Hai: The Challenge of China's Blue Water Navy," Center for a New American Security (Washington DC, 2017).

25. Xi Jinping, "Decisive Victory."

26. McDevitt, "A Chinese Dream," 127.

27. Sam van Schaik, *Tibet: A History* (New Haven, 2011).

28. Robert D. Kaplan, *Asia's Cauldron: The South China Sea and the End of a Stable Pacific* (New York, 2014), 41.

29. State Council, "China's Military Strategy."

30. "China Accuses US of Militarizing South China Sea," *Military.com, 2019,* https://www.military .com/daily-news/2016/02/20/china-accuses-us-of-militarizing-south-china-sea.html (accessed January 9, 2018); "China 'installs cruise missiles on South China Sea outposts'," *South China Morning Post,* 2018, https://www.scmp.com/news/china/diplomacy-defence/article/2144456 /china-installs-cruise-missiles-south-china-sea-outposts (accessed January 9, 2018).

31. Admiral Philip Davidson, "Advance Policy Questions for Admiral Philip Davidson, USN Expected Nominee for Commander, U.S. Pacific Command," *Senate Armed Services Committee,* 2018. Emphasis added.

32. Ian Easton, *The Chinese Invasion Threat: Taiwan's Defense and American Strategy in Asia* (Arlington, 2017), 28.

33. See Pillsbury, *Hundred-Year Marathon.*

34. State Council, "China's Military Strategy."

35. "Full Text of White Paper on China's Space Activities in 2016," *The State Council Information Office of the People's Republic of China,* 2016, http://www.scio.gov.cn/wz/Document /1537091/1537091.htm (accessed December 11, 2018).

36. Ibid.

37. Ibid.

38. Ibid.

39. Anthony H. Cordesman and Joseph Kendall, "Chinese Strategy and Military Modernization in 2016," *Center for Strategic and International Studies* (Washington DC, 2016).

40. State Council, "China's Military Strategy."

41. Cordesman and Kendall, "Chinese Strategy," 12.

42. State Council, "China's Military Strategy."

43. Cordesman and Kendall, "Chinese Strategy," 12.

44. Kevin Pollpeter, Eric Anderson, Jordan Wilson, et al., "China Dream, Space Dream: China's Progress in Space Technologies and Implications for the United States; A Report Prepared for the U.S.–China Economic and Security Review Commission" (2015), iv.

45. Ibid., iv.

46. See Elbridge Colby, "From Sanctuary to Battlefield: A Framework for a US Defense

and Deterrence Strategy for Space," *Center for New American Security, 2016, for discussion of US vulnerabilities in space.*

47. See Cordesman and Kendall, "Chinese Strategy," for a review of both C4ISR and ASAT capabilities. As Cordesman explains, "China is developing counterspace capabilities that affect the country's entire spectrum of warfighting capacities, from the tactical to the strategic levels," "Chinese Strategy," 22.

48. Ethan Meick, "China–Russia Military-to-Military Relations: Moving toward a Higher Level of Cooperation," *US–China Economic and Security Review Commission* (Washington DC, 2017), 4.

49. Jonathan Broder, "Why the Next Pearl Harbor Could Happen in Space," *Newsweek, 2016,* http://www.newsweek.com/2016/05/13/china-us-space-wars-455284.html (accessed December 11, 2018).

50. Namrata Goswami, "Waking Up to China's Space Dream," *The Diplomat, 2018,* https://thediplomat.com/2018/10/waking-up-to-chinas-space-dream/ (accessed March 3, 2019).

51. Ibid.

52. Ibid. See *CSIS Asia Maritime Transparency Initiative on Scarborough Shoal,* https://amti.csis.org/scarborough-shoal/ (accessed March 3, 2019).

53. Stephen Chen, "Will China's new laser satellite become the 'Death Star' for submarines?" *South China Morning Post, 2018,* https://www.scmp.com/news/china/science/article/2166413/will-chinas-new-laser-satellite-become-death-star-submarines (accessed March 3, 2019).

54. Ibid.

55. Pilot National Laboratory for Marine Science and Technology (Qingdao), http://www.qnlm.ac/en/page?a=1&b=2&c=221&e=1&p=detail (accessed March 3, 2019).

56. Ibid.

57. Chen, "laser satellite."

58. Author's conversation with Rear Admiral (Ret.) Michael McDevitt, 2019.

59. Burgess Laird, "War Control: Chinese Writings on the Control of Escalation in Crisis and Conflict," *Center for a New American Security* (Washington DC, 2017), 13.

60. Cited in ibid., 12.

61. Ibid., 4.

62. State Council, "China's Military Strategy."

63. "A New Nuclear Review for a New Age," *CSIS,* 2017, https://www.csis.org/events/new-nuclear-review-new-age (accessed January 9, 2019).

64. Laird, "War Control."

65. Adapted from Jonathan D. T. Ward, conference paper for National Bureau of Asian Research, October 2016.

66. Author's conversations in China. See also Dale C. Rielage, "The Chinese Navy's Missing Years," *Naval History,* December 2018; State Council, "China's Military Strategy"; and James Mulvenon and David Finkelstein (eds.), *China's Revolution in Doctrinal Affairs:*

Emerging Trends and Tactics in the Operational Art of the Chinese People's Liberation Army (Washington DC, 2002), on the principles of "active defense."

67. Kathrin Hill and Richard Waters, "Washington unnerved by China's 'military-civil fusion'," [sic], Financial Times, 2018, https://www.ft.com/content/8dcb534c-dbaf-11e8-9f04-38d397e6661c (accessed March 15, 2019).

68. Kathrin Hill, "Chinese military researchers exploit western universities," Financial Times, 2018, https://www.ft.com/content/ebe95b76-d8cc-11e8-a854-33d6f82e62f8 (accessed March 15, 2019).

69. Ibid.

70. Chiang Kai-shek, *China's Destiny and Chinese Economic Theory* (New York and London, 1947), 36.

71. See van Schaik, *Tibet*.

72. See "Timeline of Chinese History and Dynasties," Columbia University, for dates, http://afe.easia.columbia.edu/timelines/china_timeline.htm (accessed January 20, 2019).

73. State Council, "China's Military Strategy."

74. Qiang Zhai, *China and the Vietnam Wars,* 20–23, 45–48. See also Jonathan D. T. Ward, "China–India Rivalry and the Border War of 1962: PRC Perspectives on the Collapse of China–India Relations, 1958–62," D.Phil. thesis, University of Oxford, 2017.

75. "China's Military Regrouped into Five PLA Theater Commands," *Xinhua, 2016,* http://www.chinadaily.com.cn/china/2016-02/01/content_23346907.htm (accessed January 20, 2019).

76. Zhang Tao, "PLA Special Operations Members Shine in South America," *China Military Online, 2016,* http://english.chinamil.com.cn/news-channels/china-military-news/2016-04/12/content_7003604.htm (accessed December 11, 2018).

77. Meick, "China–Russia Military-to-Military Relations."

78. Nadège Rolland, *China's Eurasian Century? Political and Strategic Implications of the Belt and Road Initiative* (National Bureau of Asian Research, 2017), 93.

79. "Maldives: Trouble in Paradise," *Japan Times, 2018,* https://www.japantimes.co.jp/opinion/2018/02/13/editorials/maldives-trouble-paradise/ (accessed December 11, 2018).

80. "China's Naval Presence Deterred Indian Intervention in Maldives Crisis: Sources," *The Japan Times, 2018* https://www.japantimes.co.jp/news/2018/03/08/asia-pacific/politics-diplomacy-asia-pacific/chinas-naval-presence-deterred-indian-intervention-maldives-crisis-sources/ (accessed January 20, 2019).

81. Ibid.

82. James Kynge et al., "How China Rules the Waves," *Financial Times, 2017,* https://ig.ft.com/sites/china-ports/ (accessed December 11, 2018).

83. Ghulam Ali, "China/Pakistan Naval Cooperation: Implication for the Indian Ocean," *South Asia Watch,* 2016, http://southasiawatch.tw/china-pakistan-naval-cooperation-implication-for-the-indian-ocean (accessed December 11, 2018).

84. Shazia Hasan, "Navies of Pakistan, China Begin Their Fourth Joint Exercise," *Dawn,*

2016, https://www.dawn.com/news/1297067 (accessed December 11, 2018).

85. Ely Ratner, Elbridge Colby, Andrew Erickson et al., "More Willing and Able: Charting China's International Security Activism," *Center for a New American Security,* 2015. Also, author conversation with Dr. David Brewster, Australian National University.

86. Chris Kay, "Karachi Murder Raises Red Flag on $50 Billion Projects," *Bloomberg,* 2018, https://www.bloomberg.com/news/articles/2018-02-12/karachi-murder-raises-red-flag-on -china-s-50-billion-projects (accessed December 13, 2018).

87. Adapted from Jonathan D. T. Ward, "The Emerging Geopolitics of the Indian Ocean Region," *East West Center (Washington DC, 2017).*

88. Kiran Stacy, "China Signs 99-Year Lease on Sri Lanka's Hambantota Port," *Financial Times, 2017,* https://www.ft.com/content/e150ef0c-de37-11e7-a8a4-0a1e63a52f9c (accessed December 13, 2018).

89. Michael Safi and Amantha Perera, "The Biggest Game Changer in 100 Years: Chinese Money Gushes into Sri Lanka," *The Guardian, 2018,* https://www.theguardian.com/world /2018/mar/26/the-biggest-game-changer-in-100-years-chinese-money-gushes-into-sri -lanka (accessed December 13, 2018).

90. Chaitanya Giri, "Mapping China's Global Telecom Empire," Gateway House: Indian Council on Global Relations, 2018, https://www.gatewayhouse.in/china-global-telecom-tentacles/ (accessed January 12, 2019).

91. 杜德斌, 马亚华, "一带一路": 中华民族复兴的地缘大战略, 地理研究2016年6月 Du Debin and Ma Yahua, "'The Belt and Road': The Grand Geostrategy of the Great Rejuvenation of the Chinese Nation," *Geographical Research,* June 2015, http://www.dlyj .ac.cn/EN/10.11821/dlyj201506001#1 (accessed January 12, 2019).

92. Reprinted with permission from Mercator Institute for China Studies.

93. 杜德斌, 马亚华, "一带一路": 中华民族复兴的地缘大战略, 地理研究2016年6 月 Du Debin and Ma Yahua, "'The Belt and Road': The Grand Geostrategy of the Great Rejuvenation of the Chinese Nation," Geographical Research, June 2015, http://www.dlyj. ac.cn/EN/10.11821/dlyj201506001#1 (accessed January 12, 2019).

94. Ellen Barry, "U.S. Proposes Reviving Naval Coalition to Balance China's Expansion," *New York Times,* 2016, https://www.nytimes.com/2016/03/03/world/asia/us-proposes-india-naval -coalition-balance-china-expansion.html?_r=0 (accessed January 9, 2019). Professor Shen's academic home is the "China–America New Model of Great Power Relations Collaborative Innovation Research Center" at Fudan University's Center for American Studies.

95. Joel Wuthnow, "Chinese Perspectives on the Belt and Road Initiative: Strategic Rationales, Risks, and Implications," *Institute for National Strategic Studies,* 2012; Yun Sun, "March West: China's Response to the U.S. Rebalancing," *Brookings,* 2013, https://www .brookings.edu/blog/up-front/2013/01/31/march-west-chinas-response-to-the-u-s-rebal ancing/ (accessed January 9, 2019).

96. See, for example, Walter Russell Mead, *Special Providence: American Foreign Policy and How It Changed the World* (New York, 2009), 104-7 and George C. Herring, *From Colony to Superpower: U.S. Foreign Relations since 1776* (Oxford, 2008) on US geography, foreign policy, and power.

97. See Nicholas J. Spykman and George F. Kennan for American thinking on Eurasian grand strategy. See also Michael J. Green, *By More Than Providence: Grand Strategy and American Power in the Asia Pacific Since 1783,* (New York, 2017), 208-9 for a discussion of Spykman and Mackinder in Asia.

98. "Vision for Maritime Cooperation under the Belt and Road Initiative," *Belt and Road Portal, 2017,* http://www.yidaiyilu.gov.cn/wcm.files/upload/CMSydylgw/201706/20170620 0153032.pdf (accessed January 9, 2019).

99. "China Global Investment Tracker," *American Enterprise Institute,* http://www.aei.org/ china-global-investment-tracker/ (accessed January 21, 2019). Author's calculations. NB: Indian Ocean Region, as defined by this author, includes littoral countries of the Indian Ocean Rim, as well as those of the adjoining Persian Gulf and Red Sea.

100. Jonathan D. T. Ward, "Chinese Analysts Interpret Modi's New India," *Jamestown Foundation China Brief,* Vol. 14, No. 12 (2014).

101. Globe courtesy of Jason Davies Maps https://www.jasondavies.com/maps/, trade routes and graphic design added.

102. "Full Text: China's Arctic Policy," *Xinhua, 2018,* http://english.gov.cn/archive/white _paper/2018/01/26/content_281476026660336.htm (accessed January 10, 2019).

103. Graham Webster, Rogier Creemers, Paul Triolo et al., "China's Plan to 'Lead' in AI: Purpose, Prospects, and Problems," *New America (2017).*

104. Elsa Kania and John Costello, "Quantum Leap (Part 1): China's Advances in Quantum Information Science," *Jamestown Foundation,* China Brief, Vol. 16, No. 18 (2016). Italics added.

105. Ibid.

106. Pillsbury, *Hundred-Year Marathon,* 138–39.

107. Aaron L. Friedberg, *A Contest for Supremacy: China, America, and the Struggle for Mastery in Asia* (New York, 2011).

Part III: Catch up to America, Surpass America

1. 毛泽东年谱 1949-1976, *Record of Mao Zedong,* Vol. 2, October 29, 1955, 460.

2. Fu Ying, Chair of the Foreign Affairs Committee of China's National People's Congress, "The US World Order Is a Suit That No Longer Fits," *Financial Times,* 2016, https://www. ft.com/content/c09cbcb6-b3cb-11e5-b147-e5e5bba42e51 (accessed January 10, 2019). Madame Fu Ying also served as China's Vice Foreign Minister.

3. Xi, "Decisive Victory."

4. Jonathan Eckart, "8 Things You Need to Know about China's Economy," *World Economic Forum, 2016,* https://www.weforum.org/agenda/2016/06/8-facts-about-chinas-economy / (accessed January 9, 2019); original source: Our World in Data (ourworldindata.org).

5. Sun Tze, *The Art of War,* quoted in Hu Angang and Men Honghua, "The Rising of Modern China: Comprehensive National Power and Grand Strategy," *Strategy and Management,* No. 3 (2002).

6. Hu and Men, "Grand Strategy."

7. Shu Guang Zhang, "Constructing 'Peaceful Coexistence': China's Diplomacy toward Geneva and Bandung Conferences, 1954–55," *Cold War History*, Vol. 7, No. 4 (November 2007), 512.

8. Roderick MacFarquhar, *The Origins of the Cultural Revolution* (Oxford, 1997), Vol. II, 51, 217.

9. Douglas Brinkley and Luke A. Nichter, *The Nixon Tapes: 1971–1972* (New York, 2014), 189.

10. Hu Jintao, "Firmly March on the Path of Socialism with Chinese Characteristics and Strive to Complete the Building of a Moderately Prosperous Society in All Respects," Report to the Eighteenth National Congress of the Communist Party of China, November 8, 2012, *Embassy to the People's Republic of China in the United States of America*, 2012, http://www.china-embassy.org/eng/zt/18th_CPC_National_Congress_Eng/t992917.htm (accessed December 13, 2018).

11. Bruce A. Elleman, *Modern Chinese Warfare: 1795–1989* (London and New York, 2001). See also James Polachek, *The Inner Opium War* (Cambridge, 1991).

12. Hu Jintao, "March on the Path of Socialism."

13. State Council, 中国制造2025, "Made in China 2025" (2015), translation: IoT ONE.

14. Ibid.

15. "The Fat Tech Dragon: Baseline Trends in China's Innovation Drive," *Center for Strategic and International Studies*, 2017, https://www.csis.org/events/fat-tech-dragon-baseline-trends-chinas-innovation-drive (accessed January 9, 2019).

16. Ibid.

17. "Made in China 2025."

18. "Japan Overtakes South Korea in Ranking of Biggest Ship Building Nations," *Gcaptain*, 2017, http://gcaptain.com/japan-overtakes-south-korea-in-shipbuilding/ (accessed December 13, 2018).

19. Rana Mitter, *A Bitter Revolution: China's Struggle with the Modern World* (Oxford, 2004).

20. Odd Arne Westad, *The Global Cold War: Third World Interventions and the Making of Our Times* (New York, 2007), 73.

21. *Chronology of Mao Zedong*, Vol. III, 408.

22. Ibid., Vol. III, 555.

23. John W. Garver, *Foreign Relations of the People's Republic of China* (New Jersey, 1993), 138.

24. See Zheng Bijian, *Economic Globalization*, Wang Yiwei, *The Belt and Road Initiative: What Will China Offer the World in Its Rise?* (Beijing, 2016), and Liu Houbin, *The Historical Root and Cultural Deposit of National Rejuvenation* (Beijing, 2017) for examples of this discourse.

25. See for example Martin Jacques, *When China Rules the World* (London, 2012) and Gordon Chang, *The Coming Collapse of China* (Toronto, 2001).

26. See Niall Ferguson, *Civilization: The West and the Rest* (New York, 2012).

27. Damien Ma, public lecture, Beijing, 2014.

28. "Global Trends 2030: Alternative Worlds," *National Intelligence Council*, 2012.

29. Steven Levine, "The Big Layoff in China," *Axios, 2017*, https://www.axios.com/the-big

-layoff-in-china-2511630146.html (accessed December 13, 2018).

30. Xi Jinping, "Decisive Victory."

31. Ibid.

32. Ibid.

33. Ibid.

34. Ibid.

35. Ibid.

36. George S. Yip and Bruce McKern, *China's Next Strategic Advantage: From Imitation to Innovation* (Cambridge, MA, 2016).

37. AmCham China, "2018 China Business Climate Survey Report," 2018 中国商务环境调查报告.

38. "China's Technological Rise: Challenges to U.S. Innovation and Security." Hearing before the Subcommittee on Asia and the Pacific of the Committee on Foreign Affairs House of Representatives, No. 115–22, *Committee on Foreign Affairs,* 2017, https://docs.house.gov/meetings/FA/FA05/20170426/105885/HHRG-115-FA05-Transcript-20170426.pdf (accessed December 13, 2018).

39. See William C. Hannas, James Mulvenon, and Anna B. Puglisi, *Chinese Industrial Espionage: Technology Acquisition and Military Modernization (Asian Security Studies)* (New York, 2013).

40. David E. Sanger, "Chinese Curb Cyberattacks on U.S. Interests, Report Finds," *New York Times*, 2016, https://www.nytimes.com/2016/06/21/us/politics/china-us-cyber-spying.html (accessed December 13, 2018).

41. Sanger, "Chinese Curb Cyberattacks."

42. Alexander Stubb, "For China, Europe Is the New Africa," *Financial Times*, 2016, https://www.ft.com/content/49081fde-9241-3ffc-bedb-4f39200ca1dd (accessed December 13 2018).

43. Brian Wang, "China Starting Construction of Supercarrier with Electromagnetic Launch But Using Older Heavier Fighter Jets," *Next Big Future,* 2017, https://www.nextbigfuture.com/2017/11/china-starting-construction-of-superaircarrier-with-electromagnetic-launch-but-using-older-heavier-fighter-jets.html (accessed January 28, 2019).

44. Meia Nouwens and Helena Legarda, "Emerging Technology Dominance: What China's Pursuit of Advanced Dual-Use Technologies Means for the Future of Europe's Economy and Defence Innovation," *The International Institute for Strategic Studies, 13*.

45. Ibid., 18.

46. Alex Hollings, "Counterfeit Air Power: Meet China's Copycat Air Force," *Popular Mechanics, 2018*. https://www.popularmechanics.com/military/aviation/g23303922/china-copycat-air-force/ (accessed January 12, 2019).

47. The Oxford China Lecture, "Quantum Technology: A New Era in Computing," July 22, 2017, Beijing.

48. Jie Chen and Bruce J. Dickson, *Allies of the State: China's Private Entrepreneurs and*

Democratic Change (Cambridge, MA and London, 2010).

49. Keith Zhai and Alfred Cang, "Xi's Warning to Investors: Any Chinese Billionaire Could Fall," *Bloomberg, 2018,* https://www.bloomberg.com/news/articles/2018-03-01/xi-s-warning -to-investors-any-chinese-billionaire-could-fall (accessed January 12, 2019).

50. Chen and Dickson, *Allies of the State*, 38–67.

51. Ibid.

52. Gregor Stuart Hunter and Steven Russolillo, "Now Advising China's State Firms: The Communist Party," *Wall Street Journal, 2017,* https://www.wsj.com/articles/now-advising -chinas-state-firms-the-communist-party-1502703005 (accessed January 10, 2019); Alexandra Stevenson, "China's Communists Rewrite the Rules for Foreign Businesses," *New York Times, 2018,* https://www.nytimes.com/2018/04/13/business/china-communist-party-foreign -businesses.html (accessed January 10, 2019).

53. 3D模拟夺岛战役中国军力全景展现, 腾讯军事, 腾讯网 "3D Simulation of Military Tactics for Island Seizure: A Panoramic Display of China's Military Strength," Tencent Military, Tencent Web. https://news.qq.com/zt2015/ddzy/index.htm?tu_biz=1.114.1.0

54. "Global Top 100 Companies by Market Capitalization," *PwC,* March 31, 2018 update.

55. Li Yuan, "Jack Ma, China's Richest Man, Belongs to the Communist Party. Of Course," *New York Times, 2018,* https://www.nytimes.com/2018/11/27/business/jack-ma-communist -party-alibaba.html (accessed December 29, 2018).

56. AFP, "Sinister or Safe? China Takes the Lead in Using Facial Recognition Technology," *Hong Kong Free Press,* 2017, https://www.hongkongfp.com/2017/10/21/sinister-safer-china-takes- lead-using-facial-recognition-technology/ (accessed 13 December 2018).

57. "Wang Jianlin Talks about China Dream at Fortune," *Wanda Group, 2013,* http://www. wanda-group.com/2013/chairmannews_0529/271.html (accessed May 5, 2018). This post has since been removed from the Wanda Group website.

58. Ibid.

59. David Whitford, "What's Driving One of China's Richest Men?" *Fortune,* 2013, http:// fortune.com/2013/05/23/whats-driving-one-of-chinas-richest-men/ (accessed December 13, 2018).

60. Ibid.

61. Joseph Riley, "Hedging Engagement: America's Neoliberal Strategy for Managing China's Rise in the Post-Cold War Era," D.Phil. thesis, University of Oxford, 2016.

62. Liu Xiaohong, *Chinese Ambassadors: The Rise of Diplomatic Professionalism since 1949* (Seattle and London, 2001), 13, 132.

63. Scott DeCarlo and Nicolas Rapp, "This Chart Shows the World's 500 Largest Companies," *Fortune,* 2016, http://fortune.com/global-500-companies-chart/ (accessed December 13, 2018).

64. Fortune Global 500, http://fortune.com/global500/list/ (accessed January 19, 2019).

65. "The World's 100 Largest Banks," S&P Global, 2018, https://platform.mi.spglobal. com/web/client?auth=inherit#news/article?id=44027195&cdid=A-44027195-11060 (accessed March 3, 2019).

66. Scott Cendrowski, "China's Global 500 Companies Are Bigger Than Ever—and Mostly State-Owned," *Fortune,* 2015, http://fortune.com/2015/07/22/china-global-500-government-owned/ (accessed December 13, 2018).

67. Sara Salinas, "Six Top U.S. Intelligence Chiefs Caution against Buying Huawei Phones," *CNBC,* 2018, https://www.cnbc.com/2018/02/13/chinas-hauwei-top-us-intelligence-chiefs-caution-americans-away.html (accessed December 13, 2018).

68. Nic Fildes, "BT to Strip Huawei Equipment from Its Core 4G Network," *Financial Times, 2018,* https://www.ft.com/content/c639aaf4-f7c9-11e8-8b7c-6fa24bd5409c (accessed January 19, 2019). Also, author conversations with relevant parties.

69. China Energy Engineering Group, "Company Brochure," 2014, http://en.ceec.net.cn/col/col131/index.html (accessed January 19, 2019). The company is also known as Energy China.

70. Author's travels, Indian Ocean Region, 2016.

71. "Meeting Asia's Infrastructure Needs," *Asian Development Bank (Manila, 2017).*

72. "Constructing a New Global Order: Western and Chinese Infrastructure Abroad," *CSIS, 2017,* https://www.csis.org/events/western-and-chinese-infrastructure-development-abroad (accessed January 19, 2019).

73. See Xue Gong, "The Role of Chinese Corporate Players in China's South China Sea Policy," *Contemporary Southeast Asia 40, No. 2 (2018),* 301-26.

74. "Land Reclamation Completed for China-Funded Port City in Sri Lanka," *Xinhua, 2019,* http://www.xinhuanet.com/english/2019-01/17/c_137750757.htm (accessed January 19, 2019). China Harbor Engineering Company (CHEC) is owned by China Communications Construction Company (CCCC).

75. China Energy Engineering Group, *Company Brochure.*

76. "Alibaba Annual Report," United States Security and Exchange Commissions (Washington DC, 2016).

77. Ibid.

78. Ibid.

79. Sinopec Corp., *2016 Annual Report and Accounts, 9.*

80. Ibid.

81. Ibid., 17.

82. China National Offshore Oil Corp., *2016 Annual Report, 2.*

83. Ibid., 3.

84. Ibid.

85. Ibid., 46.

86. Ibid., 50.

87. "TV Docu Stimulates More Open Attitude to History."

88. Ibid.

89. "Profile: Xi Jinping and His Era," *Xinhua, 2017,* http://www.xinhuanet.com//english/2017-11/17/c_136758372.htm (accessed December 13, 2018).

90. Ibid.

91. Ibid.

92. Ibid.

93. Ibid.

Part IV: The Ceaseless Expansion of National Interests

1. "Xi Jinping and His Era: Strategist behind China's Reform," *Global Times, 2017,* http://www.globaltimes.cn/content/1075709.shtml (accessed December 13, 2018).

2. Xi Jinping, "Decisive Victory."

3. State Council, "China's Military Strategy"; Chinese-language version: http://www.mod.gov.cn/auth/2015-05/26/content_4586723.htm (accessed January 11, 2019).

4. "BP Statistical Review 67th Edition," *BP Statistical Energy of World Energy, 2018* (author's calculations).

5. "BP Energy Outlook: Country and Regional Insights China," *BP Statistical Review of World Energy and BP Energy Outlook*, 2018.

6. "Study Says China-Backed Dam Would Destroy Mekong," *CNBC, 2018,* https://www.cnbc.com/2018/05/17/study-says-china-backed-dam-would-destroy-mekong.html (accessed December 13, 2018).

7. Xi, "Decisive Victory." Original Chinese-language version: "扎实做好各战略方向军事斗争准备." See also US Defense Intelligence Agency, "China Military Power: Modernizing a Force to Fight and Win," 2019.

8. Ed Crooks, "The Global Importance of China's Oil Imports," *Financial Times*, 2017, https://www.ft.com/content/e7d52260-a1e4-11e7-b797-b61809486fe2 (accessed December 13, 2018).

9. US Energy Information Administration, *Annual Energy Outlook 2015: With Projections to 2040*, DOE/EIA-0383 (Washington, DC, 2015).

10. US Energy Information Administration, *China: International Data and Analysis,* (Washington, DC, 2015).

11. See, for example, Wu Sike (Ministry of Foreign Affairs, People's Republic of China), "The Strategic Docking between China and Middle East Countries under the 'Belt and Road' Framework," *Journal of Middle East and Islamic Studies (in Asia)*, Vol. 9, No. 4 (2015), and Andrew Scobell and Alireza Nader, "China in the Middle East: The Wary Dragon," RAND Corporation, 2016.

12. See Cole, "Reflections on China's Maritime Strategy."

13. Crooks, "Global Importance of China's Oil Imports."

14. "China's Arab Policy Paper," *Xinhua*, 2016, http://www.xinhuanet.com/english/china/2016-01/13/c_135006619.htm (accessed December 13, 2018).

15. Wu Sike, "Strategic Docking," 1.

16. Ibid., 2.

17. "Interview: Syria Welcomes China in Investments, Reconstruction Process: State

Minister," *Xinhua*, 2018, http://www.xinhuanet.com/english/2018-09/11/c_137461257
.htm (accessed January 20, 2019).

18. Chaoling Feng, "Embracing Interdependence: The Dynamics of China in the Middle
East," *Brookings Doha Center* (2015), 1.

19. Ibid., 2.

20. Ibid.

21. Andrew S. Erickson and Austin M. Strange, *Six Years at Sea . . . And Counting: Gulf of
Aden Anti-Piracy and China's Maritime Commons Presence* (Washington DC, 2015). See also
Ratner et al., "More Willing and Able."

22. Data: Johns Hopkins China–Africa Research Initiative.

23. "China's Second Africa Policy Paper," *Xinhua, 2015,* http://www.xinhuanet.com/
english/2015-12/04/c_134886545.htm (accessed December 13, 2018).

24. Ibid.

25. "China's Expanding Military Presence in Africa," *The China Africa Project,* 2015, https://
soundcloud.com/chinatalkingpoints/chinas-expanding-military-presence-in-africa
(accessed December 13, 2018).

26. Fatoumata Diallo, "Private Security Companies: The New Notch in Beijing's Belt and
Road Initiative?" *Institute for Security and Development Policy, 2018,* http://isdp.eu/private-
security-companies-new-notch-beijings-belt-road-initiative/ (accessed on January 11, 2019);
Charles Clover, "Chinese Private Security Companies Go Global," *Financial Times, 2017,*
https://www.ft.com/content/2a1ce1c8-fa7c-11e6-9516-2d969e0d3b65 (accessed on January
11, 2019).

27. "'Chinese Dream' and 'African Dream' Resonate," *People's Daily Online,* 2013, http://
en.people.cn/102774/8375199.html (accessed December 13, 2018).

28. "Chinese Dream Resonates with Africa Dream: Former UN Official," http://en.people
.cn/90883/8363651.html 2013 (accessed December 13, 2018).

29. "China's Expanding Military Presence." See also https://www.cfr.org/backgrounder
/china-africa

30. Ibid.

31. Chris Buckley, "In China, an Action Hero Beats Box Office Records (and Arrogant
Westerners)," *New York Times*, 2017, https://www.nytimes.com/2017/08/16/world/asia
/china-wolf-warrior-2-film.html (accessed December 13, 2018).

32. Ibid.

33. See the following articles for controversy around tagline: Su Tan, "BBC Sees *Wolf
Warrior II* through Western Bias," *Global Times,* 2017, http://www.globaltimes.cn
/content/1059939.shtml (accessed January 10, 2019); Beijing Bureau, "*Wolf Warrior 2*: The
Nationalist Action Film Storming China," *BBC,* 2017, https://www.bbc.com/news/blogs
-china-blog-40811952 (accessed January 10, 2019).

34. "China's Second Africa Policy Paper."

35. Howard W. French, *China's Second Continent: How a Million Migrants Are Building a*

New Empire in Africa (New York and Toronto, 2014).

36. "China's Second Africa Policy Paper."

37. Author's calculations, based on AEI "China Investment Tracker" and World Bank data.

38. "China's Second Africa Policy Paper."

39. Ibid.

40. Brook Larmer, "Is China the World's New Colonial Power?" *New York Times Magazine,* 2017, https://www.nytimes.com/2017/05/02/magazine/is-china-the-worlds-new-colonial -power.html (accessed January 9, 2019).

41. Ibid.

42. Ibid.

43. Dambisa Moyo, *Winner Take All: China's Race for Resources and What It Means for the World* (New York, 2012), 29.

44. Ibid., 30–31.

45. Ibid., 31.

46. Ibid., 35.

47. Ibid., 41.

48. Elizabeth C. Economy and Michael Levi, *By All Means Necessary: How China's Resource Quest Is Changing the World* (New York, 2014), 63.

49. Ibid., 64.

50. Fabian Cambero and Dave Sherwood, "China Invites Latin America to Take Part in One Belt, One Road," *Reuters, 2018,* https://www.reuters.com/article/us-chile-china/china- invites-latin-america-to-take-part-in-one-belt-one-road-idUSKBN1FB2CN (accessed January 9, 2019).

51. "Cooperation Plan (2015–2019)," China–CELAC Forum, 2015, http://www.china celacforum.org/eng/zywj_3/t1230944.htm (accessed January 9, 2019).

52. Katherine Koleski and Alec Blivas, "China's Engagement with Latin America and the Caribbean," *U.S.–China Economic and Security Review Commission,* 2018.

53. Ibid.

54. Alicia Bárcena, "Second Ministerial Meeting of China–CELAC Forum," *Economic Commission for Latin America and the Caribbean, 2018,* https://www.cepal.org/en/speeches/ second-ministerial-meeting-forum-china-celac (accessed January 9, 2019).

55. Margaret Myers, "China's Belt and Road Initiative: What Role for Latin America?" *The Dialogue, 2018,* https://www.thedialogue.org/analysis/chinas-belt-and-road-initiative-what -role-for-latin-america/ (accessed January 9, 2019).

56. "Chile Joins China's Belt and Road Initiative," *The Santiago Times, 2018,* https:// santiagotimes.cl/2018/11/04/chile-joins-chinas-belt-and-road-initiative/ (accessed January 9, 2019).

57. Jiang Shixue, "China–Argentina Ties Move towards a New Era," *CGTN, 2018,* https:// news.cgtn.com/news/3d3d774e3555544f30457a6333566d54/share_p.html (accessed January

9, 2019).

58. "Xi Stresses China–Mexico Strategic Synergy," *Xianhua, 2017,* http://www.xinhuanet.com//english/2017-09/04/c_136583000.htm (accessed January 9, 2019).

59. "China's Policy Paper on Latin America and the Caribbean," *Ministry of Foreign Affairs of the People's Republic of China, 2016,* https://www.fmprc.gov.cn/mfa_eng/wjdt_665 385/2649_665393/t1418254.shtml (accessed December 13, 2018).

60. Ibid.

61. Ibid.

62. Ibid.

63. Ibid.

64. Ibid.

65. Ted Piccone, "The Geopolitics of China's Rise in Latin America," *Geoeconomics and Global Issues* (Brookings, 2016).

66. Victor Robert Lee, "China Builds Space Monitoring Base in the Americas," *The Diplomat,* https://thediplomat.com/2016/05/china-builds-space-monitoring-base-in-the-americas/ 2016 (accessed December 13, 2018).

67. Ellis Evan, "The Strategic Importance of Brazil," *Global Americans, 2017,* https://theglobal americans.org/2017/10/strategic-importance-brazil/ (accessed December 13, 2018).

68. Zhang Tao, "China, Brazil Vow to Strengthen Military Ties," *China Military,* 2016, http://english.chinamil.com.cn/view/2016-11/16/content_7362708.htm (accessed December 13 2018).

69. Lu Hui, "China, Brazil Agree to Further Advance Comprehensive Strategic Partnership," *Xinhua,* 2017, http://www.xinhuanet.com//english/2017-09/02/c_136575462.htm (accessed December 13, 2018).

70. "China, Brazil to Advance Comprehensive Strategic Partnership to New Heights," *Xinhua, 2016,* http://www.xinhuanet.com//english/2016-09/02/c_135655442.htm (accessed December 13, 2018).

71. Nengye Liu, "China's New Silk Road and the Arctic," *The Diplomat,* 2017, https://thediplomat.com/2017/05/chinas-new-silk-road-and-the-arctic/ (accessed December 13, 2018).

72. Ibid.

73. Richard Milne, "China Wins Observer Status in Arctic Council," *Financial Times,* 2013, https://arctic-council.org/index.php/en/about-us/arctic-council/observers (accessed December 13, 2018).

74. Nengye Liu, "China's Emerging Arctic Policy," *The Diplomat, 2016,* https://thediplomat .com/2016/12/chinas-emerging-arctic-policy/ (accessed December 13, 2018).

75. Ibid.

76. Ibid. Italics added.

77. "Keynote Speech by Vice Foreign Minister Zhang Ming at China Country Session at

the Third Arctic Circle Assembly," *Ministry of Foreign Affairs of the People's Republic of China,* 2017, https://www.fmprc.gov.cn/mfa_eng/wjbxw/t1306858.shtml (accessed December 13, 2018).

78. Ibid.

79. Ibid.

80. Zhao Lei, "3 Sea Routes Planned for Belt & Road Initiative," *State Council for the People's Republic of China,* 2017, http://english.gov.cn/state_council/ministries/2017/06/21/con tent_281475692760102.htm (accessed December 13, 2018). Origin: *China Daily.*

81. Ibid.

82. Ibid, "document" refers to "Vision for Maritime Cooperation under the Belt and Road Initiative."

83. Peter Buxbaum, "China Moves Belt and Road Initiative to Arctic," *Global Trade,* 2017, http://www.globaltrademag.com/global-logistics/china-moves-belt-road-initiative-arctic (accessed January 9, 2019).

84. Heidar Gudjonsson and Egill Thor Nielsson, "China's Belt and Road: Where Does the Arctic Angle Stand?" *The Diplomat,* 2017, https://thediplomat.com/2017/09/chinas-belt -and-road-where-does-the-arctic-angle-stand/ (accessed December 13, 2018).

85. Camilla T. N. Sørensen and Ekaterina Klimenko, "Emerging Chinese–Russian Cooperation in the Arctic: Possibilities and Constraints," *SIPRI,* 2017, v.

86. Sørensen and Klimenko, "Emerging Chinese–Russian Cooperation." See also James Henderson and Tatiana Mitrova, "Energy Relations between Russia and China: Playing Chess with the Dragon," *The Oxford Institute for Energy Studies,* 2016.

87. Anne-Marie Brady, *China as a Polar Great Power* (Cambridge, 2017), 33.

88. Ibid., 34–35.

89. Edward A. Alpers, *The Indian Ocean in World History* (New York, 2014), 19–39.

90. Chen, "Camel Bells."

91. US Pacific Command (US PACOM) was renamed US Indo-Pacific Command (US INDOPACOM) in 2018 in light of a changing geopolitical situation.

92. "Vision and Actions on Jointly Building Silk and Economic Belt and 21st-Century Maritime Silk Road," *National Development and Reform Commission (NDRC) People's Republic of China,* 2015, http://en.ndrc.gov.cn/newsrelease/201503/t20150330_669367 .html (accessed December 13, 2018).

93. AEI Investment Tracker. Author's calculations.

94. Jonathan D. T. Ward, "Real Vision, Rise of India and China," *Atlas Organization,* 2018, https://atlasorganization.com/realvision (accessed January 9, 2019).

95. William Mellow, "Influential Thais in Push for Kra Canal Project," *Nikkei Asian Review,* 2017, https://asia.nikkei.com/Politics-Economy/Economy/Influential-Thais-in-push-for-Kra -Canal-project (accessed December 13, 2018).

96. Shihar Aneez, "Sri Lanka to Sell 80 Percent of Southern Hambantota Port to Chinese Firm," *Reuters,* 2016, https://www.reuters.com/article/us-sri-lanka-ports/sri-lanka-to-sell-80

-percent-of-southern-hambantota-port-to-chinese-firm-idUSKCN12S12R (accessed December 13, 2018).

97. "Vision for Maritime Cooperation."

98. Tamara Renee Shie, "Rising Chinese Influence in the South Pacific," *Asian Survey,* 2007, https://www.jstor.org/stable/10.1525/as.2007.47.2.307?read-now=1&seq=1#page_scan _tab_contents.

99. Larry Diamond and Orville Schell, *Chinese Influence and American Interests: Promoting Constructive Vigilance* (Stanford, 2018).

100. See, for example, Secretary Robert O. Work, "So, This Is What It Feels Like to Be Offset: How America's Strategic Competitors Are Trying to Beat Us at Our Own Game," *Center for a New American Security,* 2018, https://www.youtube.com/watch?v=U9iZyDE2dZI (accessed January 20, 2019), and US Defense Intelligence Agency, "China Military Power: Modernizing a Force to Fight and Win," 2019, http://www.dia.mil/Military-Power-Pub lications/ (accessed January 28, 2019), for examples of Chinese approaches to US military power, especially in the space, cyber, and maritime domains, and with regard to advanced military technologies.

101. Zheng Bijian, *Economic Globalization,* 130.

102. "Xi Instructs Army to Improve Its Combat Readiness," *Xinhua,* 2017, http://www .chinadaily.com.cn/china/2017-11/04/content_34110126.htm (accessed December 13, 2018).

103. Ibid.

104. Michael Green, Kathleen Hicks et al., "Countering Coercion in Maritime Asia: The Theory and Practice of Gray Zone Deterrence," *CSIS (2017).*

105. See Work, "So, This Is What It Feels Like to Be Offset."

106. 中国首次具备对美国有效的水下战略核威慑 Original source: *Global Times.* Also distributed in major state-owned outlets including *China Daily* and *China News Service.* With thanks to Professor Miles Yu, US Naval Academy, for the original Chinese-language version.

107. J.D. Simkins, "'We'll see how frightened America is' – Chinese admiral says sinking US carriers key to dominating South China Sea," *Navy Times, 2019,* https://www.navytimes .com/news/your-navy/2019/01/04/well-see-how-frightened-america-is-chinese-admiral -says-sinking-us-carriers-key-to-dominating-south-china-sea/ (accessed February 26, 2019).

108. 美中對抗 中國鷹派退將：美國怕什麼就打什麼, *Central News Agency (Taiwan),* 2018, https://www.cna.com.tw/news/acn/201812230157.aspx (accessed February 26, 2019).

109. Jamie Seidel, " 'Sink two aircraft carriers': Chinese Admiral's chilling receipt to dominate the South China Sea," *news.com.au, 2019,* https://www.news.com.au/technology/innovation/ military/sink-two-aircraft-carriers-chinese-admirals-chilling-recipie-to-dominate-the-south -china-sea/news-story/aaa8c33d57da62e7d5e28e791aa26e0f (accessed February 26, 2019). See also James Holmes, "Yes, China Could Sink a U.S. Navy Aircraft Carrier. But Don't Bet On It," *The National Interest, 2019,* https://nationalinterest.org/blog/buzz/yes-china-could -sink-us-navy-aircraft-carrier-don't-bet-it-41227 (accessed March 3, 2019).

110. DD Wu, "Russia–China Relations Reach a New High," *The Diplomat,* 2017, https:// thediplomat.com/2017/07/russia-china-relations-reach-a-new-high/ (accessed December 13, 2018).

Part V: The Ceaseless Expansion of National Interests

1. "Xi's World Vision: A Community of Common Destiny, a Shared Home for Humanity," *Xinhua, 2017,* http://www.xinhuanet.com//english/2017-01/15/c_135983586.htm (accessed January 26, 2019).

2. "Xi and His Era," *China Daily*, 2017, http://www.chinadaily.com.cn/china/2017-11/17 /content_34642960_23.htm (accessed January 26, 2019).

3. John K. Fairbank, "A Preliminary Framework," in John K. Fairbank, ed., *The Chinese World Order* (Cambridge, 1968), 2.

4. Ibid., 1.

5. Ibid., 2.

6. *Pleco Chinese Dictionary. See also Julie Kleeman and Henry Yu, The Oxford Chinese Dictionary,* (Oxford, 2010).

7. Ibid.

8. Fairbank, "A Preliminary Framework," 2.

9. Ibid.

10. Ibid., 3.

11. Ibid., 6.

12. Ibid., 2.

13. See Rory Stewart, "World Order: *Reflections on the Character of Nations and the Course of History by Henry Kissinger," The Sunday Times,* 2014, https://www.thetimes.co.uk/article/ world-order-reflections-on-the-character-of-nations-and-the-course-of-history-by-henry -kissinger-8fjpbdzzkhl (accessed January 26, 2019).

14. Fairbank, "A Preliminary Framework," 1–2.

15. Ibid., 4.

16. Ibid., 5.

17. Ibid., 9.

18. Ibid., 7–8.

19. Ibid., 8.

20. Ibid., 10.

21. Ibid., 12–13.

22. Ibid., 13.

23. Pankaj Mishra, *From the Ruins of Empire (*New York, 2013), 25. Emphasis added.

24. Qiang Zhai, *China and the Vietnam Wars*, 25.

25. Lien-Hang T. Nyugen, *Hanoi's War: An International History of the War for Peace in Vietnam* (Chapel Hill, 2012), 116.

26. Wang Yiwei, *The Belt and Road Initiative: What Will China Offer the World in Its Rise?* (Beijing, 2016), 12. Wang's book is not official policy, but its importance is acknowledged at the highest levels of the CCP, and it appears to be officially circulated among CCP officials

and cadres.

27. Ibid., 18.

28. Fu Ying, "China's Vision for the World: A Community of Shared Future," *The Diplomat,* 2017, https://thediplomat.com/2017/06/chinas-vision-for-the-world-a-community-of-shared-future/ (accessed January 9, 2019). See also Nadège Rolland, "Beijing's Vision for a Reshaped International Order," *The Jamestown Foundation,* 2018, https://jamestown.org/program/beijings-vision-reshaped-international-order/ (accessed March 2, 2019).

29. Fairbank, "A Preliminary Framework," 3.

30. Samantha Hoffman, "Managing the State: Social Credit, Surveillance and the CCP's Plan for China," *The Jamestown Foundation,* 2017, https://jamestown.org/program/managing-the-state-social-credit-surveillance-and-the-ccps-plan-for-china/ (accessed January 9, 2019).

31. Ibid.

32. Rogier Creemers, "Party Ideology and Chinese Law," *SSRN, 2018,* https://papers.ssrn.com/sol3/papers.cfm?abstract_id=3210541 (accessed January 26, 2019), 8.

33. Liu Houbin, *The Historical Root and Cultural Deposit of National Rejuvenation* (Beijing, 2017), 8.

34. Ibid., 9.

35. Ibid., 112.

36. See Zheng Wang, "National Humiliation, History Education, and the Politics of Historical Memory: Patriotic Education Campaign in China," *International Studies Quarterly (2008)* 52, 783-806, on the Communist Party's use of "a new 'victimization narrative,' which blames the 'West' for China's suffering."

37. Rogier Creemers, "China's Social Credit System: An Evolving Practice of Control," *SSRN, 2018,* https://papers.ssrn.com/sol3/papers.cfm?abstract_id=3175792 (accessed January 26, 2019), 13, 22.

38. Creemers, "Ideology," 11.

39. Ibid., 11.

40. Samantha Hoffman, "Programming China: The Communist Party's Autonomic Approach to Managing State Security," *MERICS,* 2017.

41. Ibid.

42. Ibid.

43. 钟国安, "以习近平总书记总体国家安全观为指引谱写国家安全新篇章," 求是, 2017, http://www.qstheory.cn/dukan/qs/2017-04/15/c_1120788993.htm "A New Chapter in National Security Guided by General Secretary Xi Jinping's Overall National Security Concept," *Quishi,* 2017, (accessed January 29, 2019).

44. Ibid.

45. Ibid.

46. Xi Jinping, "Work Together to Build a Community of Shared Future for Mankind," *Xinhua,* 2017, http://www.xinhuanet.com/english/2017-01/19/c_135994707.htm (accessed January 9, 2019).

47. Fairbank, "A Preliminary Framework," 6.

48. Ibid.

49. Creemers, "Ideology," 25. Italics added.

50. "Constitution of the People's Republic of China," *The National People's Congress of the People's Republic of China*, 2004, http://www.npc.gov.cn/englishnpc/Constitution/2007-11/15/content_1372964.htm (accessed January 9, 2019).

51. Creemers, "Ideology," 21.

52. Samantha Hoffman and Elsa Kania, "Huawei and the Ambiguity of China's Intelligence and Counter-Espionage Laws," *The Strategist*, 2018, https://www.aspistrategist.org.au/huawei-and-the-ambiguity-of-chinas-intelligence-and-counter-espionage-laws/ (accessed January 9, 2019).

53. Ministry of National Defense of the PRC, "National Security Law of the People's Republic of China (2015) [Effective]," http://eng.mod.gov.cn/publications/2017-03/03/content_4774229.htm (accessed January 26, 2019).

54. See also Hoffman and Kania.

55. Fu Ying, "The U.S. World Order Is a Suit That No Longer Fits," *The Financial Times*, 2016, https://www.ft.com/content/c09cbcb6-b3cb-11e5-b147-e5e5bba42e51 (accessed 13 December 2018).

56. Liu Houbin, *The Historical Root and Cultural Deposit*, 2.

57. Fu Ying, "China's Vision for the World."

58. Hannah Beech, "China Campaigns against 'Western Values,' But Does Beijing Really Think They're That Bad?" *Time*, 2016, http://time.com/4312082/china-textbooks-western-values-foreign-ngo/ (accessed December 13, 2018).

59. Jamil Anderlini, "'Western Values' Forbidden in Chinese Universities," *The Financial Times*, 2015, https://www.ft.com/content/95f3f866-a87e-11e4-bd17-00144feab7de (accessed December 13, 2018).

60. "Communiqué on the Current State of the Ideological Sphere (Document No. 9)," 2013, Rogier Creemers, trans., https://chinacopyrightandmedia.wordpress.com/2013/04/22/communique-on-the-current-state-of-the-ideological-sphere-document-no-9/ (accessed January 26, 2019).

61. Ibid.

62. Ibid.

63. Ibid.

64. Ibid.

65. Creemers, "Ideology," 23.

66. Samuel B. Griffith trans., *Sun Tzu: The Art of War*, (New York, 1963), 111.

67. Lionel Giles trans., *The Art of War by Sun Tzu*, http://classics.mit.edu/Tzu/artwar.html (accessed March 2 2019).

68. "Communiqué on the Current State of the Ideological Sphere."

69. "Document 9: A ChinaFile Translation," http://www.chinafile.com/document-9-chinafile-translation (accessed January 26, 2019).

70. "President Xi Jinping's Speech on 'One Country, Two Systems' and How China Rules Hong Kong," *South China Morning Post,* 2017, https://www.scmp.com/news/hong-kong/politics/article/2100856/full-text-president-xi-jinpings-speech-one-country-two (accessed January 9, 2019) Italics added.

71. Ibid.

72. Ibid.

73. Kwangmin Kim, "Xinjiang under the Qing," *Oxford Research Encyclopedias,* 2018, http://oxfordre.com/asianhistory/view/10.1093/acrefore/9780190277727.001.0001/acrefore-9780190277727-e-13 (accessed January 9, 2019).

74. Adrian Zenz and James Leibold, "Chen Quanguo: The Strongman behind Beijing's Securitization Strategy in Tibet and Xinjiang," *The Jamestown Foundation,* 2017, https://jamestown.org/program/chen-quanguo-the-strongman-behind-beijings-securitization-strategy-in-tibet-and-xinjiang/ (accessed January 21, 2019).

75. Ibid.

76. Ibid.

77. Ibid.

78. Khaled A. Beydoun, "China Holds One Million Uighur Muslims in Concentration Camps," *Al Jazeera, 2018,* https://www.aljazeera.com/indepth/opinion/china-holds-million-uighur-muslims-concentration-camps-180912105738481.html (accessed January 21, 2019).

79. Ibid.

80. Simon Denyer, "Former Inmates of China's Muslim 'Reeducation' Camps Tell of Brainwashing, Torture," *Washington Post,* 2018, https://www.washingtonpost.com/world/asia_pacific/former-inmates-of-chinas-muslim-re-education-camps-tell-of-brainwashing-torture/2018/05/16/32b330e8-5850-11e8-8b92-45fdd7aaef3c_story.html (accessed January 21, 2019).

81. "China's State Media Defends Xinjiang Muslim Crackdown," *Al Jazeera, 2018,* https://www.aljazeera.com/news/2018/08/china-state-media-defends-xinjiang-muslim-crackdown-180813055304359.html (accessed January 21, 2019).

82. Ibid.

83. Denyer, "Former Inmates."

84. Chun Han Wong, "China Applies Xinjiang's Policing Lessons to Other Muslim Areas," *The Wall Street Journal,* 2018, https://www.wsj.com/articles/china-applies-xinjiangs-policing-lessons-to-other-muslim-areas-11545566403 (accessed January 21, 2019).

85. Ibid.

86. Joshua Lipes, "Uyghur Former Xinjiang University Vice President Detained for 'Two-Faced' Tendencies," *Radio Free Asia,* 2018, https://www.rfa.org/english/news/uyghur/professor-09242018164800.html (accessed January 21, 2019).

87. Chiang Kai-shek, *China's Destiny, 36.*

88. The Belt and Road Research Team, Chongyang Institute for Financial Studies of Renmin University, *Pivot Cities on the Belt and Road* (Beijing, 2017), 94. Italics added.

89. Ibid.

90. Ibid., 217.

91. Ibid., 181. The authors refer to CPEC and also to the Chengdu–Xinjiang–Europe railway as a foundation for "the westward passage to the sea."

92. Ibid., 217.

93. "China's Military Strategy."

94. Xi Jinping, "Work Together" (accessed January 21, 2019).

95. See, for example, report by the Chinese Foreign Ministry, "Some Existing Issues in and Suggestions for the Asia–Africa Conference," 1955, FMA 207-00004-06, 59-62, CWIHPDA. See Shu Guang Zhang, "Constructing 'Peaceful Coexistence,'" Ward, "China–India Rivalry," and also John W. Garver, *Foreign Relations of the People's Republic of China* (Upper Saddle River, NJ, 1993), 43-50, on the strategic properties of Chinese "peaceful coexistence" policy during the founding decades of the PRC.

96. FMA 207-00004-06, 59-62.

97. *White Paper, Vol. VI,* 216.

98. Cheng Li and Lucy Xu, "Chinese Enthusiasm and American Cynicism over the 'New Type of Great Power Relations'," *Brookings,* 2014, https://www.brookings.edu/opinions/chinese-enthusiasm-and-american-cynicism-over-the-new-type-of-great-power-relations/ (accessed January 9, 2019). "President Xi Jinping's Speech on 'One Country, Two Systems'." Italics added.

99. "Full Text: China's Policies on Asia-Pacific Security Cooperation," *The State Council of the People's Republic of China,* 2017, http://english.gov.cn/archive/white_paper/2017/01/11/content_281475539078636.htm (accessed December 13, 2018).

100. Ibid.

101. Ibid.

102. Ibid.

103. Ibid.

104. See Kaplan, *Asia's Cauldron,* and Bill Hayton, *The South China Sea: The Struggle for Power in Asia* (New Haven, 2014).

105. Louise M. Simeon, "China Lifts Import Ban on Philippine Bananas," *Phil Star Global,* 2016, http://www.philstar.com/business/2016/10/07/1630958/china-lifts-import-ban-philippine-bananas (accessed December 15, 2018). See also CSIS, "Maritime Coercion."

106. Fairbank, "A Preliminary Framework," 9.

107. Ibid.

108. Robert A. Manning and James Przystup, "Stop the South China Sea Charade," *Foreign Policy* (2017).

109. "Xi's World Vision" (accessed December 13, 2018). Italics added.

110. John Garnaut, "Australia's China Reset," *The Monthly, 2018,* https://www.themonthly .com.au/issue/2018/august/1533045600/john-garnaut-australia-s-china-reset (accessed January 20, 2019).

111. Yan Xuetong, *Ancient Chinese Thought, Modern Chinese Power* (Princeton, 2011).

112. Isaac Stone Fish, "The Other Political Correctness," *The New Republic,* 2018, https:// newrepublic.com/article/150476/american-elite-universities-selfcensorship-china (accessed January 20, 2019). Also, Marshall Sahlins, "China U.," *The Nation,* 2013, https://www .thenation.com/article/china-u/ (accessed January 9, 2019).

113. Sahlins, "China U."

114. Simon Denyer, "Gap Apologizes to China over Map on T-Shirt That Omits Taiwan, South China Sea," *Washington Post, 2018,* https://www.washingtonpost.com/news/ worldviews/wp/2018/05/15/u-s-retailer-gap-apologizes-to-china-over-map-on-t-shirt-that -omits-taiwan-south-china-sea/?noredirect=on&utm_term=.53794a68efb1 (accessed January 9, 2019).

115. Pei Li and Adam Jourdan, "Mercedes-Benz apologizes to Chinese for quoting Dalai Lama," *Reuters, 2018,* https://www.reuters.com/article/us-mercedes-benz-china-gaffe/ mercedes-benz-apologizes-to-chinese-for-quoting-dalai-lama-idUSKBN1FQ1FJ (accessed January 9, 2019).

116. Ibid.

117. See also Orville Schell, *Wealth and Power: China's Long March to the Twenty-First Century* (New York, 2013).

118. Chen Jian, "China and the Bandung Conference: Changing Perceptions and Representations," in See Seng Tan and Amitav Acharya, eds., *Bandung Revisited: The Legacy of the 1955 Asian–African Conference for International Order* (Singapore, 2008), 133.

119. Qiang Zhai, *China and the Vietnam Wars,* 4.

120. See Hays Gries, *China's New Nationalism,* Mitter, *A Bitter Revolution,* and Zheng Wang, *Never Forget National Humiliation* for a discussion of the many sides of modern Chinese nationalism.

121. Xi Jinping, "Decisive Victory."

122. Zheng Wang, *Never Forget National Humiliation, 1–2.*

123. See, for example, Li Yuan, "China's Entrepreneurs Are Wary of Its Future," *The New York Times,* 2019, https://www.nytimes.com/2019/02/23/business/china-entrepreneurs-con fidence.html (accessed February 26, 2019).

124. Tom Phillips, "Chinese Student Abused for Praising 'Fresh Air of Free Speech' in US," *Guardian, 2017,* https://www.theguardian.com/world/2017/may/23/china-yang-shuping -free-speech-university-of-maryland-us-student (accessed May 15, 2018).

125. Yang Shuping, "Shuping Yang's Freedom Is Oxygen University of Maryland Speech," *University of Maryland Commencement Speech,* 2017, http://lybio.net/shuping-yangs-free dom-is-oxygen-university-of-maryland-speech/speeches (accessed December 15, 2018).

126. Harry Shukman, "Student Bullied off Social Media for Criticizing China in a Commencement Speech," *The Tab, 2017,* https://thetab.com/us/2017/05/23/shuping

-yang-umd-68973 (accessed December 15, 2018).

127. Ibid.

128. Simon Denyer and Congcong Zhang, "A Chinese Student Praised the U.S. and 'Fresh Air of Free Speech,' at U.S. College. Then Came Backlash," *Washington Post*, 2017, https://www.washingtonpost.com/news/worldviews/wp/2017/05/23/a-chinese-student-praised-the-fresh-air-of-free-speech-at-a-u-s-college-then-came-the-backlash/?utm_term=.2395 05d3b591 (accessed December 15, 2018).

129. Shukman, "Student Bullied off Social Media."

130. Ibid.

131. Julia Hollingsworth, "Chinese Student Who Praised U.S. Fresh Air and Freedom Apologizes after Backlash in China," *South China Morning Post*, 2017, http://www.scmp.com/news/china/society/article/2095319/chinese-student-who-praised-us-freedoms-apologizes-after-backlash (accessed December 15, 2018).

132. "No Flouting of China's Core Interests Will Be Tolerated," *China Daily*, 2018, http://www.chinadaily.com.cn/a/201801/14/WS5a5b4f65a3102c394518f19e.html (accessed January 9, 2019).

133. *White Paper, Vol. VII, 36.*

134. Xi, "Decisive Victory."

135. David Bandurski, "A History of 'Hurt Feelings' in China," *China Media Project*, 2016, http://chinamediaproject.org/2016/01/29/a-history-of-hurt-feelings-in-china/ (accessed December 15, 2018).

136. Ibid.

137. Tom Phillips, "A Human Rights Activist, a Secret Prison and a Tale from Xi Jinping's New China," *Guardian*, 2017, https://www.theguardian.com/world/2017/jan/03/human-rights-activist-peter-dahlin-secret-black-prison-xi-jinpings-new-china (accessed December 15, 2018).

138. Ibid.

139. Sahlins, "China U."

140. Tom Phillips, "Love the Party, Protect the Party: 'How Xi Jinping Is Bringing China's Media to Heel'," *Guardian,* 2016, https://www.theguardian.com/world/2016/feb/28/absolute-loyalty-how-xi-jinping-is-bringing-chinas-media-to-heel (accessed December 15, 2018).

141. "Xi Jinping Asks for 'Absolute Loyalty' from Chinese State Media," *Guardian,* 2016, https://www.theguardian.com/world/2016/feb/19/xi-jinping-tours-chinas-top-state-media-outlets-to-boost-loyalty (accessed December 15, 2018).

142. Anne Nelson, "CCTV's International Expansion: China's Grand Strategy for Media?" *Center for International Media Assistance (2013), 6.*

143. Ibid.

144. Ibid.

145. Paul Farhi, "In D.C., China Builds a News Hub to Help Polish Its Global Image," *Washington Post,* 2012, https://www.washingtonpost.com/lifestyle/style/china-building-news-hub-in-dc/2012/01/12/gIQAh2Ps3P_story.html?utm_term=.cd95844

f744c (accessed December 15, 2018).

146. Ibid.

147. Ibid.

Conclusion

1. Hugh White, Mary Kay Magistad, and Zha Daojiong, "It Is Time for America to Consider Accommodation with China," *Foreign Policy* (2015).

2. Natalie Liu, "Prominent Scholars Debate US—China Relations and Thucydides Trap," *Voice of America,* https://www.voanews.com/a/scholars-debate-us-china-relations-and-thucydides-trap/3926813.html, 2017 (accessed December 15, 2018). See Graham Allison, *Destined for War: Can America and China Escape Thucydides's Trap?* (New York, 2017) for original text.

3. Liu, "Prominent Scholars Debate."

4. Ibid. Adapted from VOA interview, 2017—includes author interview and segments from *Destined for War.*

5. Odd Arne Westad, *Decisive Encounters: The Chinese Civil War, 1946–1950* (Stanford, 2003).

INDEX

CPSIA information can be obtained
at www.ICGtesting.com
Printed in the USA
LVHW020303270419
615789LV00007B/76